SPRINGTIME

IN

LITHUANIA

Hypatia Yčas

SPRINGTIME IN LITHUANIA

Youthful Memories 1920 – 1940

Illustrated by Peggy Zuris

SECOND PRINTING

Springtime in Lithuania
Copyright © 2005 by Hypatia Ycas

International Standard Book Number: 1-929612-19-2
Library of Congress Control Number: 00-192952

PRINTED IN THE UNITED STATES OF AMERICA

ADAMS PRESS
CHICAGO, ILLINOIS

MAP OF LITHUANIA

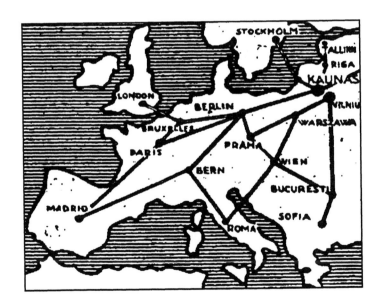

Maps are from a publication by
the Lithuanian Tourist Association, Kaunas, 1938.

Dedicated to the Memory of My Parents

photograph taken in Vilnius, Spring 1918

Hypatia Šliupas Yčas
Born Shenandoah, Pennsylvania, USA, 1894
Died Albuquerque, New Mexico, USA, 1987

Martynas Yčas
Born Šimpeliškiai, Lithuania, 1885
Died Rio de Janeiro, Brazil, 1941

Contents

Part I
Kaunas in the 1920s

Part II
Tales of Turkey Lurk

Part III
The Widening World

Acknowledgments

I would like to express my appreciation to several persons for their unfailing support and encouragement. These include the Honorable Anicetas Simutis, Ambassador of Lithuania to the United Nations; his wife Janina; and Prof. Aleksandras Shtromas. They all knew Kaunas very well in the olden days. Professor Shtromas, a scholar in Political Science at Hillsdale College, Michigan, give me valuable advice. Regretfully, he passed away in June 1999, before the completion of this work. I consider it a great compliment that he told me I had made a good beginning in describing everyday life and political undercurrents in the land he loved so well.

As to practical matters, I wish to acknowledge the help given me by my sister, Evelyna, who had the good will and patience to transcribe my text over its many revisions; and to Dolores Hance for proof-reading the manuscript. Also much appreciated is the work of the artist, Peggy Zuris, for her illustrations in this book and for permission to reproduce her oil painting, "Poppies and Cornflowers," on the cover. For me this painting captures the spirit of springtime.

Above all, my hearty thanks to Geraldine Mosher for serving as my editor and for converting a shapeless mass of material into what we both hope is a readable whole.

Introduction

This book by Hypatia Yčas is a welcome source of information about a small country of Northern Europe getting on its feet after many years of subjugation by its larger and stronger neighbors. The author's father and other relatives were actively involved in the struggle for freedom of the Lithuanian people. Hypatia was too young to be a participant, but old enough to understand what was going on in her surroundings.

The author is fluent in Lithuanian and in English. As a journalist, she has written many articles in both languages. She is also conversant with French, Spanish and Russian. Educated in Europe and in this country, she completed graduate studies in political science at the University of Michigan. Later she obtained a second Master of Arts degree from Columbia University School of Library Science. The author's background includes six years of service at the Lithuanian Embassy in Washington, D.C. as secretary, translator and information officer.

In her account of private and public life in the land where she spent her youth, the author combines keen observation of people and events with splendid reportage on the re-establishment of Independent Lithuania between the two World Wars. Her story continues through the extinction of freedom by the Soviet Russian occupation and her own extraordinary escape to the USA, the country of her mother's birth.

As a former resident of Kaunas, I knew the author's family quite well. I also knew a number of personalities appearing in these pages who played a role in the emergence of modern Lithuania. The author's brief character sketches of people who impressed her as well as her readable style of presentation add to the interest of this work.

ANICETAS SIMUTIS
Ambassador and Special Adviser to the Mission
of Lithuania, United Nations, New York, NY
December, 1999

Preface

The years 1920-1940 could be called the springtime of my life. By coincidence, these same years were springtime for Lithuania as well - a period of regeneration and hope. After the devastation left by World War I, the country was reborn in a burst of creative energy and enthusiasm. Between World Wars I and II, it was my good fortune to have lived in Lithuania's capital, the scene of stirring events. After barely two decades, the careful work of years was swept away. Bright hopes for the future vanished when Soviet Russian tanks rolled in that fateful summer of 1940. The coming of the Red Flood was an event to which I happened to be a witness.

A brief reading list of helpful publications appears at the end of this work. There is also an index of names of personalities mentioned in the text. My thumbnail sketches may help to make them come alive. These are people who do not deserve to be forgotten. These reminiscences, written with the help of my notes and diaries, were reinforced by historical facts and by tales told by my parents. My book was long years in the making and achieved final form only at the dawn of the New Millennium. In my young days, people were living in what could be termed "the horse and buggy age," in great contrast with life amid the technological advances of the computer era of today.

To my knowledge there is no exactly comparable book in the English language, which is a good reason for presenting these informal memoirs. True, there are numbers of publications on Lithuanian subjects, but they are generally far too scholarly for the general reader. Hopefully, my personal impressions of growing up in another place and time may be of some value in understanding a small nation's struggle for existence in a long-vanished world.

HYPATIA YČAS

Prologue

Much happened to my parents before they settled down to a peaceful life in Kaunas, provisional capital of Lithuania. Life had been anything but stable for the Yčas (pronounced "Eechas") family before they got there in the summer of 1920. There had been stirring events ever since the marriage of Martynas Yčas and Hypatia, nee Šliupas, in New York City's Reformed Church of St. Nicholas in November 1916. The newlyweds journeyed to Europe. World War I (1914–1918) had already erupted. Through an ocean infested with German submarines, their ship made it safely to Southampton, England, and later to the Baltic port of Haparanda. An overland trip via Finland brought them to St. Petersburg, Russia, where Father had important parliamentary responsibilities.

The young couple was not at all alike in their personal characteristics, their temperament or their life experiences. When they were married, Hypatia was a student not yet out of college. Born of Lithuanian parents, she was brought up in a small Pennsylvania town in a sheltered and rather old-fashioned atmosphere. She had never traveled more than a few hundred miles from the family home. By contrast, Martynas, then a rising young statesman, was knowledgeable in the ways of the world and was well traveled. He had visited far-flung corners of the Russian empire and countries of Western Europe. He had crossed two oceans, both the Atlantic and the Pacific. Despite their obvious differences, Martynas and Hypatia had at least one thing in common. They were great raconteurs endowed with exceptional memories and liked to talk about their experiences, if you could catch them in the right mood.

The voyage to St. Petersburg, or Petrograd as people called it then, was fairly routine and left few memories. Mamma remembered the town of Haparanda in Finland for here she had her first—and probably her last—taste of bear meat, a local delicacy. She commented that it was "so tough and stringy that I would never order it again." Later she got the distressing news that her heavy luggage, following in a separate ship, had been lost in a storm at sea and would never reach her. She never ceased regretting the loss of this trunk containing many books she had loved in her girlhood, and over the years spent much time in trying to remember what the books had been and writing to America for replacements.

Mamma's experiences as a young bride seeing Europe for the first time were among the memories she treasured the most. Tumultuous happenings in times in Petrograd and Voronezh left an indelible impression. Her husband had such exuberance and love for life that Mamma felt there could never be a dull moment while she had him as a life companion.

As for Father, closest to his heart must have been the days when he was starting his public career as a parliamentarian. In the Russian *Duma* (Parliament) he had been elected as a representative from the state of Lithuania, then still under Russian domination. After the revolution of 1905 against Czar Nicholas' autocratic regime, a Duma was allowed to assemble. Heretofore the Czar had ruled by decree without benefit of a parliament. Father served in the fourth and final such body right up to the worldshaking events of the Bolshevik Revolution of 1917.

When elected, Father was less than 30 years old, full of youthful enthusiasm and confidence that great things could be done for his native land. A measure of his self-assurance and optimism were incidents like the following. Months before his election, he had no doubts about the outcome. He happened to be in Petrograd and visited the Duma chambers in the Tauride Palace. Going upstairs to the Visitors Gallery, he viewed the meeting hall and selected the seat he would like to occupy as a future member of that body. When war broke out, the outlook for Lithuania was very uncertain. The armies of Germany and Russia were locked in deadly combat. Pessimists were saying that foreign rule for Lithuania was inevitable no matter which side was the winner. Father, always the optimist, said, "We must hope that Kaiser Wilhelm's Germany and Czar Nicholas' Russia will both collapse." This seemed quite incredible at the time and yet it was exactly what came to pass.

The war was a disaster for Russia, and other calamities were looming ahead. Some Duma members realized that revolution might be imminent. Opposition leaders hoped to stem the tide with reforms long overdue, but these came far too late. Martynas Yčas was among those joining the Cadet Party led by P. Miliukov, a respected statesman of liberal views. Duma colleagues were largely ignorant of the many nationalities within Russia's boundaries. Father was always ready and willing to inform them about his people. His statement of demands for Lithuanian autonomy was accepted by his party. According to Father, this very vocal Cadet group would have brought the matter to a vote on the floor of Parliament if events of the Revolution had not intervened. Later, as a member of the Duma delegation touring Western Europe, Father had the opportunity to make the Lithuanian case known in Britain, France, Sweden, and elsewhere. This delegation of a dozen members included his mentor P. Miliukov.

It was winter in Petrograd when the Yčas couple arrived. Mamma remembered the music of bells on the harnesses of the horses as sleighs glided through the snowy streets. The bridges spanning the canals were glistening with icicles. She had no memories of attending any Duma sessions. Public unrest was already rife in the streets and in the Tauride Palace. One clear memory remained of walking in the endless circular corridors around the assembly hall. Masses of people were milling about or standing in groups, agitating wildly, or even shouting at each other. When asked the reason for such behavior, Father replied with a wry smile, "They had better get their shouting done in the corridors rather than at the Duma session inside."

Father, who loved fine food, had a low opinion of the Duma restaurant. Mamma, however, never once had the chance to dine there. One of Father's tales concerned the restaurant, and he swore it was absolutely true. Bolshevik troops surrounded Tauride Palace after the revolution started. They refused to let Duma members out while they deliberated their fate: should they be shot or set free? There was little food in the restaurant, but quantities of champagne and caviar were discovered to everyone's delight. Their imprisonment lasted many hours and a consistent diet of these luxury foods became disgusting beyond words. After their release some of the members, including Father, could not bear the smell or taste of caviar and champagne for quite some time.

Years later, some tangible evidence remains in the family archives from those days. Among Mamma's precious souvenirs was a briefcase used by Father for his papers, notes and writings. Mother, not Father, was the one who accumulated souvenirs, squirreled away in trunks that nobody was allowed to open. This valuable relic was given to the Yčas relatives for safekeeping during the upheavals of the 1940s. The briefcase traveled with them when they became refugees, going through Western Germany and to the USA. The leather is so worn that it is falling to pieces, but one can still make out the words "Yčas"and "DUMA" In Cyrillic script with an almost illegible date. In wartime Germany one of our aunts used the briefcase to carry potatoes. When she presented it to Mamma with the above explanation for its tattered condition, Mamma was so overcome that she laughed and shed tears at the same time. So many glorious memories, now profaned by a foolish old lady who could think only of mundane things like potatoes.

Besides his parliamentary duties, Father was active in organizations aiding the refugees who were flooding Russia. Lithuanians established committees to aid thousands of their compatriots fleeing the German advance. Many settled in towns like Voronezh and were in need of food, clothing and shelter. Important for getting needed funds was the Russian Refugee Aid Committee under the honorary chairmanship of Princess Tatiana, daughter of the Czar, who tried to be more than just a figurehead. Father attended meetings at the Winter Palace and had tales to relate about his contacts in exalted circles. Rumors grew that he was seen riding around town in the Czar's own carriage. If Father really had access to such royal transportation, one would think that he would have told his family about it, but none of us remembers any such thing.

Social life was at a high ebb during that last winter before the Great Revolution. The Yčas couple received invitations to balls, theater parties, dinners and other events. Mamma said she was not enthusiastic about accepting, as she was shy about meeting strangers. Besides, she knew very little Russian. However, she found society ladies very welcoming and even met a few who wanted to learn English. Soon after her arrival, Mamma almost had an encounter with Rasputin, who as a protégé of the Czarina (wife of the Czar) had entrée into society. He was a miracle worker and a holy man to some people, but to others he was a dangerous charlatan, boding no good for the Romanov dynasty or the Empire. Mamma had heard about his hypnotic effect on women and had no desire to be anywhere near him. Father laughed at her fears, and so they went to a gathering where he was expected. However, the "Mad Monk of Siberia" did not appear. Perhaps he knew he had many enemies. Shortly afterwards, Rasputin was murdered by a group of patriotic Russians.

When spring came, there was outright revolt, and the Czar had to abdicate. It was a time of general chaos as new governments rose and fell. All sorts of groups were marching and demanding their rights. One freezing day in March Mamma was amazed to see completely naked men demonstrating for equal rights for nudists and trying to board the streetcars. Besides such comic moments, there were shootings, arrests and executions. In 1917, it was no longer safe to be in Petrograd. Martynas and his wife moved to the Russian interior, going south to Voronezh where they lived for almost a year.

It was a time of hurried journeys and separations. Somehow they always managed to get together and eventually reach safety. In Voronezh Mamma had the joy of welcoming her sister from the USA, Dr. Aldona Šliupas. As a physician, she was invaluable in organizing medical facilities and hospitals for her stranded countrymen. Better than that, she was on hand when Mamma gave birth to her first child, Martynas, Jr. in December 1917. Just about this time she had an odd experience: somebody left a newborn baby on her doorstep. She was much tempted to keep it but her husband said "No." Years later, there were times when Mamma wondered whether she had done the right thing in sending the little boy to the orphanage. Would he not have made a nice companion for her one and only son?

One of Father's great concerns was schooling for the young refugees. In view of his efforts, the Voronezh high schools were known as the Martynas Yčas schools. Their graduates, as well as those who completed adult courses in a variety of subjects, were important for Independent Lithuania (1918-1940). Here was a ready-made cadre of government employees, teachers, accountants and every kind of professional so much needed at the time.

Everyone hoped for an early return to the homeland, but revolutionary events intervened. The White (or Czarist) armies appeared, hotly pursued by the Reds (or Bolsheviks). There were also roving bands of various nationalities who were little better than bandits. Father and other leaders had to negotiate with military groups for the safety of the refugee community. Father left few recollections about these unsettled times when he was often in danger of his life, but fortunately there are Mamma's memories to rely on.

By this time Mamma was more confident about speaking Russian. She liked to go shopping in the outdoor market and noticed some strange foods. Stored in large barrels were pickled green tomatoes, salted mushrooms and beans prepared in many different ways. As time went on, food supplies became scarce. One day at the Yčas apartment (at the corner of Leather Alley and Butcher Street), a merry party of friends and relatives was enjoying a lunch of a bean concoction with tomatoes. Suddenly, the doorbell rang and in marched some young men wearing high school uniforms. They announced, "Citizen Yčas, you are under arrest." Some students from his own school had evidently gone Communist. Father showed no fear and calmly prepared to leave with his captors. He told Mamma to wipe away her tears, saying, "I shall soon be back. You will see."

Father and some other Lithuanians were imprisoned for over a month. Each time Mamma came to visit, carrying baskets of provisions, she would talk to Father through the prison bars. His words were always the same, "Cheer up and stop crying." The danger of execution was very real, but eventually the prisoners were allowed to go free. Father related that unknown benefactors contributed large sums of ransom money for their release. For years to come, this fearsome experience kept coming back to Father in his dreams. He would wake up from sleep, moaning and shivering, tortured by recurrent nightmares.

Meanwhile, plans were being laid for evacuation of the Voronezh colony. Rail transportation was disrupted and departure dates of trains were very uncertain. It was not advisable for Father to wait too long. He bade farewell to his wife saying, "See you in Vilnius later in the spring," and then he slipped away in disguise. Few details remain of his further adventures as he traveled by train, on foot, or sometimes by horse. In crossing the border into German-occupied Lithuania, his traveling companion was J. Tubelis, the same one who later became a Cabinet minister. For the "Great Escape," Father shaved off the beard and mustache he had always worn in the style of the Russian Czar Nicholas. Tubelis got rid of his toothbrush mustache and grew a beard.

One day German military detachments came to Voronezh and requisitioned rooms in the Yčas apartment building. One officer tried to be kind and considerate. He gave Mamma what he thought was a special treat. He said the crow he had just shot "would be very tasty when roasted." This officer's encouragement was important to Mamma at a turning point in her life, namely in boarding that all-important train. Everybody referred to it as "the Echelon," meaning railroad cars in special formation. Rev. J. Jasenskis, a Roman Catholic priest, led the expedition and always remained a hero in the eyes of Mamma and others.

Rev. Jasenskis collected funds to bribe the engineer who would drive the train and organized people to help in arrangements for the trip. Men, women and children rode in baggage cars when regular seats were not available. They carried household goods and food supplies for a journey that could last for weeks. Mamma and Aunt Aldona got hold of a horse and wagon and were off to the station with baby Martynas, Jr. As Mamma said, it does not always pay to have a famous name. There was an unexpected hitch when she was not allowed to board the train. The leader said to come back another time when there would be a different set of railway officials on duty. She went home in great agitation, fearing she would never make it. The above-mentioned German officer told her not to despair and to try again.

In fear and trembling she returned to the station, hoping that the Echelon had not pulled out without her. This time she got in without difficulty. Like many others, she brought a *samovar* (tea urn) for preparing hot water and said her baby never once missed his daily bath. Cooking was done on kerosene stoves. The trip lasted ten days and many fellow passengers became fast friends by sharing in the daily joys and hardships. The train moved slowly and unforeseen dangers made it stop many times. When in territory controlled by the Reds, the red flags went up on the railroad cars. White flags were displayed in White-controlled areas. Many years later, when safely in the USA, Mamma cried on seeing *Dr. Zhivago*, that remarkable movie of Russian revolutionary times. The scenes of railroad travel, display of flags and all, were exactly what she had seen on the Voronezh Echelon.

Sometimes the train would stop so the passengers could get some fresh air and exercise. One time Mamma almost got left behind. Picking flowers in a beautiful meadow in the woods, she was enjoying herself too much to notice the time. She looked up to see the Echelon moving away. "I almost had heart failure and never ran so fast in my life," Mamma said, "I had just one thought—my baby was on the train." Standing on the rear platform was a man with arms outstretched. This was the educator K. Šakenis. He literally pulled her onto the moving train. The entire trip was unforgettable, but this was one of Mamma's fondest memories. The Echelon reached its destination, and the Yčas couple were reunited. Father had found a beautiful apartment, as Mamma said, much better than the one in Voronezh. Germany was on the brink of defeat, but their troops did not withdraw until months later.

The Great War, as people called it, left a state of confusion. There were disagreements over national boundaries, and maps had to be redrawn. In Vilnius and its eastern borderlands remnants of German and Polish armies, above all Bolshevik troops from Russia, continued to cause trouble for some years. When the dreaded

Bolsheviks occupied Vilnius, there was a mass exodus from the city. Mamma vividly recalled her dismay at having to abandon the spacious apartment with its oriental rugs and oak furniture and the city where they had begun to make a circle of friends. Salvaging a few possessions, Martynas and his wife boarded the train for Berlin and later Paris. Father was a delegate to the Peace Conference with A. Voldemaras, E. Galvanauskas, then Prime Minister, and others. In Berlin there were loans to negotiate for the fledgling State obtained largely through Father's efforts. This was not his first visit to Berlin, a gateway to places such as Sweden and Switzerland. These countries had remained neutral in the war and were convenient places for Lithuanians to hold conferences. Father's talents and diplomatic skills were put to good use in those early years.

Despite difficulties of travel in those days, Father took his family with him whenever possible, also including his mother-in-law, Liudvika Šliupas. Many hours of discomfort were endured in old, dilapidated trains. Supplies of food and water had to be taken along, not to mention soap, towels and toilet paper. It was a weary road to Berlin, then in the throes of economic depression and revolution. The value of currency was so low that Mamma saw wheelbarrows piled high with paper money in the streets, all to purchase a single item like a loaf of bread. As she was out walking one day accompanied by a Lithuanian Army officer, bullets started whistling overhead. The officer shouted, "Get down! Get down!" And there was Mamma lying in the gutter, ever so glad not to have been killed in a revolt organized by the "Spartacus" group.

Father and his colleagues stayed at the Adlon, a renowned hotel in Berlin. Father enjoyed the ambience of fine hotels when traveling abroad. On the occasion of his wedding in New York, he was glad to entertain his guests at the prestigious Waldorf Astoria. Paris and London might have their Crillon and their Ritz, Lausanne might have its Beau Rivage, but you could tell by the way he talked about it that the Adlon was Father's top favorite. Situated near the Brandenburg Gate, it was a place where one could rub shoulders with princes, dignitaries and even kings from the world over. Father said that, despite wartime conditions, the hotel's restaurant managed to continue serving magnificent repasts.

Years later, when I was a teenager on a European trip with Father, we sat in the impressive Adlon lobby, amid the potted palms and the marble fountains. He reminisced about times gone by. I remember some remarks he made with a twinkle in his eye, "Very likely some of the people milling about here are only pretending to be guests at the hotel. They know the value of a good address and sometimes come here to pilfer notepaper embellished with the Adlon crest, to be used later for their own purposes." Sad to say, I never saw the Adlon again. In the 1940s, bombs of World War II destroyed the venerable old building. However, it was recently reopened in the mid-nineties under the famous name of its original owners.

Lithuania had placed great hopes in the Paris Peace Conference held in 1919 by the Great Powers that redefined the map of Europe. The delegates were well supplied with maps, pamphlets and books upholding the Lithuanian cause. These were publications of the information office set up by E. Galvanauskas and especially by J. Gabrys, best described as an eccentric expatriate. On the whole, Father said the Peace Conference was a disappointment. Lithuania, like other small nations, did not get a fair hearing from President Woodrow Wilson and other world leaders.

The Yčas couple lived in a Paris suburb called St. Cloud. The parks were abloom with chestnut blossoms. Mamma enjoyed taking her baby son there for outings. At the time he was just beginning to walk. She remembered that this was where he took his first steps. Soon it was time to move on as there were important conferences in Switzerland with leaders and diplomats to discuss the future course for Lithuania. Father and his family settled in Lausanne, on the shores of Lake Geneva, expecting to stay for several months, and it was there that the writer of these reminiscences was born.

Part I

Kaunas in the 1920s

Horse-drawn Tram on Laisvės Alėja

Chapter One
Kaunas Becomes the Provisional Capital

The first permanent home for the young Yčas family was in Kaunas, which had recently become the de facto capital of Lithuania. The years 1920–1940 spent there must have made it seem like a peaceful haven after the exciting events of earlier days. The family included my brother Martynas Jr., two years older than I, and Grandmother Šliupas who also came from Switzerland with us. I was about six months old when we arrived from my birthplace in Lausanne. This makes me a product of the early 1920s and about as early as you can get. January 6, my birthday, is also the Feast Day of the Three Kings (The Wise Men of the Bible) who bring gifts according to the folk beliefs of some countries. Mamma liked to say that the Three Kings brought her a wonderful present on that day.

Certainly, I do not have personal memories of what life in Kaunas was like in those first few years and must rely on the reminiscences of family members and others. Mamma in particular, who was never at a loss for words, had much to draw upon. She was deeply sentimental about the past. Some of what she remembered was very touching, but she also had a sense of humor and liked to make you laugh. Mamma lived well into her nineties and had a vast store of memories. Besides her European experiences, there were five decades in the USA, land of her birth, where she returned to spend the second half of her life. It is remarkable that she remembered the Lithuanian years with such clarity of vision. Even more remarkable is that her children managed to write something down while there was still time. As for Father, he was long gone before I thought of writing this work. He left this world quite early, in his mid-fifties, but some of the stories he liked to tell, many of them with a humorous twist, are firmly imbedded in my memory. I have no trouble in bringing them to life even though I wrote down very little at the time. Father left

1

important writings, but few of them are about Lithuania in these formative years.

The term Provisional Capital is used here to describe Kaunas. The true capital was, and continues to be Vilnius, as it has been through the ages. This is where the Declaration of Independence was issued on February 16, 1918. Father was not yet in Vilnius when the Lithuanian National Council published this document. While some leaders were in Russia taking care of national interests, others had remained in the German-occupied homeland to set the nation on the road to freedom. Achievement of full independence took time. The government was established soon after Germany's defeat in November 1918, but remnants of its army remained in the country for some months afterward. Lithuania's first government was headed by A. Smetona as President and A. Voldemaras serving as Prime Minister. In the first three cabinets, Father was the Minister of Finance and Communications.

It was a time of turmoil. Armies of foreign powers and roving bands of bandits were ravaging the country. A volunteer army for self defense had to be raised. Here is a quotation, in free translation, from the Call to Arms issued by the government in early 1919: "As the German forces retreat, the Russian Bolsheviks are advancing, making our rivers run with blood and tears...Today, our fate is in our own hands...Let us show the world that we are worthy of the freedom for which our nation has strived for so long." Lithuanians had to fight for their independence in wars lasting well into 1920 when peace treaties were signed with neighboring countries.

Throughout history, Vilnius had been the capital of the Lithuanian Kingdom up to the time it joined Poland in a Dual Commonwealth. This happened in the year 1569 and was not unlike the joint Kingdom of Austria-Hungary of a later day. Keeping national identity intact was difficult because of the great discrepancy in the size of the two and especially their cultural differences. It was not long before the larger partner established hegemony over the lesser, making it socially desirable for people to speak the Polish language and to imbibe Polish culture. With the dawn of new freedom after World War I, most Lithuanians considered the former union with Poland an unfortunate aberration and tried hard to get out from under that all-pervasive influence.

Not surprisingly, Vilnius had cultural ties with Poland. Lithuanians said that to the Poles it was just one more provincial city and could not be very meaningful, but the Poles thought otherwise. Several armies tried to get control of Vilnius after World War I. Lithuanian troops tried to defend the city but could not hold it for very long. Vilnius changed hands so many times that this tangled web of events is best left to the historians.

It was clear that the government should move elsewhere, and there was no alternative but Kaunas. How the transfer took place is related in memoirs of some of the participants. Germany was already defeated. In January 1919, the German occupants were getting ready to evacuate Vilnius, loading weapons and equipment into railroad cars at the station. It was in one of these freight cars that members of the Lithuanian government hitched a ride. About a dozen of them traveled for many hours, sitting on their suitcases in a slow freight train that made many stops. They left the Lithuanian flag flying on the tower of the castle of Gediminas where it had been hoisted when the German emblem was taken down.

Many of the Cabinet members were not with the group. The President, the Prime Minister, the Minister of Foreign affairs and the Minister of Finance were absent. They were either in Paris or Berlin for important diplomatic negotiations. Thus, the group had to make independent decisions, issuing orders on behalf of the government. They arrived in Kaunas sleepless and exhausted. Fortunately, they found rooms at the Hotel Metropolis, albeit not adequately furnished. There were seven vacant rooms and much joking about assignment of beds. The lone lady, a secretary traveling with all these men, was given a single room. Three men were left with a room that had only one bed, a sofa and a long table.

M. Šleževičius, acting vice-president and leader of the expedition, jokingly related that he made a great sacrifice and chose to sleep on the long table. Fortunately, apartments were soon found for them and for other government workers. By April 1919, adequate premises for offices were found, public employees were hired and the government was supposedly in working shape.

Some people may have been expecting an early return to Vilnius, but conditions there remained unsafe because of the Russian Bolshevik invasion. It was not to be under Lithuanian rule for years to come. On the eve of signing a Peace Agreement in October 1920, leaving Vilnius to Lithuania, Polish troops had already seized and occupied the city and its region. Supposedly, the deed was done by rebels without the knowledge of the Polish High Command. However, it is likely that Marshal J. Pilsudski himself, the "Strong Man of Poland," was behind the scheme.

From this time on, Lithuania closed its borders and severed relations with Poland. Lithuania referred the case to international tribunals and to the League of Nations, but it was never truly resolved. The Polish-Lithuanian quarrel became so tiresome that finally the Conference of Ambassadors decided to keep the status quo, i.e., to leave Vilnius in Polish hands. Marshall Pilsudski, who lived for some years in Vilnius, wanted to show the world how truly Polish it was. He left instructions in his will that his heart be buried in a Vilnius cemetery, whereas his body was given a hero's burial in Cracow. Years later, as I stood by the monument marking the burial place of his heart, I thought about this unusual request. It was said that Marshal Pilsudski remained angry over Lithuania's so-called anti-Polish attitude to the end of his life, and this could have been his way of getting his revenge.

All this, however, is quite another story. The important fact here is that members of the brand-new Lithuanian government were forced to withdraw from Vilnius. For want of a better choice, Kaunas became the provisional capital. Interestingly enough, though called "provisional" in English, the word used to describe it in Lithuanian always was *Laikinoji Sostinė* (temporary capital*)*, signifying that dreams of the return of Vilnius would never actually fade.

So strong were public feelings about the loss of Vilnius, that a song by the writer P. Vaičiūnas *"Ei Pasauli...Mes Be Vilniaus Nenurimsim"* (Listen, World...We Cannot Rest Without Vilnius) became one of the most popular of the day. The song was a favorite at public gatherings right up through my high school years. In 1991, these words came true. Vilnius is once again the capital of a free and independent Lithuania.

Today, in the 1990s, Kaunas has grown so much that it is hardly recognizable to those who knew it long ago. To go away and then come back again makes one aware of changes. For Father, the changes he saw in the 1920s must have seemed like great improvements. He lived there as a young law school graduate before World War I. He said that the buildings in Kaunas were unimpressive, but the natural setting was unusually lovely. A popular saying of the time was "Kaunas is like a bad painting set in a beautiful frame." One never got tired of exploring the wooded hills and vales. One of these valleys was associated with the great 19th century poet Adomas Mickevičius (Adam Mickiewicz) who wrote on Lithuanian themes in the Polish language. According to legend, he composed some of his most notable poetry while sitting on a rock in this "unspoiled corner of Paradise." It was known forever after as *Mickevičiaus Slėnis* (Vale of Mickevičius). The poet was in Kaunas for several years, and one could still see the modest house where he had lived. At the confluence of two mighty rivers, the Nemunas and the Neris, was Old Town with a crumbling 13th century castle and vestiges of the important port that had once been there. A splendid stand of oak trees covering several acres called *Ąžuolynas* (Oak Park) overlooked the town from a hill and is still in existence today.

Father was returning to a town he knew quite well since he had lived there in years past, but Mamma had never been there

5

before. It was a shock for her to see wooden sidewalks amid the mud of *Laisvės Alėja* (Freedom Avenue) the most important street of a town that was supposed to be the capital of the country. She had been raised in well-kept small towns in Pennsylvania. Her later travels had taken her to New York, London and Paris, all so vastly different from what she was seeing now. True, she had seen deplorable conditions in Russia, and she spoke with disgust about the masses of bedbugs, lice and cockroaches she had seen there. She was inclined to be very critical but had to admit that Kaunas was a lot cleaner and had far fewer pests. Adjustment to these new circumstances was not easy for Mamma. She did not have Father's happy-go-lucky temperament that enabled him to take everything in his stride.

When Father was less than five years old, our paternal grandfather, also named Martynas, left for America to seek his fortune. Father learned to be self-reliant and to make his own way in the world. Furthermore, he believed that one could conquer the greatest difficulties with a smile rather than an angry word. He liked to be with people who were enjoying themselves. He was always welcome since he had a great sense of the ridiculous and an endless store of anecdotes and funny stories. The phrase "positive thinker" had not yet been invented, but this would describe him well.

It is not easy to describe one's parents with a proper degree of objectivity. In the words of an eminent psychologist, we begin by loving our father and mother. Later, we judge them, and sometimes we forgive them. At this late date, I have nothing to forgive. They were products of their times and their own family upbringing, as we all are. They were the best parents they knew how to be. Better than this, they were people of sterling character and high moral principles. Their loyalty, honesty and courage are qualities to be admired. What is needed today is not to adopt a judgmental attitude but to try to understand them better.

Mamma spoke both Lithuanian and English fluently and believed that no one should forget the language of their parents. As the youngest in the family, she was used to being petted and spoiled, especially by her father. Unlike her brother and sister, she was not inclined to scholarly pursuits. She majored in Liberal Arts at Cornell University but never finished, something she always regretted. One semester before graduation, my father, a rising young statesman, came on the scene. Father was in haste to return to his parliamentary duties in St. Petersburg, Russia. He assured his bride that she could always graduate from college later on, but this never came to pass.

Married life started with unexpected adventures. Russia was about to explode into the Great Revolution. The young couple had to flee several times, leaving their possessions behind. Mother was indulged by her husband almost as much as she had been by her parents. She had great courage and, when left without him, she knew how to proceed alone.

In a comparatively short time Kaunas got a new face, and even critics like Mamma had to agree that it became a capital worthy of the name. Much of the credit for modernization is due to J. Vileišis, longtime mayor of the town, especially in installing an efficient water and power system. Before that, in the poorer areas, there were people employed as water carriers. One of my childhood playmates remembers a little old man with a wooden bar across his shoulders. On this he balanced two buckets of water, taking them to homes that had none. Most of the larger homes and apartment houses generally got their water from a well on the property, brought indoors either by hand, or piped in, if you were lucky enough to have an electric pump.

Great strides were made in transforming Kaunas into the center of the country's cultural, political and social life. Of course, it could never equal Vilnius. People tried not to make comparisons, but to make the most of obvious advantages. Unlike Vilnius, Kaunas occupied the geographical center of the country and was not somewhere far out to the East. Although distances in mileage between the two were not that great, some people never had a chance to see Vilnius and its wonders. Many spoke of going there, but kept putting off the trip until it was too late.

Chapter Two
Settling Down

The Šliupas grandparents, especially Grandma, were an important part of the family. The children had never known their Yčas grandparents, who had both died young. Grandma Šliupas actively participated in settling into the spacious apartment at No. 15 *Laisvės Alėja*. Like many older houses of the time, this was built around a large courtyard with ample room for a garden. On the first floor, several stores faced the street. Steep stairs went up to the apartment on the second floor.

Grandma Šliupas had never seen Vilnius and was eager to go there. She refused to believe the rumors of danger, since she had made many perilous journeys of much greater distances, even crossing the Atlantic Ocean several times. Having made arrangements with a friend named Mikas Petrauskas to accompany her, she calmly packed her suitcase with gifts for her sisters who were living there. They were preparing to go to the railroad station when the news came that trains were no longer running. This was October 1920. Vilnius had fallen and the borders were closed. Grandma died some years later, never realizing her dream of seeing that fabulous city.

In the days of national renewal after World War I, much needed to be done throughout the land to rebuild, refurbish and reorganize. The whole country, Kaunas in particular, was recovering from the ruins left by German-Russian combat in the recent war. In the Provisional Capital there was excitement in the air. Not so long ago, it had been an out-of-the-way garrison town, a military outpost. And now, it had to be given the semblance of an important metropolis. In clearing out the rubble and making all things new, many imposing buildings arose, parks were landscaped, and streets were widened and paved. This was a period of remarkable vitality and enthusiasm.

Father liked to relate his personal experiences in organizing the country's finances. The coffers were empty for a long time because the newborn state had no money. Many government employees were willing to work for free, sometimes going without their paychecks for as long as six months. Public enthusiasm was such that there were few complaints. People felt they were making an important contribution and tried to keep up a cheerful front. Progress was difficult without those hard-to-obtain international loans, and it took some time to establish a stable currency. Meanwhile, people managed to surmount the hardships and hoped for better times.

One of the treasures in my personal library is entitled *Pirmasis Lietuvos Dešimtmetis, 1928* (Lithuania's First Decade) Among the essays in this book by various statesmen is one by Father on the newborn country's financial travails. It is a very slim volume and many questions remain unanswered. This was a creative period of learning about how to run the country. Surprisingly ingenious methods were devised and one would like to know more. In many instances, experience was lacking. The people trained in the schools of Voronezh or elsewhere, as mentioned in the Prologue, most certainly filled a gap in the ranks of public employees. Military officers, who formed the core of the Lithuanian Army, as well as other professionals, had received their training mainly in schools of Czarist Russia.

At that time, Kaunas was a town of moderate size of less than 100,000 in population (the entire country had barely three million inhabitants). Vilnius, so much larger, was the only true city in the international sense. Kaunas could not begin to compare with that multi-cultural and multinational metropolis with long historical traditions. Kaunas was a provincial and rather dilapidated town in those days. Among the nationalities in the town were a number of Jews, Poles, Russians and Germans, some of whom had trouble learning the prevailing language. Some shopkeepers had signs in their own languages above their stores. Patriotic campaigns to substitute signs in Lithuanian were conducted by the authorities. However, minorities were all free to have their own schools and churches. Kaunas had a Russian, a Polish, a Jewish and a German high school, called Gimnazija. Jews were numerous in newly independent Lithuania and were of importance to economic life because of their business acumen. For a time, the Lithuanian Cabinet included a Ministry for Jewish Affairs.

One of my early memories is of a Jewish bakery that refused to close on the Sabbath (nobody seemed to make bread taste so good as the Jewish bake shops). One evening, while out for a walk with my nurse, we stopped to see what a loud argument was about. A uniformed policeman was shouting, "I am telling you to close your store. Don't you know it's the Sabbath? It's the law!" And the baker unwillingly shut his doors. So powerful were the Orthodox rabbis that they could enlist the help of the legal authorities. The venerable long-bearded rabbis kept tight control.

Russians constituted a fairly large minority. They were either longtime residents or new arrivals who settled here as refugees from the Great Revolution of 1917. Memories of the unspeakable butchery and savagery of the Bolshevik regime were still fresh in Lithuanian minds. Someone close to them, or someone they had heard about, had been subjected to these horrors. The wholesale slaughter of the Russian Czar and his family at Ekaterinburg was still a recent memory. This tale of needless cruelty was frequently told in my childhood and never failed to arouse feelings of consternation and dread. My parents had been in Russia at the time and felt the tragedy keenly. The Soviet Union was a threat and the very thought of Communism caused revulsion or outright fear. Those who knew about international politics thought that a *Cordon Sanitaire* (French term meaning sanitary barrier) between us and them might be a good idea.

Father came to the provisional capital as a member of the Council of Ministers. In the days of his distinguished position, he was frequently away from home. My earliest memories include parties and social gatherings. On the days when Father was home and not socializing with great numbers of people, one could find him

11

at his desk, reading, writing and positively swimming in a sea of papers. He liked to write articles for the press and was trying to complete a book.

Father had a facility for expressing himself with equal ease either verbally or in writing. Public speaking and journalism were his chosen avocations. With law as his field of specialization, he was well on his way to a career in public life. In his Russian Duma days, this young man, not yet thirty years old and an outsider as far as nationality was concerned, was outstanding enough to be selected as a member of the parliamentary delegation touring Western Europe. This group was received by national leaders and heads of state of Sweden, Great Britain, Belgium, Italy, and other countries. All this and much more are related in Father's *Atsiminimai* (memoirs), published in Kaunas in three volumes in 1935 and, unfortunately, never completed. So far, they have not been translated into English. Father's memoirs were reprinted in their original language in Chicago, Illinois, in 1990. Subtitled *Nepriklausomybės Keliais* (On the Road to Independence), they are important to scholars of the history of those times.

While in Kaunas, the Yčas family increased. In 1923, twin daughters Evelyna and Violetta were born. Although the Red Cross Hospital was not far from our home, the family doctor, Aldona Šliupas, Mamma's sister, decided that the birth should take place at home. Her specialty was gynecology and the training of medical personnel, including midwives, much in vogue at the time. Home delivery of babies was not unusual, often without the supervision of a physician. Hospital care for routine or ordinary cases of childbirth was not considered essential. The twins, born in June on the day of St. Peter and St. Paul, might have been named Petra and Paulina, according to local custom, had not the other and more romantic names been chosen.

Father was not at home at the time of my sisters' birth, having gone to Biržai in the North Country. Nearly every midsummer he would attend the annual Synod of the Lithuanian

Reformed Church, an institution he loved and supported throughout his life. He visited Biržai whenever he could as he had been born in a small country village nearby. He was overjoyed at the news that he had become the father of twins, calling for champagne for everybody present. This was something hard to find in that small town. The traditional Biržai drink was, and still is, a particularly intoxicating beer home brewed by the country folk. However, somehow, he found some champagne. There are a few people living today who still remember the festive party held in honor of the twins.

Despite his busy schedule, Father found time to be with his children. He liked to carry the twins around and sing them to sleep. I have a clear recollection of him on a night with moonlight streaming through the window, singing an F. Schubert lullaby with words in Lithuanian *"Tylu, Ramu, Mėneselis Šviečia..."* ("In Silence and in Peace, the Moon is Shining..."). Since I was very young when my sisters were born, I cannot say whether I truly remember their birth or not. There is a picture in my mind's eye of two big dolls lying in a wing-back chair. But it may be just a photo, preserved in old family albums that I remember. Their arrival caused a great stir, and a special nurse came to look after them. This was Liuda, a red-cheeked young girl from Palanga by the sea.

Mamma loved all her children but was inordinately proud of having given birth to twins. Relating memories of those days, she told of her joy in taking the twins for a ride on the Avenue in their high-wheeled perambulator. She did not allow anyone to do this but herself—no grandmas, aunties or nannies. Naturally, people she met, perfect strangers as well as friends, would stop to speak to the proud mother.

One day she had an unexpected and not altogether pleasant encounter. It was a fine sunny day as she set out on her customarily triumphant journey under the linden trees (a walkway for pedestrians in the middle of the street). A certain busybody rushed up and told her that such behavior on the Avenue was not allowed. Mamma was startled, but was resolved to stand her ground. She calmly stated that she had a perfect right to continue pushing her perambulator if she so desired. The other woman lost her temper and started shouting. Soon a policeman came by and asked what the trouble was. Two well-dressed and cultured ladies having a squabble right on the Avenue was unheard of.

By the time the policeman came up, Mamma was no longer calm. One loud angry voice kept saying, "Go home! I forbid you to push that perambulator!" The other kept repeating, "And who are you to order me around?" Mamma was not about to take orders from this woman, Mrs. Celina Mošinskis, who set herself up as the social arbiter in town. Madame Celina, as she was known, was feared by some and hated by others, because of her acid tongue and her know-it-all attitude. She was an avid card player, a pastime for which Mamma had no use whatsoever. Besides, Mme. Celina did not hesitate to broadcast her opinions about foreigners to all who would listen. Here was Mamma, an American, and worse yet, she was insisting on her rights. The policeman was highly amused when he realized what the "incident" was about. He told both ladies to go on about their business, a solution which suited Mamma very well.

This was only one of such interesting happenings on Main Street. There were still no real sidewalks, and pedestrians had to thread their way through the mud stepping carefully on loose wooden boards. One other time, when Mamma was out walking, she saw a well-dressed gentleman, complete with hat, walking stick and leather briefcase, laid low by a billy goat trotting along behind him. Suddenly the goat changed his pace. Running at a full gallop, he lowered his horns and struck from behind. Imagine the gentleman's consternation when he lost his balance and how muddy (and angry) he was when he got up! I must add here that I have no memory of mud and wooden boards on the Avenue. Proper sidewalks and concrete paving, as Mamma said, were one of the first improvements to be made in Kaunas. As early as I can remember, the Avenue was no different from streets to be seen elsewhere.

However, the walkway of linden trees in the middle is still in existence today (in the 1990s) and is a distinctive feature which few cities possess.

Chapter Three
On the Avenue

*L*aisvės *Alėja* or Freedom Avenue was the principal thoroughfare of the town and the center for all great happenings of the time. It was the local equivalent of New York's Fifth Avenue. What occurred on a side street never seemed to be as important as what was happening on the Avenue. Many houses, including ours, had balconies with railings of black ironwork. We children, together with Grandma, often stood on the balcony to see the sights. There were hardly any buses or motor cars on the street. For transportation you used your own two legs, or you could choose a horse-drawn conveyance drawn by one or two horses (never by three, as the Russian-style three-horse *Troika* was never popular in Lithuania). If in a real hurry, you could get a *Droshky*, a one-horse carriage with a hood, which served as a taxi. There was also a tram of sorts running up and down the Avenue, drawn by a slow-trotting horse, for people who had plenty of time. To us the *Konkė* (a popular name of Russian origin for the horse-drawn tram) seemed so fascinating that we were determined to ride it one day. We had to wait a long time, however, before we realized our desire.

Some of the sights seen from our balcony were parades and special ceremonies. We would hear military music as soldiers marched or rode by on horseback. I was impressed to see Antanas Smetona, President of the Republic, going by in an open carriage, followed by an honor guard of red-trousered Hussars mounted on prancing horses.

There were religious services at the huge St. Michael's church that was close to our home. It was called the Sobor but now had another, non-Russian, name. Although still called by most people by its old name, it had been re-christened to the Lithuanian *Įgulos Bažnyčia* (garrison church). An imposing structure, quite the largest in town, it was the scene of public gatherings, especially on national holidays.

This had been a Russian Orthodox church built in Czarist times to serve the religious needs of the troops. Though it looked ancient to us, it actually dated back only to the mid-19th century. In our time, the author of a book on old Kaunas days wrote about his great grandfather's recollections of a swamp on the edge of town where the Sobor now stood. Hunters used to shoot wild duck there not so long ago. The church, built in the typical Russian style of many domes was considered an architectural ornament by some, but to others it was an abomination and a reminder of times of oppression. After all, this was not Kovno any more, as the Russians had called it, but Kaunas, the ancient name of a town founded by Lithuanians centuries ago. There was talk of sweeping out every single Russian word and expression that had crept into the language and of tearing this building down as well. However, common sense prevailed and such projects were given up. Besides, wrecking the Sobor would have been more trouble than it was worth.

The Sobor underwent conversion several times, an outstanding example of what can happen due to the prevailing winds of change. Lithuanians transformed it into a Roman Catholic church to serve the needs of the army. When Russian rule came again in the 1940s, Communist fanatics converted it into a museum. After Lithuania regained its independence in 1990, it again became a Roman Catholic church. During five decades of Communist Russian rule, churches were desecrated and monuments to national heroes destroyed. In their turn, Lithuanians too destroyed Russian reminders of the past when they had the chance. The Sobor, however, evaded such a fate and still stands as a landmark in Kaunas today.

Our nurse, Elena Nikitishna, was a Russian refugee from the town of Pskov. Her experiences during the Great Revolution had been so terrifying that she never spoke of them. We later found out that most of her family had been killed. Perhaps this was why she did not wish to be known by her true last name, Timofeyeva. Elena preferred to be known by her Russian patronymic, Nikitishna, i.e., the daughter of Nikita. Elena seemed happy to have found peace and quiet in her position with us. She was interested in what was going on in the world and often tried to take us children on some excursion or other. Such events, however, were rare as our Mamma liked to keep us close to home.

Elena had some special projects in mind. She was determined to take us for a ride on the horse-drawn tram, an experience, she said, we would never forget. This vehicle, a relic of former days, was not likely to last much longer. Many people thought it was a disgrace and were clamoring to have it removed. They said it delayed progress and, besides, it was reminiscent of old Russian days. Somehow Mamma was persuaded to let us go on this dangerous ride. So off we went in great excitement, looking into unfamiliar store windows, past the Theater Gardens, and the Post Office, enjoying the sights from one end of Main Street to the other.

Later, I learned that horse-drawn trams were used in the USA until the turn of the century. After many years and thousands of miles away, I rode in one that was almost an exact replica of the *Konkė* (the one at California's Disneyland, however, was not nearly as much fun). The days of the *Konkė*, this ancient relic, were numbered, and it had to go. When Kaunas authorities delayed in removing it, it was forcibly overturned by an enthusiastic band of university students amid cheers and applause.

The town mayor and other dignitaries attended the grand farewell ceremony. The mayor's wife was presented with a bouquet of flowers. This was an occasion for public celebrations with much partying and general merriment. Our personal excursion took place just shortly before this happened so our ride had historic importance in more ways than one. Father had many business interests. Surprisingly enough, he was a part owner of the *Konkė* enterprise. His partner was V. Frenkelis, a jovial Jewish man and a longtime friend of the family. How the two partners felt when this antiquated conveyance collapsed is not recorded. However, since both of them

19

had a keen sense of humor, there surely must have been a certain amount of laughter.

Horses serving our family's transportation needs were kept in stables at some distance from Main Street. Those who could afford it kept horses and carriages as well as a staff of domestics. Having servants was not at all unusual, even among people of less than average income. There were plenty of country girls who considered it a privilege to have a job in town, no matter how low the salary. The *Konkė* stables had the usual horse smells mixed with the overpowering odor of a billy goat, at least as obnoxious as the aroma of a skunk. For some reason (perhaps for good luck), horses were assumed to need this smelly type of companionship.

Our coachman was named Valiukas. He lived in a small apartment near his beloved horses. He had a white beard and whiskers much like Santa Claus and wore a green velveteen uniform with silver buttons. His visor cap gave him a military appearance. When transportation was needed (a carriage at most times and a sleigh in winter), one of our maids would run over to tell Valiukas that it was time to harness the horses. Calling by phone was not feasible as telephones were scarce, though we did have one. It was number 17, one of the earlier phones in town. There were real live operators in those days, making it possible for humorously-inclined persons to play practical jokes. How many hours Valiukas spent just sitting and waiting until he was needed, and what he did in his spare time, who can tell? He loved his horses and spoke of them more than he did of his wife, family, or anything else. Everyone called him "Valiukas." He must have had a first name, but I never heard it.

Many pleasant childhood memories are associated with Valiukas, especially the sleigh rides in winter. If my memory is not playing tricks on me, winters at that time were colder and lasted much longer than today. The Nemunas River would freeze and remain solid well into the spring. Melting ice often resulted in flooding in the streets, particularly in the low-lying Old Town area.

Barriers of bluish ice blocks, sparkling like crystal, would pile up on the river. Sometimes, dynamite had to be used to explode the ice. It seemed winter would never end. For months, there was the sound of sleigh bells in the streets heard above the gentle swish-swoosh made by sleigh runners coasting over hard-packed snow.

There were many trips in the sleigh with coachman Valiukas at the reins, going here and there to visit friends or on pleasure rides outside town into the woods. Everyone bundled up in their warmest overcoats, caps and gloves. We covered our knees with a bearskin rug—the long hair inside, green velveteen on the outside. There was also a bearskin coat known by its Russian name Shuba, always taken along in case somebody felt particularly cold. Leg coverings of felt, worn with galoshes, protected our feet. These were particularly effective if one put newspapers inside. There were tried-and-true remedies like goose grease in case of a frostbitten nose. Frostbite was no laughing matter as it could have serious consequences. Some people we knew took their hot water bottles, the kind made of rubber, wrapped in flannel bags of many layers. Many ladies had fur muffs to protect their hands.

One elderly lady, Mrs. Volfas of the well-known Volfas-Engelmanas beer brewing family, had novel ways of keeping warm. She said with great delight, "I always take a live chicken with me. Putting my hands under the wings of the chicken is better than any muff!" This spirited Jewish mother was not like other women. She had five grown sons, some of whom were grey-haired and had children of their own. Mrs. Volfas ruled her household with a rod of iron. Her sons listened to her advice with great respect. If they did not do what she told them, she wanted to know the reason why.

Valiukas had served as coachman to several famous folk including the last Russian governor of Kaunas *Guberniya* (province) in Czarist times. In fact, our family inherited the coachman from Governor P. Veriovkin. Valiukas liked to remember those days and still wore the same green uniform with pride. Governor Veriovkin seemed to have been a benign gentleman who had many Lithuanian friends, including Father. On losing his post when the Russian Revolution came, the Governor chose to live at his estate near town on the banks of one of the two rivers. There he lived contented with his lot until the 1940s. In a sense, his presence was still felt in Kaunas because his gubernatorial residence had been converted into Lithuania's White House (Palace of the President of the Republic).

Sad to relate, when the end came for the coachman Valiukas, it was not as happy an exit from this life as it had been for his employer, the former Governor. Valiukas loved his horses to distraction. There were two horses, a mismatched pair of varying color, held in high regard by Father who on occasion enjoyed riding one or the other. One was a black horse named Smigly; the other named Orlikas was a light golden, maybe Palomino, color. It happened that Orlikas became terminally ill because someone had fed him too many oats when he was overheated. Veterinarians said there was no hope for recovery and the animal would have to be destroyed. Valiukas took the death of Orlikas so hard that his mind became unhinged and he could no longer serve as coachman. He disappeared into retirement at a rest home and never come back. He had not recovered from mental illness when he died shortly after he lost his favorite horse.

Though the rest of the world might think that man's best friend is his dog, Lithuanians held such attachment for horses that their best friend might be the horse. Folk memory retained songs and legends aplenty about the swift and noble steed. Motorized transportation or any kind of farm machinery was very scarce. Most people got around by using horse power. In a horse-oriented society such as ours, the tragic story of Valiukas and his love for his horse was quite understandable.

Chapter Four
From the Old House to the New

Everybody called our home at No. 15 on the Avenue the Donskis House after the name of its owner. The garden in the courtyard had apple trees, vegetables and flowers. As in most such houses, there was a caretaker or porter in charge of the sweeping, cleaning and other maintenance tasks. One of our earliest playmates was Pauliukas (Little Paul) Rutkauskas, the caretaker's son, who was the same age as my brother. There was plenty of room for playing hide-and-seek among the currant and gooseberry bushes. Since I was younger, I was frequently left out of their games. One day there was a terrible sight in the gardening shed, talked about for days. Hanging from the rafters was a hairy animal's hide with a huge head and curled-up tusks. What could it be? The grownups explained that this was a boar, rather like a large wild pig that Father had shot out in the woods. Father was no great hunter, but very occasionally he would bring home a long-eared hare (wild rabbit, European variety). This was everybody's favorite especially if served with oven-roasted potatoes and grated beets, prepared with plenty of sour cream. Roast hare was in a class with goose or duck, all considered delicacies very suitable for guests. Savory dishes could be prepared with beef but, on the whole, people preferred pork in the form of pork chops, ham, sausage, or bacon. There was no talk of calorie-counting or cholesterol then. Enjoying good food constituted one of the pleasures of life, most Lithuanians being big eaters.

There were always people at our house, but I was not of an age to remember many of the guests. One already mentioned was just a name to me. Mikas Petrauskas, musician and composer, sometimes came to see Grandma. They had become friends long ago while living in America. Chiefly remembered today as a brilliant choir leader and early popularizer of folk music, Mikas Petrauskas was the brother of Kipras, star singer of the Lithuanian Opera. In imitation of his famous brother, Mikas tried for years to be an operatic singer. Unfortunately he had a weak voice, a great disappointment to him.

Another guest at No. 15, not even dimly remembered, was certainly noteworthy if only because Mamma spoke of him with great amusement. This was a music conservatory student making his home with us at the request of his parents. They were members of our Evangelical Reformed Church and lived in Biržai in the North. His mother said he would not be a bit of trouble, but she was wrong. Vladas Jakubėnas (who later became a famous composer and music critic) loved bread and butter. He had a ravenous appetite, and there never seemed to be enough bread in the house to satisfy him. He had all sorts of amorous adventures, sometimes with married women. One time while he was conducting a secret romance with the wife of a military officer, the outraged husband came to the house, brandishing a pistol and threatening to shoot the lover dead. At this point, according to Mamma, young Vladas was politely asked to find a room elsewhere.

Images of family members like Grandma and Aunt Aldona, warming themselves by the high tile stove in the living room, stand out in my memory. These stoves of shiny pure white tiles, fueled by wood, reached from floor to ceiling. This was the standard way of heating a house. One opened the little black iron door to reveal the grate within. What possessed me to place my hand on the red-hot grate I cannot tell, but this happened to me exactly once and certainly never again. After all these years, there are still traces of the scar on my left hand to remind me of the time when my screams of pain were loud enough to alarm the whole neighborhood.

When I was five, we moved to a new residence as Father had bought a house at No. 4 on the same street. The great job of packing began weeks, maybe months, before we actually moved. Mamma did not want to leave any of her favorite possessions. She still had vivid memories of losing the contents of her home several times in a few short years of married life. The first time she had to abandon her possessions was in Voronezh, southwestern Russia during the Great Revolution. The second time was in Vilnius escaping from the Bolsheviks. Mamma, so very sentimental about her things, took her wedding dress with her while abandoning many valuables, like jewelry, which would have been more useful. When moving to our new house, she made sure that nothing of value was left behind. Nobody could have foretold that years later, yet another Russian invasion would leave her homeless again. When safely in the USA in the 1940s, Mother said she hoped never to have another such experience for the fourth time.

Though it seemed like half a world away, we actually did not move very far. The distance from No. 15 to No. 4 was not that great even for children walking all the way. The Avenue went on for a few long blocks and ended at the entrance to Vytautas Park. You only had to circle the Sobor and go past the Red Cross Hospital, an imposing building painted white. One wide street to cross, and there was No. 4, only a few houses away. Going past the hospital, whether walking or driving, meant being reminded of relatives on Mamma's side of the family who worked there. These were great-Uncle Rokas and Aunt Aldona, both physicians named Šliupas, together with some other relatives.

My first recollection of the new house was that it seemed like a really vast building with many people running around. They were firemen trying to pump out the water from the flooded basement. I have no idea whether any of the periodic spring floods caused by the ice blocking the river were to blame as I do not know what time of year it was. It was no use asking Mamma as she could remember little about our move. When asked about it years later, the question released a flood of memories about Moving Day in her own childhood days in Philadelphia, Pennsylvania, and that was all she wanted to talk about.

I still remember the firemen with their hoses and their red machines, so they must have made a big impression. My uncle, Prof. Keistutis Šliupas, was in command of the operation. The firemen did exactly as he told them. This was the first time I had

25

seen Uncle K in such a position of power. Everybody complimented him on doing an efficient job of getting the water out. I had the greatest admiration for Uncle K partly because he was seldom too busy to find time for us children and he seemed to enjoy our company in a way that his sister, our Aunt Aldona, never did. He had a great sense of fun and enjoyed jokes. Later, when he was asked why he was chosen as "Director of the Firemen," he replied, "I am supposed to know all about water problems. Am I not a professor of physics?"

There was much more room in the new house than in the old one. Everybody got used to having more space, adjusting without difficulty to the spacious and comfortable quarters. The bedrooms were upstairs on the second floor. On the first floor were the dining room, a living room large enough for a ballroom, and other reception rooms. It seemed to have been a good move for everyone except for our two cats who missed their old home. Elena Nikitishna dearly loved her coal-black Pintzus with the yellow eyes. Housekeeper Petrusia's very special pet was Rotzelis, also black but with white paws, white shirtfront and the most delightful long white whiskers. The two cats kept running back to No. 15.

Elena and Petrusia were the only two domestics who moved with us. A cook who came later was a new person in the household. Petrusia Grauslytė came to us as a maid-of-all-work from Palanga and stayed on for years. She was so helpful and trustworthy that she was soon promoted to housekeeper. Petrusia, though not formally educated, had natural intelligence and genuine organizational skills. She was much loved by the family, indeed she was considered "one of us." She had a way with children. We had more affection for her than we did for Elena who was far less lovable. In a sense, owing to differences in language and customs, Elena remained outside our family circle.

There were times when I would walk with either Elena or Petrusia back to our old home in search of the missing cats. Luckily, they were always to be found and were carried back, meowing pitifully all the way. They would be petted and fed their favorite foods in their new abode. Hopefully, they would make up their minds to stay. Rotzelis of the long white whiskers was the one who got used to his new home first, but Pintzus continued to run away. Eventually, Elena found a solution. Someone told her that if you spread butter on a cat's paws, he would never run away again. This turned out to be true. Licking his buttered paws at No. 4, Pintzus forgot all about his old home.

Among the many features of the new house that I found remarkable was the second-floor balcony, running practically the full length of the building. This balcony of wrought ironwork opened into our parents' bedroom. It was so solidly constructed that it was still standing, though slightly battered, when I went back to see the old home place in the 1990s. Also remarkable to me was that the house had not one, but two front doors. The one on the right was for everyday use. The front door on the left side of the house was for special occasions only. Visitors entered through the hall and were ushered into the reception room, which everybody called *salionas* (from the French word *Salon*). Across the hall was Father's private room where he retreated to do his reading and writing. The hall had a winding staircase leading up to a guest room with an odd-shaped and medieval looking window.

In front of the house was a small park lined with trees growing so straight and tall that they seemed to be reaching for the sky. These were Lombardy poplars with branches that grew straight up and not sideways like those of other trees. Across the way were large nursery gardens where Grandma and Mamma frequently went to purchase plants or flower and vegetable seeds. They took me along in early spring to see the pansies, daisies, bachelors' buttons, and especially lettuce and radishes coming up. In time, the nursery and its attractive greenery disappeared to make way for apartment houses that were beginning to be built all over Kaunas. The acreage around our new home was eventually built up, becoming a maze of streets and buildings.

The orchard, as everyone called it, was large enough to contain not only fruit trees and beds of flowers and vegetables, but an unfinished tennis court and several other structures as well. A garage and storehouse had living quarters for the caretaker and his family. There was an old tumble-down chicken house with green moss growing on the roof on one side. Our land climbed steeply uphill on one side, separated by a high fence from Vytautas Park. Further on, there was a winding street named *Parodos gatvė* (Exhibition Street). A newly built and handsome red brick building stood there, within walking distance of our house. It was the home of our grandparents.

On their return from the USA, our grandparents, Jonas and Liudvika Šliupas, lived at first with one or the other of their children, but always wanted a place of their own. Grandma spent most of her time with us and could not tear herself away from her beloved grandchildren. Father generously donated the land and even the bricks needed for construction. As he used to say later on, he did it in a spirit of so called enlightened self-interest, hoping in this way to see less of his mother-in-law. Whether this story was true or not, Grandma and her son-in-law, my father, actually liked each other. Nobody could be happier than she was when her daughter married a rising young statesman—and a Lithuanian at that. For his part, Father admired Grandma's wisdom and political acumen. They both liked humorous stories and enjoyed many good laughs together.

A number of chickens lived in the chicken house. I considered it a privilege to be allowed to collect the eggs. There was a rooster that would sometimes crow loudly and frighten me just as I was reaching for an egg hidden in the hay. One of the great marvels was a bisexual chicken, known as *Vištgaidis* (hen-rooster), which unbelievably enough could crow like a rooster and also lay eggs like a hen. I remember him, her or it, as rather big with fluffy white feathers. In later years, I learned that people of indeterminate sex also exist and wondered whether there were certain parallels between the world of chickens and of human beings.

There were other remarkable birds living here. Grandfather Šliupas kept his beloved guinea hens in our chicken yard. Their pen was roofed by wire netting so they would not fly away. They had queer looking heads somewhat like a turkey's with rather unusual black and white speckled feathers. Their voices were loud and piercing, making an unearthly racket. When I later learned English, I was told that the cackle of guinea hens sounds like the words "come back, come back," a good approximation. By the way, they laid cute, teeny tiny eggs.

The following tale shows how Grandpa Šliupas loved his guinea hens. Once one of them got very sick, refused to eat, and took no interest in life. Grandpa called the veterinarian. Dr. Sokolskis examined the patient and said that no amount of medicine would help because death was a sure thing. The veterinarian (who happened to be an old family friend) gave Grandpa a very large bill for his house call, even though the guinea hen died. Grandpa was quite upset, but everyone else thought it was very amusing that a personal friend should have seen fit to present such a bill.

Chapter Five
Treasure Trove

All the rooms in the new house offered endless opportunities for enjoyment. The drawing room with its eight long windows facing the street had several fat white columns holding up the ceiling. It was great fun for my brother and me to chase each other, running round and round the columns. I remember the laughter and shrieks of joy until out of sheer exhaustion we would collapse in a heap on the floor. This was parquet flooring and its oaken surface had to be polished by someone with felt slippers skating across it. Beer, not water, was used for cleaning it in order to keep the shine and the color. Nobody ever mentioned the workers stopping their work to have a swig of beer.

There was a huge Turkish rug in the standard colors of red and blue with little birds, plants, and animals all over it. The rug covered less than half of the floor. When we moved to our next home which was smaller by far, the rug went with us, and even in the biggest room, the rug was a tight fit. Mamma used to say that the rug, purchased at some auction of antiques from old Russia, must have been a wall hanging in some forgotten princely palace. As she pointed out, there were tiny brass rings sewn all along one length that no one had bothered to remove. In Kaunas, many such rare items were then being sold locally by Russian refugees fleeing the Great Revolution.

In the dining room there were art objects of glass and china that we children were not allowed to touch. On rare occasions, we were invited to join in family gatherings around the large mahogany table with leaves that could be extended to accommodate well over a dozen people. On the sideboard stood a silver samovar with a coronet and a ducal coat of arms engraved upon it. They are generally made of brass so this one was unusual. Years later, I learned that, though the samovar is considered a Russian institution, it was the wandering folk of the mountains of Afghanistan who initiated it. With this portable tea urn, they could enjoy hot water for tea anywhere they chose to travel. Lighting a samovar without setting fire to the house (from sparks flying upward) was quite an involved process. The teapot, like a decorative item, always sat on the very top to keep the tea hot.

The correct way to drink tea in this part of the world is with lump sugar and a slice of lemon, often from a glass rather than a cup. There was a set of decorative silver holders for glasses in which tea was served in the Russian manner. The elegant holders protected your fingers from the scalding hot liquid. Two candelabra with intricately carved branches stood on either side of the samovar. To see them gleaming yellow in the candlelight was an enchanting sight. For years I believed that the candelabra were made of pure gold.

As mentioned, children were not always welcome in the dining room. Another room I loved where I could not always gain admittance was Father's den. If the door with curtained glass panes was tightly closed, that meant he was there working and should not be disturbed. I could hardly wait for the door to open. Even at that early age I loved books. I could be happy for hours with a book, stretching out on the tiger rug with one in hand, whether I could read or not. Looking for pictures was my main task. Since nobody had ever told me whether this was the fur of a real tiger, or just a fake, lying on that rug was not a really comfortable experience. What would I do, I used to wonder, if the tiger should suddenly come to life? Father's desk was piled high with papers that no one was allowed to touch. I could not really understand it then, but Father was writing something he called Memoirs. There were huge floor-to-ceiling bookcases containing works in many languages. Some had glass fronts and others had roll-top mechanisms to be pulled up or down that I thought amazing.

Brother Martynas, Jr., doubtless influenced by all this reading and writing, decided to write a play called "Drama about Explorers in the Jungle." The stage directions said, "There are all

sorts of animals here, even crocodiles, but they cannot be seen."
Neither he nor I could fully understand why the grownups
considered this statement so amusing. I had few original ideas of my
own and was content to follow in my brother's footsteps. If he
wanted to play "riding the bus," chairs would be pushed together
and off we would go with our teddy bears and dolls as passengers.
The bus conductor was always my brother handing out slips of
paper as tickets and sounding his toy trumpet when it was time to
depart. If we played "store," he was the manager and chief salesman
whereas I was the buyer of toys and candies. We loved the
gleaming foil that candies were wrapped in and used the "silver" as
money for our games.

None of us was going to school and we knew few children
to play with, so we had to make do with each other's company. The
twins were too small to participate and besides, we had no patience
with them. My brother had several ideas on making money. One
that I thought just great was making perfume out of tangerine peel
which to us had a heavenly smell. When he grew older, he said his
ambition was to be the owner of a factory making musical records.
Our record player, a Victrola, was housed in a cabinet of polished
wood and was the kind that you had to wind up by hand. There was
a picture inside of a dog listening to "His Master's Voice" coming
out of a trumpet. Everyone enjoyed listening to the records, young
and old alike. The "gramophone," as we called it, was our earliest
introduction to classical music. Since our parents were partial to
opera, we heard many golden voices. The only ones I can clearly
remember were the Italian tenor Enrico Caruso, the soprano Amelita
Galli-Curci, and the folk songs of Mikas Petrauskas.

My brother's favorite toys were a Meccano set for building
tall towers or bridges out of long metal strips, or that wonder of
wonders, an electric train running around the room on its own
railroad tracks. I could not follow him in these games. First, I had
no mechanical ability whatever and, second, I sat down in the wrong
place one time and got a terrible electric shock. From that time on,

my brother had the train all to himself. We had a rocking horse and several toy animals on little wheels that I liked much better. It was fun to take teddy bears for a ride (strangely, none of us girls liked dolls as much as we liked our teddies). After the ride was over, the animals had to be tethered, as we said, to prevent them from running away. They were strapped to the great mahogany legs of the grand piano in the living room.

The grand piano was a Knabe made by an American firm. It reached us not from the USA, but by way of Warsaw. It had been the property of the famed orchestra conductor E. Mlynarski, the father-in-law of the world-famous pianist, Arthur Rubinstein. During World War I, the Knabe was brought for safekeeping to Mrs. Mlynarski's ancestral estate in Lithuania. Anna Mlynarski was a friend of the family and visited us often. Her estate, *Ilguva*, was some distance away on the river Nemunas, easily reached by steamboat. All through the War, the Mlynarski's butler kept the Knabe piano in hiding for fear that destructive soldiers would damage it. Aunt Aldona, quite a pianist in her youth, heard about this remarkable instrument and eventually bought it. How it was shipped to Kaunas, one can only imagine, most probably upriver by steamboat. Our aunt, after going to all that trouble, found the Knabe too big for her small dwelling and decided that the Yčas family should have it. That is how it came to grace our living room. Fortunately, its extensive travel experiences had not damaged its quality or musical tone in the least.

Several of the animals on wheels were too big to be housed in the "stable" under the grand piano. One was a huge teddy bear, "King of the Bears," as my brother called it. Another was a grey felt elephant with a red saddle and bridle. More remarkable, however, was a donkey, large enough for a grown-up person to ride on. This donkey came all the way from Paris, one of the first very large toys bought for my brother who had lived there as a small boy. According to family legend, the cabinet minister A. Voldemaras, then a frequent visitor to our home, liked the donkey and thought he would go for a ride. And crick crack, he broke the donkey's back. Fortunately, the damage could be repaired.

We had perhaps entirely too many toys. Like many children, we would get tired of them after a while. I cannot recall whose idea it was to "send the toys to Siberia" every so often, but it was certainly a good one. They would get stored in a trunk and taken up to the attic. After maybe six months, they would be brought down again. They were greeted with joy as by that time, we had forgotten most of them. Besides "old friends," we would find others which seemed completely new. We were not encouraged to go to the attic by ourselves. It was a dark and mysterious place full of strange looking bundles, boxes, and trunks. On rare occasions Petrusia might invite us to pay a visit to her room under the eaves. To our great delight, there was a magnificent view from her window of what we thought was the entire town of Kaunas. People, horses and wagons in the streets below looked unbelievably small.

The toys we played with were not quite like those of other children. We were never allowed to play with guns, cannons, or other warlike toys because Mamma was very much against this sort of thing. Battles with tin soldiers were about as far as we were allowed to go, but there was to be no shooting. There was also a revolving top which hummed a melody when you wound it up. What also stays in the memory are exquisitely carved wooden figures representing a farmstead with small buildings, tiny animals, and people. These had been made in Germany, the toy capital of Europe at that time.

Educational toys as such were not thought of back then, but there were toys from which a great deal could be learned. Perhaps the most memorable of these was a large model of an ancient Roman villa. There was an atrium or courtyard in the middle with a basin for water where you could play at having a real fountain. There were rooms under a colonnade going all the way around. This was a gift from a friend of our Father's from old days in the Russian Duma (was his name Demidoff or Adjemoff?) who now lived in

35

Paris, France. Some of these Russian friends would send us presents. Clearly remembered is one that was a vast disappointment: a whole crate of oysters in the shell. They had not been properly refrigerated and were spoiled on arrival. For a time, we had many of these shells to play with and used them for various construction projects.

Father kept up with friends from pre-Revolution days. Many thousands of Russian refugees had settled in Paris, and once in a while another old Duma friend, such as P. Gronsky, might visit us in person and bring us unusual gifts. Above all, I remember that gleaming white doll house in the style of ancient Rome. It stimulated our interest in learning about people who lived long years ago and gave us some idea of the passage of time, a concept of which we were not aware. It gave me a desire to study Roman history later on. I remembered that doll house when I saw a real Roman villa many years later at the John Paul Getty Museum in Malibu, California.

Chapter Six
Our Household Helpers

Closest to us was Elena, our nurse. It is not surprising that there remain more impressions of her than of any of the others. Elena Nikitishna was very pious, often telling us, "But for the mercy of God, I would not be alive today." Mornings and evenings she would get down on her knees and recite prayers without end. Much of her off-time was spent going to her church where she wanted us to go too. This was not a popular idea with our staunchly Protestant parents, but she did succeed on more than one occasion. Going with Elena left indelible memories of candlelight shimmering in the darkness, priests garbed in gold-embroidered robes, and sonorous choir music. Surely Elena had no thought of converting us, but even if she had, there was no danger of that as the services were so boring. There were no chairs for anyone to sit on and long hours of standing made our feet sore.

Once in a while, Elena would take us to see Russian friends, a family called Voynich who had a remarkable grocery store. Their oranges, grapes, tangerines, and bananas smelled absolutely delicious. Exotic fruits were a rarity, very expensive due to the high customs duties imposed. Later on, there was quite a government campaign against imported foods in general. The public was told that native products were much more healthful than anything coming from a far distant country. "Eat carrots. They are every bit as nutritious as oranges" was the official line. Perhaps this made some sense in an agricultural country like Lithuania with its wealth of every type of produce. When we visited the Voynich home, we were given home-brewed *kvass* to drink (a typical Russian drink, tasting like a sour lemonade).

I admired the bright-colored *kilims* (carpets) that decorated their living room walls and, most of all, the guitar with a gypsy shawl draped over it. When I asked what a guitar was, the answer was "Well, it's not a *balalaika*." This did not tell me much since I was not acquainted with either one. Much later, I learned that the balalaika is a Russian stringed instrument of triangular shape, not curved like a Spanish guitar.

In the nursery, the rule was "early to bed and early to rise." The stories Elena told us at bedtime did not always have a calming effect, but we liked the shivers of horror that "Baba Yaga" gave us. She was a terrible old woman who lived in a hut made of skulls and bones into which she enticed little children to roast them and eat them. "The Firebird" evoked a bonfire and tongues of flame consuming a magical bird that could always come back alive. "The Flying Carpet" of Persian tales was equally fascinating. Stories read to us by Father from a book by the German writer W. Hauff, especially about a winged horse and a Caliph of Bagdad who could change into a stork, and Maeterlinck's "Blue Bird" were top favorites. At that time Father, always interested in book publishing, had just issued some works in a Lithuanian translation, including the unforgettable "Blue Bird." Searching all over the world, a little boy and a little girl come home at last, only to find the Blue Bird of Happiness they had been looking for singing in the window.

Elena liked to get up early. A little Russian rhyme she taught us still stays with me, "Get up, children, the rooster has crowed already and the sun is looking in." When she came to my bedroom to wake me at six o'clock, I was usually awake. A loud siren, so punctual that you could set your clock by it, had already sounded. It was calling factory workers to another day of labor in the Tilmans ironworks miles away. Already the sound of wagon wheels and horses' feet going clop-clop-clop could be heard from the street. I would lie in bed wondering what the weather outside was like. The windows had thin yellow drapes, and the light filtering through was just like sunshine. This did not come our way very often, and skies were often grey in that northern climate.

Our day generally started listening for the music of the coffee grinder. We knew it was time to come downstairs when we heard Cook grinding coffee in the kitchen. This was real coffee (like all imports, very rare and expensive) and always ground by hand. It was for grownups, not for children, but even the adults drank theirs mixed with roasted barley grain. Pure coffee was reserved for special guests only. As for us children, we drank barley coffee with hot milk, which seems good even today. Bread and milk the way Elena made it was delicious. We learned from her not to waste sugar, which had been scarce in Russia where she came from. When she drank tea, it was with a piece of lump sugar in her mouth "to make the sweet taste last longer." Elena convinced us (and I believe it to this day) that a slice of home-baked dark or black rye bread, thickly spread with real butter and sprinkled with sugar, is better than any cake.

Elena's word was law, but my brother was not afraid to talk back to her, being secure in his position as her favorite. When she ordered us to eat everything on our plates, he wanted to know "Whatever for?" Elena explained that there were many children in the world who did not have enough to eat. He asked, "If I eat everything up, how could it possibly help those poor children?" It is a miracle my brother did not grow up to be a totally spoiled brat. Elena thought he could do no wrong. Our parents and grandparents referred to him as "the crown prince." He was always getting complimented on his cleverness. I do not remember being jealous because, after all, I had my Grandma's love as a security blanket. The twins Evelyna and Violetta, of course, were too young to care.

Since ready-made clothes hardly existed for purchase in the town, many people had theirs made by seamstresses either at home or by dressmaking and tailoring establishments. Our seamstress was Elena who made not only the children's clothes, but also aprons, nightgowns, curtains and other household items. A vivid recollection about Elena concerns dresses. She had a soft heart for people in need and took pleasure in giving away food and clothing to the beggars who sometimes rang our door bell. One time her charitable impulses got her into serious trouble. While Mamma was away, Elena went to her wardrobe and selected some "unneeded" dresses. The beggar woman at the door was very lucky that day.

On her return, Mamma was highly indignant, especially because she thought she might have pinned an expensive brooch on one of the missing dresses. There was a to-do and a frantic search for the missing jewel, which finally turned up in an unexpected corner to the relief of everybody concerned. Elena was roundly scolded for taking things without the owner's permission. Mamma said later that it was a good lesson for her, too, not to be so careless with her jewelry. As a matter of fact, she was not too interested in jewelry as such. She could admire beautiful ornaments, mostly when other people wore them, but she did value that particular brooch. It was said to have formerly belonged to a famous Russian ballerina who was a favorite of the last Czar Nicholas II.

In a milieu where there was a patron saint for practically everything, it is no surprise to find a St. Zita, patroness of maids in service, who had supposedly lived centuries ago and had served a wealthy family. Loyal and faithful in her duties, she loved God and prayed often. One time while praying and waiting for bread to finish baking in the oven, she was much distressed for fear she had let it burn. But it had not burned, for angels descended from Heaven and removed the bread from the oven at the right time. Never had bread tasted so good or smelled so sweet. Whether or not people believed in St. Zita's powers, there was a St. Zita society to take care of the servant population. Employers and employees could register with the Society, which was not a union, but acted like an employment agency.

The Society had close ties with the Roman Catholic Church and was not always used for the best purposes. Simple country girls were much in demand as nuns for convents either locally or in foreign countries. St. Zita's Society sometimes cooperated in sending the poor young things into exile. This kind of entrapment was experienced by one of our domestics named Basia, an unlettered girl from the country. One day, when we were all assembled at the dining room table, Basia came in weeping to say she could no longer work for us. She told us she was going away to Belgium to become a nun. "I don't want to leave you but I must," she said. Father asked why she was doing this if she did not want to go. Her reply was, "I love you all. You have been so good to me. I don't know why I am going, but St. Zita's Society said so."

Basia went off to Liège, Belgium, and worked as kitchen helper and maid in a Catholic convent. She stayed in the kitchen after taking her vows and was soon promoted to chief cook. There was no news of her for some years and then *Soeur* (Sister) Jeanne (her new name) started to write us letters in beautiful handwriting in both good Lithuanian and excellent French. This uneducated woman was evidently very talented. She wrote inspirational letters, saying she remembered the Yčas family every day at evening and morning prayers. One may wonder whether Basia merely made peace with her situation or if she had truly found her vocation in the religious life.

Mamma kept up the correspondence with Soeur Jeanne for years. Events of World War II cut off communication., but in some mysterious way they found each other again. Letters from Liège continued almost up to the time of Basia's death in the early 1980s. Her love followed us for several decades and perhaps even longer, if there is room for such sentiments in Heaven. The Abbess of the convent was kind enough to notify my mother by letter that Basia was no more. We all wiped away a tear or two when reading the Abbess's words of appreciation for Basia's devoted service to God and to all human beings. She said that her gentle ways and sweet disposition would be long remembered.

Most families we knew were much attached to their loyal domestic servants. What happened to them after they left their jobs was a matter of special concern. Like other employers, our parents wished to reward their domestics for good and faithful service. Often this took the form of getting them married to a good husband and making sure there was a dowry. Girls without a so-called marriage portion were not as likely to get married. Ancient practices like setting money aside for a dowry and collecting linens for a hope chest, together with the custom of informal matchmaking, were still very much alive. Father, as head of the household, made it a point to get our faithful Petrusia married off when she left us after over a dozen years of service. He used to joke that he was no matchmaker and that his efforts were often less than successful. True enough, Petrusia's marriage had unfortunate and even tragic consequences. All this, however, happened many years later.

Among our domestic help there never was anyone quite like Petrusia. As the grownups said, running the household without her would have been unthinkable. She was from Palanga by the Baltic Sea where we spent our summers. We all looked forward to these golden days by the seashore, but Petrusia was happier than anyone else when it came time for us to go there.

Chapter Seven
Summer Interlude One
The House by the Sea

It was easy to enter the House by the Sea as the doors were generally left unlocked. In those days people lived without fear and felt no need to bolt their gates or bar their windows. There was a wall of evergreen trees around the garden. You lifted the latch of the gate, went up the gravel path and the few steps of the porch, and there you were at the front door. It used to be easy to push the door open. It is just as easy for me to return to the childhood summers spent in Palanga on the shores of the Baltic Sea.

I am now several thousand miles away on the other side of the world. It is not likely that I shall ever see the house again, and perhaps it is better so. If it is still standing, it would certainly not be as large or as enchanting as I recall it. Peopled with shadows from the past and echoing with the sound of voices so fondly remembered, why should I try to find it? Seeing it in my mind's eye as it once was is so much easier and more pleasant.

Many of those who vacationed with us many decades ago have gone to the "Land of No Return." Of those who remain, some cannot and others do not wish to remember. To have no one to share memories with is sad, but I have no regrets. Hopefully, a few readers of these pages (who have never been there and perhaps have never even heard of it) might wish that they too had been in Palanga then. Perhaps they can share in the pervasive sense of wonder and discovery of those days. Although this feeling leaves us bit by bit as we get older, some of us can still be overcome by impressions of far away and long ago. For me, the real marvel is that experiences, neither startling nor remarkable, could cast such a spell, almost as if they had been sprinkled with the magic dust described in fairy tales.

For some reason, it is the seaside summers that gleam like precious stones among memories of other times of the year. In winter there was the jingling of sleigh-bells and muffled sounds of

43

horses' feet on the snowy streets of Kaunas. In the fall, there were mushroom-hunting expeditions and picnics in the woods. In spring, there were wild violets to be picked on the hillside by our house in town. However, none of these pictures can compare with those of the fine white sands of Palanga Beach where we spent hours playing among the tall grasses of the sand dunes. Listening to the sound of the sea, I often wondered what the waves were saying. I believed that they spoke the same language as the pine trees swaying in the wind, telling fascinating stories if we could only understand them.

Preparing for the trip (always by train, the preferred mode of travel) was almost as exciting as getting there. For days and weeks the entire household would be bristling with preparations. Besides personal belongings, there was much packing of pots and pans, as well as cages for birds, cats and dogs. Lamps, rugs, easy-chairs and other furniture had to be taken along, not to speak of enormous provisions of food stuffs to protect us from starvation. Summer clothes had to be made ready which meant long sessions with the seamstress for children as well as grownups. Standing still for the seamstress, either for alterations to old dresses or to be fitted for new ones was an utterly boring experience. There was no such thing then as ready-made garments for sale.

Innumerable boxes and trunks were packed for Palanga. This caused a revolution in our home. There was always someone looking for some indispensable object which might happen to be packed at the very bottom of the trunk. There were plaintive calls for Petrusia who would be sure to know where things were. The grownups probably did not look forward to the journey that lasted from early morning to nightfall, but it was a thrill for us children—fancy being able to eat and sleep on a train!

Before we could really enjoy the trip, however, an object of horror had to be overcome. This was the terrible tunnel just outside the Kaunas railroad station. The blackness was not as awful as the eerie sound of the train whistle echoing throughout. Our favorite cat, Pintzus of the coal black fur and orange eyes, usually rode with us. Nurse Elena tried to bolster our courage, "Look, Pintzus is not afraid of the tunnel. Why should you be?" Unfortunately, Pintzus began to meow very sorrowfully just then and I could not restrain my tears. Soon my baby twin sisters were howling too. Mother, Nurse and Grandma had trouble quieting the noise. The only child who showed no fear was our brother, acting older and wiser than the rest of us.

There was much opening and closing of the picnic basket and few of the goodies (sandwiches, fruit, cheese, etc.) were left by the time we reached the town of Kretinga, our railroad stop. A long wagon with slatted wooden sides, the kind used for farm work, was waiting for us. The bottom of the cart was piled high with hay, more comfortable than any pillow and smelling a whole lot better. With a crack of the driver's whip and a *noa* (giddy-up) to his two horses, we would go off into the night, our storm lantern casting a feeble light around us. Despite the excitement of the journey, we soon drifted off into dreamland, waking up every so often to find ourselves riding in the moonlight through woods that smelled of pine needles. It would be hours after our usual bedtime when we arrived at our summer home.

Everyone called these summer homes villas, no matter whether they were elaborate structures or mere cottages. There was nothing fancy about ours, and it did not have a distinctive name like some. It was simply Dr. Joeckel's Villa, the name of its former owner. The house, slightly elevated on a brick openwork foundation, had a balcony overgrown with vines above the front porch. Inside, there were stairs leading up to the second floor. Off the hallway was a seldom-used sitting room with creaky wicker furniture. It was dark there because its windows looked out on the veranda running the full length of the house. The dining room led to a bedroom with two tiny beds for the twins and another one for Nurse. Other bedrooms were upstairs. Lighting our candles, we would go to bed, too sleepy to mind passing through the attic where a ghost or witch might jump at us from behind the trunks and bundles.

Candles and kerosene lamps were a way of life as most of Palanga was not wired for electricity. Inevitably, there were fires. A large charred mark was left on the twins' bedroom door when a candle carried in Nurse's hand set fire to a hanging towel. All water for household use had to be dipped from the well, lowering a rope with a bucket attached. Looking into the water was fascinating. It was the color of gold and had bleached pine needles floating in it. In the shade of surrounding trees, pale mushrooms and red-and-white speckled toadstools grew among the moss. Further on were clumps of flowers called Sweet Williams with a ruby red color that seemed to me the most beautiful in the world. An interesting place was the tennis court at the bottom of the garden. The adults seldom used it, so we played our own games there almost as often as we liked.

Across a sandy road seldom used by traffic was another favorite playground: a vacant lot with foundations of a house burned down before our time. Tall spikes of purple flowers grew over the charred debris. We tried to imagine how the house and its residents had looked in former times. Nearby was a gnarled old acacia tree where we collected shriveled seed pods for use as money in our games of store. Beyond lay the kitchen garden and strawberry patch, the garage (for a nonexistent car) and the washhouse. A mound of earth covered an underground icehouse or cellar. Behind that was a wire enclosed pen for chickens or other fowl, bought live in the market and kept to fatten and eat as needed. Grandma and Nurse carefully kept us out of the way when the unfortunate creatures were being killed. All these diversions notwithstanding, it was jaunts to the beach that took first place in our thoughts.

In the mornings and sometimes afternoons we would walk to the beach. Grownups carried rugs, towels, lemonade, sandwiches, etc., and sometimes the twins when they got tired.

46

Brother Martynas trotted along with his spade and bucket, ready to build sand castles. Usually I lagged behind carrying my rubber doll that was almost as big as I was, a made-in-America African chief in grass skirt and jungle headdress. Many hours were spent in trying to catch the sun. There were cloudy days, but getting a good suntan was not impossible. Towards evening we would walk the sands looking for sea shells or bits of amber, quite plentiful in those days. Grandma always had stories to tell. One of our favorites was about Jūratė, Queen of the Sea who lived in an amber palace under the water. She fell in love with a simple fisherman and fell out of favor with the gods. A thunderbolt wielded by the mighty Perkūnas smashed her palace to smithereens. The waves bring up pieces of the amber palace from time to time and you can hear the voice of Jūratė wailing in the wind.

Grandma was my favorite person because she always had time for me. Everyone else in the household, including Mamma, seemed to be preoccupied with the oldest and the youngest children. My brother, the first born, soon learned what it was like to be a "Crown Prince" and was often allowed to have his way. Perhaps I too might have become a spoiled brat if it had not been for the death of Grandma at an early age. Grandpa, although much loved, was a rare visitor. A physician and excellent storyteller, he was for us a source of learning and wisdom. Grandpa enjoyed talking to children and translating facts of history, geography, nature study, etc. into simple language. Having resided in the USA, he told us about ships and ocean voyages. I recall seeing ships at sea and asking if Grandpa was on board though everyone I knew came by land, mostly by train. Our men folk were busy in town and could not come to Palanga very often. Glad as we were to see Grandpa, nothing compared to the joy of seeing our father. He loved company, and there would be picnics, excursions and fun for everyone. There were great preparations before he came. The house was cleaned from top to bottom. Pots and pans danced on the wood stove and delightful aromas filled the kitchen. All the children had to wear their Sunday-best sailor suits, and I got a new silk ribbon for the butterfly-bow in my hair.

Father could never stay very long but wanted to enjoy every moment of his break from daily routine. There was storytelling on the veranda in the evenings when he came and parties on the tennis court (probably more partying than actual tennis games). He loved his children dearly and would toss us into the air one by one and then hug us close. It was a treat to be allowed to listen to the musical tinkle of his gold pocket watch. What tears there were when he departed! But when we saw him off at the station, there were more fun and games. Leaning out of the train window, he would hold his handkerchief to his eyes and then wring it dry pretending it was soaked with tears.

Mamma was of a different temperament, rarely taking part in our childisn games. She was not too sociable and loved to read books, mainly in English. She was totally bilingual, speaking both languages with no trace of accent. When she came from America as a bride, she had shipped a trunk full of books. However, the ship sank in a storm and Mamma spent years trying to replace those favorite old-time classic romances, cook books, and gardening books. Once Mamma got interested in a project, she made sure it was done exactly down to the last detail.

Petrusia, the housekeeper, had a genius for knowing where lost or misplaced articles were hiding. Petrusia enjoyed coming to Palanga, her old home. Her family lived in a cottage nearby, and sometimes she took me with her to visit. Sometimes Father was invited too. Once he came home highly amused because he had seen some of our possessions, like silverware, tablecloths, and dishes, in that house—somebody had been pilfering. However, Petrusia got away with just a scolding and never got fired. Where could we get another efficient housekeeper like her? She stayed with us until we were grown and a suitable marriage with dowry was arranged for her.

Summer days in Palanga went all too quickly. Though exhausted from the day's activities, we never wanted to go to bed and went unwillingly up the stairs. We would rather have stayed in the dining room where grownups gathered in the evenings around the *samovar*. It was hard to go off into the darkness, leaving the gentle hissing of the kerosene lamp that filled the room with a soft yellow glow. However, once we got upstairs with our little candles, my brother and I were happy to have made the trip. Our bedroom had pretty pink wallpaper, pine trees rustled at the window, and best of all, we could look forward to another day filled with delights. Such a feeling of anticipation is rare and hard to recapture.

Since those far off days I have seen other forests, other seas, and other beaches. I have slept in more strange rooms that I care to remember. But nowhere can I find the enchantment of those mornings when I would awake to thoughts of pure joy, "I am in Palanga again, in the House by the Sea."

Chapter Eight
Summer Interlude Two
Explorations and Discoveries

During summer vacations in Palanga, my favorite companion was my brother. The twins were still babies, far too small to be playmates. They seemed like a pair of flaxen haired and extremely fragile dolls. They were always falling down, hurting themselves, and then screaming their heads off. My brother had a scientific turn of mind. Even at that early age, he collected facts and made conclusions. Later in life he did indeed become a scholar in the natural sciences. As for me, I lived strictly on impressions of the moment. My brother seemed so infinitely clever that I was only too glad to follow where he led. On looking back, it seems that many of our games and diversions were actually learning experiences. One bright blue day with the smell of autumn already in the air, we noticed masses of dragonflies caught in the wire netting of the tennis court. The wind had evidently blown them there.

At first we were delighted. We had tried to catch dragonflies before. Now we could have a hatful without any trouble. Our joy turned to sorrow when we saw that many would never fly again. Their rainbow colored wings were maimed and broken. As usual, we went to Grandma for comfort. She said that death was no great blow to those insects since they only lived for a few days or weeks at most. The thought that dragonflies were born, flew around in the sunshine, and then perished was overwhelming. Was the same true of butterflies? I had never realized that there was such a thing as death and had no concept of time. Did not everyone and everything live forever? What was a week, a month, or a year?

I had not learned to count, except on the fingers of one hand, and could not read as yet. The older people I knew never discussed their age, not even Grandpa, unquestionably the oldest. When the question came up, he said he was not very old. And then came someone who said he had lived "for close to a hundred years." This was a little old man who sometimes came to the house with his beggar's basket and cane. Mamma would give him bread, sausage, and other good things to sustain him on his journey. He would sit on the kitchen steps telling tales of long ago. One hundred was the biggest number I had ever heard of and it seemed impossible to imagine. Another visitor who had me wondering about his years was a neighbor with a long white beard. He sometimes came, arrayed in a flowing black cloak, to bring bouquets of roses from his garden for the ladies of the house.

When the twins began to walk and talk, we started to enjoy their company. A curious fact about our baby sisters, Evelyna and Violetta, was that they ignored each other's existence for a long time (perhaps for two years). They did not play together or pay attention to one another even when sitting face to face in their high wheeled perambulator, or baby buggy. They had a language of their own and we would talk back to them in the odd words they used. That baby talk was also a language and seemed to be the most natural thing in the world. We knew that not everyone talked the same, having been exposed from earliest days to other languages. Our nurse was Russian and taught us her language. When someone asked how many languages I knew, I would answer, "Lithuanian, Russian and Baby Talk," as a serious statement of fact. If I had known the Samogitian dialect spoken locally (it was very different from standard Lithuanian), I might have added that too. From these early beginnings, I developed a lifelong interest in various languages.

One day when Father was expected to come for a visit (a great event as he could seldom leave his many concerns in Kaunas), my brother and I wanted to take part in the preparations. The house was being made ready for his coming. People would come for evening parties on the veranda, so we wanted to make sure it was clean. A tall metal container of milk brought fresh that morning was conveniently close. We reasoned that milk would clean ever so much better than water. Plunging rags and brooms into the milk can, we set to work. We felt useful and divinely contented until Mamma came out and saw the mess we had made. We were seldom spanked as our parents did not believe in the old adage "spare the rod and spoil the child." This time, however, we got a thrashing, the memory of which remains for life. I cried my heart out standing in the corner. The punishment seemed out of proportion to the crime. Furthermore, our good intentions had been misunderstood.

Another disaster of sorts was the art exhibit we decided to put on in our bedroom. The pretty pink flowered wallpaper made an ideal background for art works stuck on with paste. People would pay money to see it, we thought. The paste, a sticky concoction of rye flour and water, made a very good adhesive. On rainy days we had fun with scissors, cutting out pictures from postcards and magazines, and pasting them into collages to go on exhibit. The son of a prominent artist, Rimtas Kalpokas, who later became a painter himself, used to come by to teach us how to paint and draw. Some of his colored drawings would be the stars of our show and, amazingly, I can still see one of them in my mind's eye. Hoping nobody would see what we were doing (this was to be a surprise for the grownups), my brother and I worked like mad until the walls were properly decorated. This time, there was no spanking, only a tongue lashing for the damage we had done. Nurse Elena was also scolded for not keeping an eye on us.

In the kitchen there was always something interesting going on. If Cook was in a good mood, she would allow me to watch her at work. There usually was a crackling wood fire going in the white tile stove under the black iron top. Preparation of meals took a long time. As soon as one was served, Cook would be at work again. Tack-tack-tack went her big shiny knife cutting carrots, cabbage, and onions into tiny little pieces. If I got up early enough, I could see all sorts of activities at the back door. Countrywomen came with wicker baskets of wild strawberries, blueberries or shiny red lingonberries, picked in the nearby forest at sunup. There might also be three or four different varieties of mushrooms, so delicious when cooked with onions and sour cream, and served with boiled potatoes. Cook made marvelous things out of potatoes such as potato pancakes, *kugelis* (potato pudding), and vegetable soup with milk. Sometimes fish were delivered at the door, either freshly caught or smoked. My favorite, however, was salted herring from the barrel. What we had for lunch one day stands out in the memory (perhaps it was on the day Grandma was taking me to the fair). The long oval plate of chopped herring, garnished with carrot slices, green onions, parsley sprigs, and hard-boiled eggs, was a most attractive sight.

Provisions could be bought at the weekly markets down by the red brick church. When walking to the marketplace, Petrusia and Grandma would take baskets and a good supply of paper bags. Everybody saved paper bags, string and other scarce items. Sometimes I was allowed to go along. People in traditional peasant garb would come in their horse-drawn carts to sell cheese, butter, loaves of dark rye bread, vegetables, and other farm produce. When fairs were held, the sights and sounds were particularly exciting. The music of the *katarinka* (hurdy-gurdy) resounded. There were handmade clay pitchers and bowls on display, as well as linens and woolens woven on looms in country homes. Rows of gingerbread men, decorated with pink and white icing, and horses with chocolate manes and tails hung in the stalls.

Grandma had lived for many years in the United States and had adopted some American ideas. She was very particular about things being right and proper, especially in regard to health and cleanliness. A story she liked to tell about Palanga days was the time when she went to the market to buy some butter. An old lady began to ladle it out of a white enamel container. Grandma stared and could not believe her eyes. The container had a handle on it like a loop. It just couldn't be, but it was—a chamber pot with a new mission in life. Grandma refused to buy the butter or listen to the vendor's explanations that it was all right because the pot had been thoroughly scrubbed with soap. In those days, where there was no indoor plumbing, chamber pots were standard equipment in every household. Some were made of china, decorated with paintings of fruit and flowers, and have appeal for antique collectors of today.

One side of the garden was walled off by the stable of a cavalry detachment. There were many horses in the Lithuanian Army then. I was not tall enough to look into the narrow high windows but could hear the stamp of the horses' feet and the rustle of hay. Sometimes companies of hussars in red trousers, their sabers flashing, would come riding out, mounted on splendid horses. Having stables nearby meant there were flies buzzing about, even in the house, despite attempts to close the screen doors and windows. The grownups hated them, but to my brother and me they were a source of wonder. Some were really big with iridescent blue bodies. These clever insects eluded all our attempts to capture them alive. If they were so smart, how could they be stupid enough to be fooled by those long, sticky fly papers hanging from the ceiling? That was a good way to catch flies. There was also a glass dish of sugared milk where they could come to drink but not get out again. How could such a intelligent creature be so stupid? Needless to say, it was my brother who asked such questions. His interest in insects had us spending hours running around with a butterfly net. When captured, he would put them to sleep with drops of alcohol. To this day I cannot bear the smell of vodka and related spirits.

In our household there were not many rules such as "children, don't do this or that." We were warned about dangers to stay away from but were allowed to experiment within reason. There were some things we would have liked to do but Nurse would not let us. We thought her a spoilsport for not letting us ride those lovely bounding horses on the merry-go-round. She said "I am afraid that you might fall off." Another restriction of hers was that she could not bear to see any blood shed so she shielded us from the sight of chickens being killed. This was a sight we were very anxious to see. We had overheard Cook telling about the time she had beheaded a chicken that refused to drop dead. It had no head but ran around the shed three times before lying still. One day we were almost successful in viewing a beheading from our hiding place in the bushes, but Nurse came and snatched us away. The mystery of the headless chicken remained unsolved.

Of all the things we learned in Palanga, probably learning to read was the most memorable. A young student came to teach us our letters out of a black-and-white picture book (there was little color printing then). Our nurse also took lessons but had a hard time writing in Latin characters instead of Cyrillic script. She spoke so much Russian to us, with the excuse that her Lithuanian was poor, that our parents told her she would have to leave her job if she did not learn our language. Elena learned to read and write it in a very short time and remained with us for years.

Sitting on the swing, a board suspended by rope from a pine tree branch, I first made the exciting discovery that I could read. All of a sudden, the letters under a picture of a stork standing on one leg began to make sense. There it was, the word for stork, G - A - R - N - Y - S. Immensely thrilled at this discovery, I ran over to my brother shouting, "I can read, I would know it was a stork even without the picture." His answer was like a shower of cold water. "Nonsense, you only know what it is because the picture is there," he said crossly. He had known how to read for some time and felt very superior. I surprised him, dancing around in excitement, and spelling out other words in the book.

From reading to writing was only a step, and I dreamed of writing a letter as soon as I learned to shape the words. My thoughts turned to Grandpa who had not visited us in a very long time. Why not write to him? This was the first letter from my pen, kept for years in the archives of the family. I could not understand why the grownups were so amused by what I had written. The letter read (no punctuation marks), "Dearest Grandpa I miss you very much and today we had a smoked herring for our lunch." Reading was indeed a great thing. Later on, I was able to enjoy some of what the books and newspapers said.

Next time, when Father came, I had things to tell him. My great news was that I would soon be able to learn everything about everything in the whole world. For a long time I believed that everything that was printed was true. When I was old enough to understand, Father told me that lies could be told in print as well as through the spoken word, a thought that caused me to shed bitter tears. The notion that pain could be an accompaniment to the joy of discovery had not entered my mind.

Little by little, problems of the adult world intruded into our midst. Things considered unfit for children's ears were going on—love affairs, illicit meetings, secret romances. One day a really juicy scandal hit our household like a bombshell. Grownups whispered among themselves, refusing to tell us anything. A well-known Army physician vacationing in Palanga had been shot and killed in the woods near our house, but nobody explained why. If they had, it would have been above our heads. The facts were that J. Romanas, owner of a summer villa, grabbed a revolver and shot this Dr. Brundza, an officer in the Lithuanian Army, who had allegedly stolen his wife's affections. The days of duels, or "affairs of honor" were long since over, but such shootings did occur, especially in military circles.

Nobody was too surprised when the murderer evaded justice and later turned up in that classic place of refuge, the United States of America. The whole affair was talked about for weeks. We children found it boring and a terrible waste of time when we finally caught on to the meat of the matter. It must be said that scandalous goings-on and crimes of passion were not exactly uncommon. Though characterized as a placid people, some Lithuanians have a volatile temperament. Public opinion was inclined to condone a crime of passion, as we found out later when we were grown. In our society of tight and rather Victorian moral restrictions, scandals were kept under wraps. Stories of this kind were unlikely to get publicity in the newspapers or on the radio. There must have been plenty of nonconformist behavior going on in Palanga, as elsewhere, but well bred people did not talk too loudly about it.

Chapter Nine
Summer Interlude Three
Leisure Time

Six and more decades ago Palanga was not the bustling modern vacation resort that it is today. There was nothing resembling an up-to-date hotel. The center of social life with a restaurant, music, and dancing was at the *Kurhauzas* (pump room), where mineral waters could be enjoyed. This was not, of course, for children and though we spent many summers in Palanga, I never set foot in it. Nearly everyone who vacationed here lived in one of the villas. Usually they were wooden houses, some very elaborate and others more like cottages, built mainly in 19th century Victorian style. Many had verandas with carved balustrades, fretwork (interlaced ornamental design) decorations and balconies, if there were two stories. Some were private homes reserved for the use of the owners while others were for rent by the week or month, sometimes for the entire summer. There were some rooming houses that rented rooms and served meals, if desired, and apartments with kitchen facilities.

Some of the villas, like ours, were known by the name of the owners, but others had imaginative names. *Villa Jūratė, Birutė, Keistutis*, etc. were named after legendary or historical personalities. There was also *Jūros Akis* (Eye of the Sea), which was supposed to have a magnificent view of the Baltic waves. My own favorite was *Villa Angelas* (Angel). A large statue of an angel with wings outstretched stood on guard amid flowers that seemed so much nicer than ours. Great-Aunt Bronia (Grandma's sister) lived there the year round and was interested in tending her garden. Our villa had simple flowers like daisies, pansies and sweet Williams that grew wild, but *Villa Angelas* had great bushes of roses and clumps of lilies around the angel. Auntie Bronia and her husband, Doctor Antanas Bacevičius, were considered well-to-do. After years of living in the USA, they bought a home in Palanga where they planned to live for the rest of their lives. In a few years, however, they missed America and went back for good.

Such journeys back and forth across the Atlantic to the old homeland of Lithuania were characteristic of Mamma's family. They would live here or there for a time and then be overcome by an unbearable longing to return. Mamma left America, the land of her birth, only when she was married. Grandpa and Grandma made their home in America for years, then went to Lithuania with their son and another daughter after the country became independent in 1918. Uncle Keistutis, the professor, and Aunt Aldona, the doctor, came to stay with us in Palanga on rare occasions. Auntie, having done great things in organizing Red Cross hospitals and distributing medical supplies received from America and Britain, went back to the USA in the thirties, never to return. Other relatives also made these multiple journeys, collectively covering many thousands of miles.

Aunt Bronia was an important part of our family circle. First, she had an elegant home for us to visit, and then there was her automobile, a spacious open Benz convertible. We considered ourselves lucky if she took us for a ride. Few people had cars in Lithuania, let alone Palanga, and this was luxury indeed. Horse-drawn vehicles were the rule. Horses were not accustomed to motors of any kind. They leaped into the air and bolted at our approach. It was quite a show, as far as we children were concerned.

Because of these motor rides we got to see surroundings of our little town that were too far away to reach on foot. One of the more amazing sights was a huge gray *Villa Komoda* (chest-of-drawers), thus called because of its fancied resemblance to this piece of furniture. It stood empty and alone among grassy hillocks and marshlands close to the seashore.

Driving further north was the *Šventoji* (Sacred) River flowing into the sea. Attempts were made to build an alternative seaport there. The work had barely begun and would take many more years. The coast was flanked by a wall of evergreen forest, and there were several hills at a distance. One of tri-corner shape was called Napoleon's Hat (perhaps Napoleon was here in 1812 on his way to Russia?). The other was *Švedų Kapai* (Swedish Cemetery) thus named in memory of invaders, either Vikings or 17th century warriors from Sweden, no one knew which. Masses of black crows were usually hovering over the hill. According to local legend, they were the ghosts of the departed Vikings. Sometimes we would get out of the car for a ramble between the sand dunes and the cottages of fishermen who went out to sea with their nets. A delicious aroma came from the smokehouse where they prepared their fish for market.

The Benz also took us to Klaipėda, the only seaport on Lithuania's short Baltic coast. There were imposing buildings there, people scurrying about, and deafening noise by comparison with the peace and quiet of our summer resort, which after all was only a sleepy village. Big ships such as we had never seen (going where, perhaps to the ends of the earth?) stood in the harbor, loading and unloading packages of unknown content. Life in this city atmosphere did not attract any of us. Already the grownups were planning what we would do when we got back home.

One of the delights of Palanga was that there were places of interest within walking distance. A walk of even several miles seemed no great thing. An evergreen forest was just across the street from our villa, extending to the park and manor house beyond. A winding road led to a hill named in honor of Birutė where a red brick chapel stood among the pines. From here there was a good view of the sea and the steeple of the village church.

Birutė, raised in Palanga in pagan times, became Queen of Lithuania in the days of invasions by the Teutonic Knights. She was a vestal virgin, tending the eternal fire of the gods when the great ruler Keistutis came by on horseback. He fell in love with her and snatched her away. From their marriage came a whole dynasty of famous rulers. Somewhere near Birutė's Hill was a cave, green with

61

ferns, called *Liurdas* (after Lourdes in France). A statue of the Virgin Mary in blue cloak and a crown of stars stood here. She was surrounded by floral offerings and constantly burning votive candles. The park, consisting of over 200 acres, with many spots for rest and meditation, was considered one of the most beautiful in Lithuania.

A local aristocrat, Count Tiškevičius, built his summer home, known as the Palace, in the 1890s, carefully planning the landscaping of the estate. Though vacationers had been coming for many years, Palanga was not widely known until the Count and his titled friends made it popular. The pump room was established, but the Count's plans to fully develop the area were interrupted by World War I. His greatest legacy, left for all people to enjoy, was the park, partly laid out in formal gardens and partly left to cultivated meadows and forest land. The manor house—what a palatial structure it seemed to us then—was a private home not open to the public. In later times, it became a Museum of Amber, a much-visited tourist attraction.

A life-size statue of Christ with arms outstretched stood in front of the palace steps, surrounded by flower beds. Much later, I learned that it was a copy of a work in white marble by the famous sculptor, B. Thorwaldsen, now in a museum in Denmark. Past the vast green lawn, walks led to buildings such as greenhouses. There I saw palms and orange trees for the first time. An enchanting topiary garden had hedges clipped in the shape of birds and animals. A huge bear looked so lifelike as to be almost ready to spring at us. At the rivulet you could walk the bridge and see a man-made waterfall. A favorite resting spot for tired feet was the Mushroom, an umbrella-like roof over benches built in a circle. You could also find shade under the leafy roofs of linden trees, which I was told were planted "roots up" or upside-down.

Nooks and corners of the park made ideal meeting places for lovers or friends out on a stroll. Occasionally, we would meet people we knew without any prior arrangement. I remember a cousin of Grandma's who managed to snag a dashing military officer (named Napoleon, of all things) after she was well past middle age. She never said so, but I thought the couple must have met while strolling in the park. We liked this pair because their pockets were usually stuffed full of candy, and they would give us some. They believed in eating candy as an antidote to nicotine addiction (both had been heavy smokers). Another distant relative likely to be in the park was a lovable Roman Catholic priest named J. Kasperavičius. We had all kinds of religions in our family, Catholic fanatics as well as freethinkers. Our parents, staunch Protestants, liked this wise priest who never scolded anyone for his or her "heretical" notions.

Speaking of meeting people, everybody who was anybody was likely to show up in Palanga, regardless of social position. It was the thing to do. You could vacation in other places but people did not think much of you unless you could say that you also went to Palanga. If you were not affluent enough to afford it, you saved up from your meager means for as long as necessary. Some people were against Palanga and this so-called manifestation of wealth, but most of them did go there, if only out of curiosity.

You only had to go to the beach to see some of the most important people in the land, many of them without so much as a bathing suit on their winter white bodies. There were separate beaches for various types of bathers, all according to their taste in being either clothed or unclothed. So long as rules of modesty were observed, nude bathing was accepted. Some people did not even own a bathing suit. If they felt that modesty required it, they would go into the water swathed in a sheet. The beach consisted of separate areas: one for men bathing in the nude, another for women in the altogether, and a third for mixed bathing for everyone, strictly for those with suits. In addition, entire families, such as ours, could go behind distant sand dunes, clothed or unclothed as they wished.

A policeman patrolled the beaches to see that everyone obeyed the rules. Amusing stories arose over the years. An enraged woman rushed over to the policeman to tell him about a peeping Tom spying on naked women, quite forgetting she was not wearing a stitch herself. Mr. Smetona, the President of Lithuania, was often seen holding court, i.e., having a cabinet meeting on the beach, with nobody wearing any clothes at all. I saw Aunt Aldona, a very forceful lady, loudly scold a young man in military uniform. He had been observing nude women from behind a sand dune through his long range spyglass—surely a criminal offense.

Our well-loved Palanga was an ideal rest and recreation spot for practically everyone. Whether true or not, people believed that its aura was good for what ailed them. In the words used in American advertisements, they went back to wherever they came from "relaxed, refreshed, and impressed." Grandma, in failing health for some years, always had high hopes that a rest in Palanga might improve matters. She was only one of many who came there for their health, whether mental or physical. Even hard-to-please Mamma really enjoyed these vacations by the sea.

A golden haired beauty with eyes of cornflower blue, Mamma was outspoken in her criticisms and did not worry about being popular. Comparisons about life "over here" and "over there in America" were quite frequent. She was not easily swayed in her opinions. According to Mamma, the house flies constantly buzzing around (no doubt attracted by the nearby horse stables) was something that would never be allowed in America. As for me, I believe that those Palanga days taught me to find joy in small things, a gift to be treasured for the rest of my life.

In this modern age of jet travel, people are frantically seeking new places to explore. There are plans to turn Lithuania (and the other two Baltic countries) into tourist attractions. Emerging from years of Soviet rule (or rather misrule), they are newly independent and their coffers are empty. How else can they make money, promoters of tourism ask? Having noted the desecration of other idyllic spots of the world, like tropical islands sleeping in the sun, the thought of what might happen to Palanga seems appalling to me. The tramp-tramp-tramp of tourists' feet might disturb the ineffable peace to be found among the swaying grasses of the sand dunes, the rustle of the forest and the sound of the sea.

Chapter Ten
Holidays and Religious Observances

Much as we loved Palanga and the long lazy days of summer, getting back to No. 4 on the Avenue in Kaunas was always a pleasure. In some ways being there again was like returning to another world. We looked forward to the joys of wintertime and the holiday celebrations. People would visit each other on these special days and would come to our house to present their greetings in person. On New Year's Day, for example, it was the custom for people to call on each other. They would either walk or come by horse and carriage. Usually there was no advance warning that they were coming, not even by those who had phones. Telephoning was not a universally accepted custom.

If our parents happened to be out, the visitors left their calling cards in a round beaded basket on a table in the hall. On holidays such as New Year's, the letters *p.f.* would be handwritten on a corner of the *vizitka* (calling card). This was abbreviated from the French words *pour feliciter* (to congratulate). In general, the French language was held in high esteem, especially among people educated in Czarist Russia. In the 19th century and well into the 20th, there were many Russians of culture who handled French better than they did their own native tongue. This was never so among Lithuanians, but still it was considered classy to know French words and expressions.

April 1st, or April Fools Day, was a day for pranksters and jokesters. It was enjoyed by many people, but jokes were made that were not always funny. Petrusia loved to make jokes whether it was April 1st or not. She would pick up the phone and have lengthy telephone conversations. Instead of saying "wrong number" she would pretend to be someone else, resulting in confusing situations. One day, after coming home from a walk in the park, I was told by Petrusia that Father was gone and would never be coming back. To me this was a terrible disaster. Father meant more to me than anybody else in the whole world, including Mamma or Grandma. I burst into tears and crawled into my favorite hiding place under the writing desk in my father's study. Maybe I would never have come out if Petrusia, loudly crying "April Fool," had not dragged me out by force.

April Fool's Day postcards, meant to be sent anonymously by mail, were much in fashion. Some, perhaps inscribed "From a Secret Admirer," were complimentary, picturing hearts and flowers in the manner of an American Valentine. Some of the postcards were not nice at all and might be downright insulting, telling people they were fat, stupid, or ugly. I remember one with a bright red devil saying, "Careful, your sins will find you out." The shiny cards with a gleaming surface and a scattering of glitter were the ones I liked best. Today such cards would be considered a leftover from the Victorian age.

A favorite pastime of mine was to put postcards in my album. The pages had little slits at the corners to insert the cards, so I didn't need paste. I wanted to save all April Fools Day cards, but the grownups would not allow me to keep some of the vulgar ones. My collection was full of birds, animals, flowers, and pretty scenes from far distant places. Anyone going away was sure to be asked to send postcards. One could exchange cards with grownups as well as children because some adults collected them as well. Some of my favorites came from Switzerland, which had a much higher grade of color photography than any obtainable locally.

One of the pleasures of winter, starting well before Christmas, was going to the ice-skating rink. There was one close by, in fact almost just across the street. For some time my brother had been going there with an older neighbor boy. Finally, I too got my high laced boots with the skates you had to screw on and remove every time. It was an adventure to be allowed to cross the street without an adult. After all, we could always be run over by the traffic, although there was the sound of sleigh bells to warn us if a sleigh was coming. The skating rink was a great place for young people wanting to escape from supervision by their elders.

According to family legend, Grandfather and Grandmother Šliupas had used a skating rink for secret meetings in their courting days. The atmosphere had not changed much since then. Waltz music one could dance to was still being played. There was cheer and laughter as skaters fell down and got up again. Gentlemen could push their lady friends around the ice on chairs with metal runners just as in days of old.

Christmas meant presents for children from Santa Claus. There was no mass exchanging of gifts and, among adults, no commercialization of this essentially religious holiday. We were not Roman Catholics but kept up some of the customs like Christmas Eve Supper. There were twelve dishes in memory of the Twelve Apostles containing no meat or fat as everyone was supposed to fast. On the table were several kinds of fish, both fresh and the ever popular salt herring, also various salads, clear beet soup and pickled mushrooms. For dessert there was milky white poppy seed soup and several dishes made with fruit. In remembrance of the Christmas star shining so bright over Bethlehem, one always looked for the first star in the sky before starting the meal. After the traditional supper, our Catholic friends went to Midnight mass.

Three days of Christmas were celebrated, the First, Second and Third Day. People did not go to work then as many offices and stores were closed. During this season, going to each other's homes to view the tree was a popular form of entertainment. For weeks we prepared decorations for the tree, usually a very tall one placed by the grand piano in the living room. Our paper chains, tiny baskets, painted pine cones, and other handmade items were shown off amid the store-bought tinsel, Bohemian glass birds, angels, shiny gold stars, and colorful balls. Real candles, not electric bulbs, were on the tree. They were lit only rarely because they were a real fire hazard. Each year we thought our tree more beautiful than any we had ever seen before.

On January 6th, known as Twelfth Night, people dressed in costumes of the Three Kings would visit houses in town as well as in the country. Sometimes they would be mounted on horses (camels, of course, not being available). They were followed by shepherds with dogs, sheep or other animals with a few angels in their train. Loudly singing religious songs, they would knock on the door asking for food and drink. Sometimes the Three Kings brought candy and other gifts for the children. The date usually coincided with Nurse Elena's Christmas since the Russian Orthodox calendar ran about ten days later than ours.

Soon after Christmas and Twelfth Night came Lithuanian Independence Day on February 16th. At nightfall people went out into the streets to admire the colorful illuminations, the fireworks, and the national tricolor flags flying from every house. There was not that much electricity to be wasted, but all those who could afford it decorated their houses with colored lights. The lights, the merriment in the streets and especially the fireballs, the flaring rockets and the shooting stars in the sky seemed to convert our town into a fairyland. Public ceremonies and military parades marked the event, but nothing seemed as impressive as the fireworks. One Independence Day was particularly memorable. A policeman rang our doorbell to announce the sad news of the death of Dr. J. Basanavičius. This great patriot, known as the Father of his Country, passed away on that very day, February 16, 1927.

The greatest of all holidays was Easter when there was much visiting back and forth. It was celebrated much more than Christmas. Easter, the Feast of the Resurrection, usually came well before the advent of spring. By this time, snowdrops would be peeking out of the ground. But it was often too cold for flowers like tulips or narcissus. Cherry, apple, pear and plum trees would wait well into late May before they would flower. Getting outfitted with brand-new clothes and hats or frilly Easter bonnets was not the custom. Easter was the most important religious observance of the year, marked by lengthy services in all Christian churches except for the Russian Orthodox whose calendar differed from ours.

To prepare for Easter, the house was given a thorough cleaning. There were almost no mechanical appliances available then. Rugs, for example, had to be taken outside, swept with brooms and beaten with long rattan paddles to get the dust out. Housewives wishing to keep up the minimum of a respectable life style had hired help to do the heavy work. Doing laundry without any washing machines was not easy, not to mention ironing done the old-fashioned way using a heavy black iron. You put red-hot coals inside through a little door. If the door was not properly closed, a coal might fall out and ruin your work. For smoothing the sheets, tablecloths and other linens there was a mangle. The linens were put in between the rollers, and then you turned the handle. Every curtain in the house had to be washed for Easter. Some, like the hand-worked ones in the living room (filet netting embroidered with baskets of fruit in an intricate design), were washed by hand with extreme care.

After the house was thoroughly cleaned, it was time for coloring the Easter eggs, in which most members of the household participated. There was nothing we children liked more. Quantities of colored eggs were needed for our own use, and others were to be given away. Each person going to someone's house had to bring at least one such egg with them. Newspapers were spread on Cook's well-scrubbed kitchen table so we could dabble with the dyes to our heart's content. One Easter, Nurse Elena decorated a white silk scarf with bursts of brilliant color. Fancy decorations done with beeswax and a pinhead (in the manner of Lithuanian folk art) were too complicated for any of us. The dyes used were generally in powdered form. Sometimes natural dyes were obtained by boiling yellow onion skins or the bark from birch and other trees.

Easter Sunday, Monday and Tuesday were three non-working days. The long period of Lent was over and this was a time for feasting, not fasting. Hostesses would vie with each other in serving as many fancy dishes as possible. There was always a variety of fish, baked, smoked, or marinated, steamed with stuffing inside, or swimming in aspic. There was likely to be a whole pike or salmon on the table, along with the inevitable herring salad, colored pink with beets, and sour cream aplenty in most dishes. There might be roast goose, duck, ham, and suckling pig, together with mounds of pork jelly, a holiday favorite that took hours to make. An unusual treat, not present in every home, was *Baumkuchen* (the German name for a "cake of many branches"). There was also the "Napoleon cake" of many layers of French pastry and the richest torte imaginable. Russian-style *Paskha* (a concoction of cream cheese and almonds) was usually made by Elena.

One superb hostess who always set a lavish table outdid herself one Easter. This was Aunt (or *Dédina*) Šliupas, the wife of Dr. Rokas Šliupas. She had prepared so many dishes that her table was not big enough. She was obliged to put some of the food on dining room chairs, benches and even under the table on the floor. She made her own "cake of many branches," explaining that it had to be made over an open fire. One turned a spit, ladling the egg mixture (almost entirely egg yolks and sugar) on to it from time to time. This would form the horns or branches with the cake ending up several feet high. Over the years, this tall cake became essential for all sorts of occasions. In present day Lithuania, there is hardly any wedding without one. Modern cooks make it on an electric rotisserie and it is even offered for export. This version, advertised in English as "tree cake," is heavily glazed with icing and decorated with shapes of colorful birds and flowers.

Almost everything was prepared at home in those days, but one might get additional items and imported delicacies such as Russian caviar, French wines, cognac and liqueurs, smoked salmon, exotic cheeses and the finest coffees from Mr. Kučinskas, the leading grocer. Marvelous almond cakes and raisin bread were obtainable at Jewish bakeries all over town because their Passover holiday came around this time. The Easter feast consisted of cold dishes somewhat like a glorious Scandinavian smorgasbord. Usually the hostess stayed home to receive guests. No special invitations were issued; everyone was welcome. The ceremony of "cracking the eggs" had to be done first to determine who held the strongest (or champion) egg in their hand. The Easter Bunny was much mentioned as the bearer of presents for the children, but no one talked of egg hunts or egg rolling on the lawn.

After Easter there were religious holidays, anniversaries, saints' name days or birthdays, to look forward to. In our house we celebrated Catholic name days and our own Protestant-style birthdays as well. Name days came on the feast day of one's patron saint. One of my names being Ona (Anne), I was entitled to a special cake called *kringelis*, baked in the shape of a large number eight on St. Anne's Day in July. But my birthday in January was celebrated too, with cake, candles, presents, and all. So many numerous holidays makes one wonder how any work got done. Office hours for public or private employees were quite short, only from 8 a.m. until 2 p.m. However, employees worked until 1 p.m. on Saturdays. They did not miss the Saturday to Monday long weekend, the accepted way of life in so many other countries. As the saying goes, you can't miss what you don't know. Life without a weekend holiday meant that they did not have to exhaust themselves trying to crowd too much housework, recreation and play into a few short hours at week's end. People returned from work early every weekday, ate their big meal of the day at 3:00 p.m. and had the rest of the day to do their chores or visit friends.

Veneration of saints was an important part of the Lithuanian national psyche, and we were all affected to some extent. Very early in life I heard about those people, whether real or imaginary, who were inspired to do great things. One of our maids had a storybook with pictures of saints that made good reading so I began to recognize them by name. Of course, I knew about St. Martin (a popular name among Protestants because of Martin Luther), the Roman centurion who met a ragged beggar and cut his cloak in half so the poor man could keep warm. Although the patron saints of

73

Lithuania was St. Casimir, a very pious prince who prayed all the time, he did not interest people as much as the valiant St. George, conqueror of evil (by coincidence, he is also the patron St. of England). St. George became associated with horses and farming equipment, and his Feast Day in April was an important date for horse fairs and for completing new yearly contracts with farm laborers.

Two other popular saints, named Izidorius and Rokas (of French origin, known elsewhere as *Roque*), were patrons of various aspects of farming like raising of sheep and the growing of rye or other crops. Most people of that day were named after a particular saints, a requirement for baptism as Roman Catholics. Many people had a second and a patriotic name selected from a list of national heroes of the past, like Vytautas, Gediminas or Birutė. Another name often mentioned in our household was saints Anthony, finder of lost articles. Even a nonbeliever like Mamma claimed that he was of help on several occasions, once in the finding of a long lost diamond ring.

Wayside shrines and crosses beside the roads or even on farmsteads near private homes were an important part of the landscape. Often the crosses were ornamented with suns, moons, stars, wheels, and similar symbols, said by scholars to be a direct link to the country's comparatively recent pagan past. Lithuania was one of the last countries in Europe to be Christianized. Years later, I learned of the wood carvings or *Santos* (saints) of New Mexico, USA, which are very much a part of the local folk culture. Their primitive style bears a strong resemblance to the works of Lithuanian woodcarvers of a former time.

The most popular image by far at these wayside shrines was a Meditating Christ (the Man of Sorrows, seated and resting his head on his hand) known as *Rūpintojėlis*, one who offers comfort and shows concern, a word not readily translatable. Often portrayed was Mary, or *Mater Dolorosa* (Suffering Mother), with seven swords piercing her heart. These naive portrayals of saintly figures were often surrounded by flowers, animals, doves and other symbols. Not surprisingly, there were likely to be angels, too, but devils were also much in evidence. Carvings of saints and angels in their simpering sweetness seemed much less interesting than the ferocious devils with their endless variety of droll facial expressions. Some resembled gargoyles, those fantastic creatures perched on the roofs of medieval cathedrals of Western Europe. Many of these carvings (like the incomparable collection of devil sculptures in the Kaunas of today) became collectors' items long ago and are now in museums.

Chapter Eleven
The Šliupas Connection

In my young years, Mamma's side of the family played a significant role, much more so than the Yčas branch of the family who lived elsewhere. Grandpa, Grandma and the other Šliupas relatives surrounded us in Kaunas in the early 1920s. (Various spellings were used by members of the family, e.g., Slupas, Szlupas etc.). Ours was a family-oriented society, and ties were close. Grandpa was away from home often, being a part-time diplomat, teacher and lecturer, whereas Grandma was near us most of the time. Grandpa was a man of many talents, a physician by profession, but not much inclined to medical practice, unlike his brother, Dr. Rokas, and Grandpa's daughter, Aunt Aldona. They were both giving their time and energy to the local Red Cross Hospital.

Jonas Šliupas, M.D. (1861–1944). Grandpa, perhaps the best known of the three Šliupas doctors, came from a small country village in northern Lithuania. He fought his way to educational achievement. All his life he was a fighter for his beliefs so the word "fought" is not inappropriate. A victim of Russian Czarist persecution because of his patriotic activities, he emigrated to the USA in 1884. He had been a contributor and editor of the underground magazine *Auszra* (Dawn), which was so influential in fostering the Lithuanian national spirit. Having started his university studies in Moscow, Russia, he overcame language barriers and pursued medical studies in America. He obtained his doctorate in medicine from the University of Maryland in 1891. Publishing newspapers and other publications on his own printing press, Grandpa worked for the education of his unlettered compatriots. Much of his life was devoted to the cause of independent Lithuania, and he raised his three children to continue in his footsteps.

After thirty-five years abroad, Grandpa Šliupas returned to the "Old Country" to help in any way possible. He was given the post of diplomatic envoy to various countries of Europe, including

England. Persons proficient in English were very scarce at that time. He was a brilliant orator and a scholar with many books to his credit (close to 70 titles in English, Lithuanian, and other languages, mostly on historical, political, and scientific subjects). Dr. J. Šliupas was the recipient of numerous honors, including three honorary doctorates from the University of Lithuania in Kaunas. Like many idealistic emigrants returning at the time, he tried to bolster the economy by pouring his savings into various, mostly unsuccessful, business enterprises.

Return to the "land of his dreams" brought much disillusionment. His uncompromising views on religion brought him many enemies and were a barrier to his political career. Dr. Šliupas was a freethinker, constantly pushing this cause in a strongly Roman Catholic society where the population was not used to an American-style free exchange of ideas. The concept of separation of church and state never did take root in Lithuania. His campaign for equality and legal protection of human rights for freethinkers and other so-called deviant groups was an uphill fight all the way.

He had no success in promoting a pet project called "Civil Metrication" under which the local governmental agency could record vital statistics including births, marriages, and deaths (even divorces in very rare cases) because it would have removed this lucrative business from the hands of church officials. Under this ecclesiastically-controlled system, people of no professed religion or church could be left entirely without such basic documents.

It must be emphasized here that Dr. J. Šliupas called himself a freethinker and not an atheist. His antireligious stance stemmed from personal experience with what he called the unjust and corrupt behavior of certain priests. His lifelong fight for liberation from the tyranny of the church was unpopular to say the least. His totally fearless attitude and his forceful personality made him a controversial figure among his countrymen on both sides of the Atlantic. Even today in the 1990s he is a controversial figure. There are those who admire him and consider themselves

*Šliuptarnia*i (followers of Dr. Šliupas). He had several clergymen, especially Protestants, among his friends and believed in freedom of self-expression. In his own family, he did not deny his children the right to associate with any religious group they liked. The two older ones grew up with no clear religious affiliation. Mamma, the youngest, attended Protestant churches, as she said, simply because her school friends happened to go there. Later, upon her marriage to Father who was of the Reformed faith, she formally accepted the Protestant religion.

Rokas Šliupas, M.D. (1865–1959). Rokas, like his older brother Jonas, surmounted many difficulties in achieving an education. Graduating in biology at the University of St. Petersburg, Russia, he obtained his medical degree at the University of Moscow in 1893. His personality and talents were unlike his brother's, but they shared some of the same interests. He grew up at a time of intense Russianization when the printing of material in the native language was forbidden. In his high school days, he was already distributing clandestine literature, including his brother's publications. As a university student, he established an underground newspaper and was put under surveillance by the Secret Police. In punishment for various patriotic activities, he was exiled to the Russian province of Kazan for a year.

As a young physician, he served with distinction in the Russo-Japanese War of 1905 and later in World War I, exhibiting a talent for organizing medical facilities. After Lithuania became independent in 1918, Dr. Rokas, as President of the Lithuanian Red Cross Society, organized several hospitals besides the one in Kaunas. He was active in promoting courses in medical training, traveling around the country and giving lectures and seminars. Under a somewhat gruff exterior, he was a humanitarian who helped needy students. He was generous in his financial contributions to various cultural enterprises like publication of newspapers and books. When Dr. Rokas retired, he was made Honorary President of the Lithuanian Red Cross Society.

Though he meant well, he had a prickly personality. Aunt Aldona told us that he was not exactly an easy person to work with, demanding discipline and strict attention to detail. Working with him at the Red Cross, she tried hard not to impose on the uncle-niece relationship. As we remember her, she herself was of quite a high-strung temperament, hardly ideal for administrative duties.

Dr. Rokas could be really dour at times. Perhaps he considered children a nuisance as he would often stalk out of the room when he saw us coming. Actually we came to his house not to see him but to be with our kind and loving great-Aunt, as different from her husband as day is from night. If consulted about our medical problems, Dr. Rokas would scare us by saying, "Give the children plenty of castor oil." Our hospitable and warmhearted great-Aunt, or Dėdina as we called her, was known far and wide for her delicious cookery. She was quite our favorite aunt.

Though seemingly harsh in manner, great-Uncle Rokas did have a heart somewhere deep down inside. A family story related that he was engaged for years to a lady he could not marry because of wartime events. His fiancée, a sister of Grandma's, never married and waited for him in Vilnius. But when he got there, she would not see him, sending him a written message instead. It said, "You knew me when I was young and pretty. I do not wish you to see me now that I am grey-haired, wrinkled and old." It was said that Dr. Rokas went away brokenhearted, but being a practical man, he soon married somebody else. He had four children, each one named in honor of Lithuanian heroes and heroines: daughters Aldona, Danutė, Gražina and son Mindaugas.

Aldona Šliupas, M.D. (1886–1980). Aldona, oldest daughter of Dr. J. Šliupas, born in New York City, had been brought up to be a doctor following in her father's footsteps. She graduated from the Women's Medical College in Philadelphia in 1908 (it later merged with the University of Pennsylvania), when there were very few women in the profession. In 1917, she joined her father and left the USA to give medical aid to Lithuanian refugees stranded in Voronezh, Russia. When independence was achieved after World War I, she remained to fight the virulent typhoid epidemic raging in western Lithuania and was awarded a Distinguished Service Medal by the Lithuanian government. Aldona demonstrated considerable diplomatic skills in getting shipments of food and medical supplies from England and the USA, notably the Lady Paget Mission, the Hoover Food Administration, and the European Red Cross Mission. These were leftover war supplies being distributed in Europe. She helped organize the Lithuanian Red Cross Hospital in Kaunas and was a member of its medical staff. It was then sadly wanting in every sort of help, especially in her chosen field of gynecology. She found time to write medical papers and to teach classes in nursing and related subjects.

There was a tragic love story in her past but she never talked about it. Mamma was the one who related this tale to us about her older sister. Aldona married very young against the wishes of her parents when she was a beginning student of medicine. Vincent Jankauskas, her husband, had a good job as Immigration Inspector on Ellis Island without ever finishing college. He saw no reason for his wife to outshine him and right away there was a conflict of wills. Aldona was determined to get her degree but Vincent would ridicule her ambitions by saying, "Give me those books in chemistry, biology and the rest. I can master these subjects in two weeks." There would be many tears and violent quarrels. Aldona would return weeping to her parents, but soon Vincent would prevail on her to come home again. Such an on-again, off-again marriage could not last. Much as Aldona loved her tall, dark and handsome husband, there had to be a divorce. Later she had many admirers but never married again.

Dr. Aldona had a great effect on our lives. She always seemed to be there, giving help and advice. Her younger sister, Hypatia , while acknowledging her virtues, did not always appreciate her domineering ways. After all, there was a difference of eight years between them. Mamma used to say that it was ridiculous to have Aunt Aldona give advice on the raising of children because she never had any. Neither did she have a husband but felt free to criticize Mamma's treatment of her spouse. If marital tiffs occurred in the Yčas family, Aldona liked to step in and give her opinion. There were instances when Grandma had to make peace between her two strong-willed daughters. It must have been hard for her because Aldona without question was her favorite, just as Mamma was "her Father's daughter."

Liudvika M. Šliupas (1864–1928). I owe much to Grandma. When I was still a baby, Grandma decided that Mother had her hands full with the other children and appropriated me for her very own. Nurses notwithstanding, it was she who was going to bring me up. She saw in me some characteristics of herself in her far-off youth. She had been a writer and somewhat of a poet and wanted me to be the same when I grew up. I loved my grandmother dearly and always ran to her—not my mother—when the world treated me ill. Unfortunately she died when I was still quite young, after having been an invalid for a long time. I have fewer memories of her loving kindness than I do of a fretful old lady in poor health, constantly reprimanding us and telling children not to do this or that.

Grandma, born Liudvika (or Liuda) Malinauskas on an estate in northern Lithuania, was a romantic soul. She also had great courage and determination. Grandma had considerable literary talent and was an early contributor to the magazine *Auszra*. As a young girl, she fell hopelessly in love with the fiery student Jonas Šliupas, considered totally unsuitable by her family, and followed him to the USA. Described by Grandma later as "an outspoken young giant with sky-blue eyes and yellow hair like a lion's mane," he was beneath her station in life. She was born into a family of gentry who had their own coat-of-arms and considered it genteel to speak Polish. This was a common phenomenon in Lithuania at that time, somewhat comparable to the prevailing fashion for Russian people of culture to speak French. Jonas was considered a misguided Litvoman, or Lithuanian fanatic, and a peasant besides.

Grandpa sailed for America, inviting his fiancée Liudvika to join him later. She did so in defiance of the wishes of her family, as soon as she reached the age of 21. Shortly after her arrival in 1885, they were married in New York City. When Liudvika sailed so courageously into New York Harbor, the world-famous Statue of Liberty had not yet been completed.

There were many hardships in Liudvika's young married life. Her husband's activities, such as printing and publishing of books and newspapers in the Lithuanian language, kept them on the edge of poverty. Liudvika went to Lithuania to claim her inheritance but had to come back empty-handed. Grandma was her husband's constant helpmate, continuing to write patriotic articles and romantic verse and bringing up three children in the process. She was an able seamstress and supported the family in this way for quite a long time, while her husband was out making idealistic speeches instead of making money.

Prof. Keistutis Šliupas (1888–1932). The second Šliupas child was Keistutis, born in Shenandoah, Pennsylvania. An only son, he was their special pride and joy. All who knew the boy, especially his teachers, were impressed by his ability to handle many different subjects—mathematics, languages, music, history—all with equal ease. He was a voracious reader. If not reading a book, one could find him outdoors, excelling in athletics. He also played the piano and composed humorous verses. When in college, he tried out many fields of interest including medicine, before becoming a physicist and mathematician.

Among the several universities he attended were those of Chicago and of Munich, Germany. Keistutis could have made his career in America or Germany but chose to go to Kaunas with the rest of the family. He gave great impetus to budding academic life while teaching theoretical physics at the newly opened School of Sciences at the University in Kaunas. He soon became Chairman of the Physics Department. Reportedly, he was one of its most popular lecturers due to his informal approach. He wrote noteworthy scientific papers and also edited a widely circulated humorous magazine. Unfortunately he died in his early forties from tuberculosis and acute alcoholism. His early death was a great loss to the family.

Uncle K played an important role in the young lives of my brother and me. He delighted in entertaining us with his stories and, above all, in the lessons he taught us in the rudiments of science. Uncle K's sense of humor sometimes took a sardonic turn. He would probably have laughed heartily had he known we are still puzzling over the "unsolved mystery" he left behind (only Uncle K would know the real answer).

Years after his death, Mamma made what she called a horrible confession. She had received a letter ages ago that she decided not to answer. A German girl wrote from Munich that she was the illegitimate daughter of Keistutis Šliupas. Mamma, so conservative she could not bear even the slightest breath of scandal about her brother, threw the letter into the wastebasket. Losing a possible relative (was the girl telling the truth or not?) was then and still is a source of great regret to those of us who loved Uncle K.

Hypatia Šliupas Yčas (1893–1987). The youngest daughter of Jonas Šliupas, born in Shenandoah, Pennsylvania. Biographical notes about her and her husband Martynas Yčas (1885–1941) are given elsewhere. How she got her rather unusual first name is a story which may hold some interest, especially since it sheds light on the household of Jonas and Liudvika Šliupas in the early years of their marriage. After much discussion, the youngest child was named not after a heroine of Lithuanian history as was the oldest child, Aldona, but after an outstanding woman of ancient Greece. Grandpa Šliupas, a defender of women's rights as well as human rights in general, was a classical scholar and a great admirer of Hypatia of Alexandria, Egypt. She was a teacher of astronomy and mathematics in the 4th century AD, a pagan and a courageous fighter for the right to choose her own beliefs. She was so outspoken that she finally died as a martyr, victim of Christian intolerance. According to Grandma, the name was chosen on the advice of a friend of the family, Rev. Vladas Dembskis, who was well educated and a classical scholar. He was a former Roman Catholic priest who had deserted his church long ago. Reverend Dembskis, fleeing persecution, found a permanent home with the Šliupas family in Scranton, Pennsylvania. He stayed with them for over a dozen years until his death in 1913. More than just a counselor and friend, he was a well-loved substitute grandfather for the children, especially the youngest. Among my mother's most precious childhood memories were those of her wise and loving "Grandpa."

Father was deeply involved in Lithuanian plans for national independence. When he came to the USA in 1913 on a diplomatic mission, accompanied by Dr. J. Basanavičius, a visit to that fiery patriot, Dr. J. Šliupas, was on the schedule. Mamma liked to tell the story about the way she first met her future husband. She was peering over the banister on the second floor landing of her family home in Scranton, Pennsylvania, trying to catch a glimpse of those important visitors from overseas. When the front door opened, she was so affected that she immediately felt she was about to meet the great love of her life. Dr. Basanavičius, an older man with a long, gray beard, looked so imposing that she thought he would be hard to talk to. But her heart went out to his young companion who radiated warmth and charm the moment he stepped into the hall.

Chapter Twelve
The World Outside

The people we came in contact with, whether family friends or strangers, were rather like visitors from outer space. They made us aware of the great big universe outside our limited circle of vision. Also influential in introducing us to the world outside our four walls were the tutors who came to teach us. Grandpa gave us lessons in history and geography, but he came seldom. Uncle K came more regularly to instill rudiments of physics and mathematics. We were fascinated with our uncle's accomplishments and his teaching methods. He could sharpen a pencil with his penknife to the finest point anyone had ever seen and do wonderful drawings like caricatures or cartoons. Uncle K introduced us to Swift's *Gulliver's Travels* and teased us by saying that some of it was not fit for children's ears. So vivid were his scientific explanations that one of them sticks in my memory even today. In illustrating the power of heat, he would make a coiled serpent cut out of paper whirl around while holding it above the flame of a candle. Having been a bachelor all of his life, Uncle K was also clever at many household tasks. One dish I often saw him cook was a large pan of ham and eggs. He said, "No trouble at all if you have three or four eggs and plenty of ham." Besides all these talents, he had a good voice and sang very well.

We had lessons in drawing and painting, and some attempts were made to teach us ballet, a subject for which none of us had the slightest talent. Sometimes, a prima ballerina from the national theater would instruct us along with a group of other children in our living room. I wish I could remember if this was the noted Russian ballerina V. Niemchinova. Like some of her compatriots who were refugees from the Great Revolution, she was the mainstay of the Lithuanian Ballet Theater and had trained a rising young generation of local dancers. However, dancing lessons did not do a thing for the untalented Yčas children.

More important for our future life was the fact that we had learned English. Since our earliest years, Mamma had attempted to teach us her language, but her lessons were not a success. Our first governess was Isabel Bain of Scotland. She was interviewed for the position by Father's good friends in Edinburgh. After all these years, I still remember some hymns this deeply religious Presbyterian lady taught us, such as "Jesus loves me, this I know, for the Bible tells me so." Miss Bain complained that Lithuanian winters were too cold and did not stay with us long. She left to join relatives in what she said was the warmer climate of Melbourne, Australia.

Our parents thought that their children should learn as many languages as possible. Father, though not technically a linguist, could make a speech in five or six languages and jokingly said he could speak Latin, a "dead language," as well. He could recite poetry in resounding Latin hexameter, a mystery to us at the time. Classical studies were very much a part of the cultural requirements of the day so we learned Latin rather early. Our earliest exposure to a foreign language was from Nurse Elena who spoke Russian to us. Our parents wanted us to learn French, which we mastered only much later. For some reason, there was no talk of teaching German in our house (Slavic languages were supposedly less alien than German). Some family members, like Aunt Aldona, wanted to teach us Polish which they spoke very well. However, Grandma put her foot down and firmly said "No." To my regret, Polish is a language I never learned.

Our parents were in total agreement about teaching us at home and not sending us to school. At that time this was considered a very odd idea. Father had entered high school only at a later age, having been prepared at home for the examinations. He said it was an experience that had done him more good than harm. As for Mamma, she was always making comparisons with the supposedly superior educational institutions of America. She regarded Lithuanian (and maybe all European) schools with distrust, if not outright dislike.

How Mamma was ever persuaded to send her one and only son to a Swiss boarding school is hard to imagine. When he was about ten years old, he spent some months (less than a year) at the International School in Geneva, which was attended mostly by British and American children. To be thrown into a school environment (especially in a foreign land) must have been rather shattering. At least there was no language problem, as by that time he was fluent in English. Sending my brother to school in Switzerland turned out not to be the best idea in the world, considering that he came down with a severe case of scarlet fever while he was there. Living in our sheltered environment and having few contacts with other children, we had not been exposed to the usual childhood diseases. My brother caught the first bug that came along. Mamma went to Switzerland to bring him home. She said that every one of his possessions had to be sterilized or thrown out altogether.

An important part of our lives was having the Yčas relatives come to town and getting to know them better. So far I have mentioned only those related to Mamma's family, i.e., the Šliupas clan who lived in Kaunas. Many other relatives were little known to us and hard to reach. Aunts, uncles and cousins lived too far away—in the USA, Poland, or elsewhere. Grandma had family members living in Vilnius, but traveling was impossible because the borders between Poland and Lithuania were closed due to the "rape of Vilnius" incident. Father's relatives and the friends who accompanied them lived mostly around Biržai in the North Country.

One of our Yčas aunts liked to say that the family was easily moved to tears and just as easily to laughter. In other words, they did not dwell on their sorrows. It was an enjoyable jaunt for them to leave their provincial home and go to the "Big City" to enjoy social life, especially the theater. The happy Yčas group with their ready laughter, humorous repartee, and sheer lightheartedness differed from some of the Šliupas relatives who were inclined to take the world too seriously.

89

Kaunas, catapulted into fame, was the nation's capital and was the scene of a vigorous social life. The National Theater was in good shape because it was a State enterprise completely supported by the Government. It had quality performers and hardly anybody in town could command the high salaries paid to opera singers. Entrance tickets cost very little and people went as often as they did to the movies. Movies were of course imported, and Hollywood productions were top favorites.

We could anticipate a visit from the Biržai relatives and friends in winter or early spring. This was timed so they could enjoy cultural activities not available in their small town. Part of the group would be our house guests for as long as they liked. Every day they would go sightseeing or attend concerts, exhibits, and lectures. They enjoyed seeing movies too, but going to the theater in the evening to see an opera was the crowning event.

Most such social diversions were naturally outside my reach, but I did see an opera before I was seven (*Carmen* by Bizet), probably with some of the Biržai relatives. About that same time, I also saw a movie (*The Last Days of Pompeii*). This was the era of the silent screen and, of course, no color film. A live piano player played scary tunes and thunderous chords as buildings collapsed and boiling lava from Mt. Vesuvius buried the town. Years later, on seeing remakes of this movie, none of them seemed quite so impressive despite the lavish technicolor and the sound effects as that first Pompeii movie seen so long ago.

Many of the older generation had seen many theatrical productions in their student days in Russia before the Great Revolution at some of the best theaters of Petrograd (St. Petersburg) or of Moscow. In those days, people went to Russia to be educated because there were hardly any high schools and no institutions of higher learning in Lithuania. Denial of educational opportunity and of employment at a higher level was a conscious policy of the Russian oppressors. Non-Russians who wished to study at universities encountered many obstacles. Lithuanians were particularly distrusted because they had participated in armed uprisings against Czarist rule as late as 1905.

Father's favorite cousin, Dr. Jokubas Mikelėnas, was the life of the party. He and Father had both attended the University of Tomsk. He was my godfather, full of affection and gaiety, and a great singer of folk songs. His sister, gentle Katrytė (Katherine), was sometimes with him, very deaf but loveable just the same. One Yčas uncle who was especially welcome was Father's older brother, Jonas (John) the Professor. Having many children of his own, he was good to us. He would tell us to look in his pockets where there was likely to be chocolate candy wrapped in those shiny foil papers that we liked so well. We had another "uncle," a bachelor Yčas cousin called Jonas the Engineer, who never brought us any presents. He was too stingy for that although he had a good government job in the Post Office. He did not even spend money to buy new clothes for himself. It was said he wore the same coat, suit, and hat that he had worn before the Great Revolution. His once black overcoat was green with age, and he carried an umbrella riddled with holes. In fact, he was an eccentric (there has to be one in every family).

Sometimes, there was another visitor, Army Col. Jonas Variakojis whom we liked much more. He would join the Biržai group, being from that area himself, if his military duties permitted. He served with distinction in the Wars of Independence (1918–1920), repulsing Russian, Polish and German invaders. He was not a blood relative, but Father loved him like a younger brother ever since Jonas' school days and entry into the Military Academy in St. Petersburg.

Among the remarkable personalities from the North Country were several ministers of our Reformed Church. One was the venerable Rev. J. Šepetys with white beard and mustachio. He was looking for adventure and excitement—not quite in keeping with his ministerial status. He liked parties and was likely to have left his wife at home. At these gatherings there was such laughter and partying, such exchange of jolly stories and anecdotes and, above all, such singing! Father would be requested to sing and to play the piano. Although not really a musician (he did not read music) he could play folk songs by ear and a polka or two. When the Biržai group gathered, the songs for which the North Country is famous made the rafters ring.

Trying to look solemn amid the merriment was the Rev. Prof. P. Jakubėnas, very conscious of his position as the highest authority in our Church. There was no Reformed Church in our town, but services were generally held at the local Lutheran church. Rev. Jakubėnas would come to officiate on special occasions. He was in Kaunas for the christening of all four of the Yčas children. This took place not in church but in our living room, and all of us were baptized at the same time. None of us were babies anymore. I was old enough to have clear memories of the twins screaming loudly as their heads were sprinkled with baptism water. Father, as we have said, was a great pillar of the Church, but very open minded. He was not pious in the least, and Mamma was even less so. In my childhood, there was no Bible reading or religious education in our house. Nurse Elena told me of the Guardian Angels who were all around us, but nobody in the family instructed us on religious matters.

While the Biržai group was at our home, the conversation was about opera more often than not. One of our top music critics (the composer, Vladas Jakubėnas) characterized Lithuanian society between the two World Wars as being "completely enamored of opera." Some opera singers were quite spoiled by all the adulation. Their romantic and often scandalous exploits were subjects for gossip among those sitting in the cafés or walking on Freedom Avenue under the linden trees. The main café was the one known as Conrad's, a gathering place for all the so-called important people in town. Our Biržai visitors would certainly be going there to see and be seen and to hear the latest tittle-tattle. Many of the group had been around and were able to compare Kaunas performances with those given elsewhere. They rejoiced that the National Theater was making great progress and that productions of opera and ballet, at least in scenery and costumes, could compare with the best.

Part of the social activities in Kaunas were, undoubtedly, the hunting parties during appropriate seasons of the year. Most of the men, whether high or low on the social scale, liked to go hunting. The game they bagged was only a short distance away from the cooking pot as it was generally cooked and eaten soon afterwards. Some brought their hunting dogs, but Father not being too serious a hunter, had no dogs. Forests were thick and game was plentiful. There was good hunting for large animals, including boars and deer. Nobody mentioned bears, so maybe they were extinct, but wolves were numerous. One extraordinarily cold winter they became a real menace. They attacked not only smaller animals such as sheep but sometimes even little children. In the mid-1920s, wolf hunts were organized in many parts of the country. A cruel custom was for beaters to go ahead for the convenience of the hunters. They stirred up the deer, hares, and many kinds of birds like quail, partridge, duck, grouse and woodcock. At these hunting parties, which were social occasions for the most part, you could meet important people, from the President of the Republic to his cabinet ministers, high-level military officers, and on down.

The renowned opera singer Kipras Petrauskas, a keen hunter, was likely to be there. He had a hail-fellow-well-met manner and could be charming when he wished. According to a family anecdote, one time he was in a foul mood and got himself laughed at. He came out with a stream of bad language in front of Martynas, Jr., who was very young at the time. One of the words was *Gyvatė* (snake). A peculiarity of the Lithuanian language is that it has no real swear words, and to call somebody a snake, toad, or a devil is considered going pretty far. My brother thought he was referring to a real snake and started shouting in great excitement, "Where? Where? Show me!" K. Petrauskas, good actor that he was, explained, "There was a snake hiding behind that stump, but now it's gone" and pretended to search for it. I can still visualize this singer, dressed for the hunt in brilliant attire. Whereas others wore plain plus fours in drab colors, Petrauskas came in a coat of shocking pink, orange hat, and wearing brightly checked pants. Father and Petrauskas were friends quite apart from hunting and operatic interests. They were also frequent partners at *preferance* (a card game as popular in Eastern Europe as bridge was in other lands).

Hunters get very hungry, and picnic food was brought to the woods by the womenfolk. Heating over a crackling wood fire one winter day, as I remember, was an iron pot of sauerkraut, ham and sausage, while potatoes were roasting in the embers. There was much jollity and drinking of liquid refreshments, the most popular being vodka, said to cheer you and to warm your bones. I remember the taste of that hearty meal and the way everyone wolfed it down. You had to eat fast before the food cooled off in the frosty weather. A vivid memory remains of a sleigh ride home from the hunt in the winter twilight with the last rays of the sun barely showing through the clouds.

Chapter Thirteen
The Social Scene

As a way of getting people together, there was nothing like having a dance (or ball as it was called in those days). Formal attire was required. Ladies were dressed in long gowns; and the men wore tail coats and stiff shirts. When the immense oriental rug was rolled up, there was ample room for dancing on the parquet floor in our living room, now turned into a ballroom. Lights blazed from the crystal chandeliers. A buffet supper of cold smorgasbord-type dishes was prepared in the dining room in the light of candles, set in the candelabra, which glittered like pure gold.

Also lit were several brass samovars, as the silver one with the ducal coronet would not be enough to provide the tea for a big crowd. The music was provided by some accomplished player at the Knabe grand piano. Sometimes people would play guitars, violins, or other portable instruments. If opera soloists were present, as they often were, they might perform, and the entire assembly would break into song. Liquid refreshments like wine and champagne were not really needed to get people to sing. They were ready to sing at the drop of a hat.

Out of my hazy recollections of social activities and great balls at No. 4 on the Avenue, only one comes completely clear. This was a grand celebration of the birthdays and simultaneous name days of Martynas, Sr. and Martynas, Jr. St. Martin's feast day came in the middle of November. There was a great array of opera singers, actors, painters, writers and others associated with the arts. Father had many friends among them and was willingly accepted into their company.

From the early beginnings of the *Meno Kūrėjų Draugija* (Creative Arts Association) in 1919, he had wholeheartedly supported their efforts. In the cultural wasteland left by World War I, this Association founded the National Opera Theater, the Conservatory of Music, the Art Academy, and many related enterprises. Our parents spoke of having attended the historic opening of the Opera, when K. Petrauskas, among others, sang in G. Verdi's *La Traviata* on New Year's Eve, 1920. In the period between the two World Wars, this opera, as a matter of tradition, was always given in Kaunas on December 31st.

K. Petrauskas was on hand to lead the singing of a special song of congratulations, "We Come to Salute Both the Father and the Son," composed by one of the group. The manuscript, signed by all present, was kept for years by Father as a treasured memento. Among the bevy of performers present, was the ballet dancer J. Vasiliauskas, a servile attendant of Petrauskas who followed him everywhere. Special friends, like the opera singers Mrs. V. Grigaitis and Mrs. V. Jonuškaitė-Zaunius, also dramatic actors Mr. and Mrs. P. Kubertavičius, were there. One could not help noticing the painter P. Kalpokas, always noisy when he had too much to drink. He was dancing with his overcoat in his arms, telling everyone that he had found a new lady friend.

Our parents and their friends were young and exuberant, delighting in the social whirl of banquets, receptions, and especially ballroom dancing. Watching our parents getting dressed for the ball was always an experience. Father would wear his forked swallowtail coat, starched white shirt and bow tie, complete with white gloves. Men wore formal clothes with different suits for daytime and for evening, when a dinner jacket or tuxedo was proper. When paying official calls on the President of the Republic, for example, or on cabinet ministers or ambassadors, one wore striped pants and a long morning coat, called a Prince Albert. On state occasions, Father wore a top hat. For everyday use, a bowler was considered suitable.

Mamma would put on a ball gown of fabulously gauzy material. A favorite gown was midnight blue embroidered with tiny silver beads. Around her neck she generally wore her long string of crystals, a present from Father that came from the far-off Ural Mountains of Russia. A big fan of fluffy white ostrich feathers completed her costume. Sometimes she wore something bright and shiny in her hair. Invitations were sometimes worded "evening attire with *tête parée*." This French term, approximately translated as head ornamented, signified that ladies were supposed to wear wreaths or something similar on their heads. Sometimes Mamma would wear a crown of rhinestones, sparkling like diamonds. To us children it made her a vision of royalty. I can still see us dancing up and down and shrieking, "Mamma looks like a queen!"

Ordinarily Mamma did not enjoy dressing up. She was not the kind of woman to spend hours primping before a mirror. Impressing people with flashy clothes or what she called outward glitter was of little concern to her. Going beyond what she considered decent and proper was deemed hardly necessary. She had good looks but was not vain in the least and used the minimum of makeup. A favorite saying of hers was "beauty unadorned is adorned the most." This did not always suit Father who liked to do things with a flair and did not mind showing off. He would have liked his beautiful Hypatia to make a big splash and deck herself out in fine clothes, expensive jewelry and furs. Her talk of being simple and modest in her tastes did not please him.

Father was much more interested than Mamma in going out in the evenings. We were far too young to understand the reasons why she was not a good social mixer. Though she spoke Lithuanian very well, a barrier existed between her and local Kaunas society. In a sense, she was always the outsider. She was very sensitive and sometimes imagined slights where none were intended, getting more distant and withdrawn as the years went on. She never felt completely at home in what she sometimes called the wilds of Lithuania, always longing for that so-called American paradise.

I have no recollection of exactly where all these dances were held. Many were charity benefits, then very much in vogue. One charity organization promoting such social gatherings is forever to be remembered because of its somewhat odd name *Pieno Lašo Draugija* (Milk Drop Society). This organization raised money to provide milk for the children of the poor and was supported by the wives of the "Powers that Be," headed by the spouse of the Prime Minister. There were always tickets sold for drawings with fabulous prizes. These could be crystal vases, silk shawls, dishes and other objects of fine porcelain, or original paintings by well-known artists. The morning after the ball, our parents had to tell us all about it and show us the prizes, if any, that they had won. And what of the food they ate? Did they by chance have caviar and champagne, did the orchestra play good music, and how did they enjoy the dancing?

Father, a great dancer, enjoyed every moment. Mamma, who did not have this talent, enjoyed the dance floor somewhat less but did not lack for good spirits. Directing some of the dances was one of Father's great joys. He used to tell us about the social events of his youth when one of the favorite dances was the Polish Mazurka, full of vigorous movements. Ladies who wanted to be graceful learned to dance this with a glass of water balanced on their heads, a story we found hard to believe.

Many of the people enlivening our parties in the long ago are now like vague shadows waltzing off into the distance. A few, however, refuse to disappear into that Never Never Land. Strangely, they included few personalities from the realm of government and politics. Of course, Father associated with politicos, but they made less impression on me than some rather flamboyant people from the artistic world. P. Kalpokas a leading artist of the day, equally known for his landscapes and portraits in either oils or watercolors. He was one of the older generation who taught at the Art Academy, guiding hopeful young artists. Father was fond of him since he was a talented and amusing compatriot from Biržai. Mother disliked him because of his drinking habits. He was the boon companion of our Uncle K, who was even then on the dangerous road to alcoholism. Kalpokas studied art in Italy in his youth and married there. All the time we knew him, his Italian wife was never around (perhaps she had died years before), but he often brought his son. Rimtas had sparkling black eyes, an olive complexion, and dark hair like his mother. This was the young student who came occasionally to give us art lessons. Later he, too, became a painter of distinction.

Kalpokas, Sr. is hard to forget also because so many of his pictures were hanging on our walls. My visual memory is such that I can still see some of his landscapes as well as an oval portrait framed in gold. That blonde and wistful cherub, floating in clouds of pink and blue, happens to be me at age three. When our parents went abroad, especially to London, Kalpokas would ask them to bring him oil paints. None would do except those made by Winsor & Newton, which he considered the best of the best. (Years later, in the 1990s, these paints are still considered to be of superior quality). Museums in Lithuania as well as in Chicago, Illinois, own some of P. Kalpokas' paintings. In some mysterious way, a huge canvas of his which we had in our Kaunas home recently turned up in Washington, D.C. It is a collective portrait of the men who signed the Lithuanian Declaration of Independence in 1918. This painting must have had some interesting adventures, but I have no details.

Another unusual person, veterinary doctor Konstantinas Sokolskis, was a frequent guest. A Russian who had settled in Lithuania in prewar times, he was fluent in both languages. A man of many talents, he had artistic leanings and was also a journalist. Dr. Sokolskis was a longtime friend of the family. He looked after our horses and other livestock, later coming regularly to our farm to give anti-tuberculosis injections to the herd of cows. Dr. S was a good pianist and had a pleasant singing voice. He loved to accompany himself on our Knabe grand piano, while regaling us with renditions of "The Flea Song," made famous by F. Chaliapin, with the Russian refrain *"Ha-Ha-Ha-Ha-Blaha* (Flea)." This always made a big hit. Dr. S was generally well liked and was a welcome guest at parties. He liked to relate anecdotes about his veterinary experiences, always described in lurid detail. "Have you heard the one about the cow that had such a difficult birth? Well, she lost so much blood that she almost died," he would say. His tales were not always in good taste. He took a wicked delight in shocking some of the more squeamish ladies in his audience. Smiling broadly, he would ask them if they were ready to hear more.

Likely to breeze in, and particularly if he heard there was a party, was Father's distant cousin , J. Aukštuolis. He loved the outward trappings of the "striped pants" set and his position in the Lithuanian diplomatic service. He was a "social butterfly" who enjoyed meeting people and was full of stories about the friends he made for Lithuania in various countries of the world. In his youth he was frivolous in the extreme and had not changed much according to those who knew him then. He was Father's somewhat younger companion during their student days at Tomsk University. Aukštuolis loved to play practical jokes and spent more time partying than in minding his books. He needed much coaching so he would not fail his examinations.

In his student days, Cousin Jonas wanted to be known as a photographer. This was an easy way to popularity, cameras being rather scarce in Old Russia. He would purposely neglect to put film in his camera and then announce to his waiting public that the pictures did not come out. He did a few brilliant things in his life, one of which was to marry a rich and beautiful heiress from Riga, Latvia. The other was to wangle an appointment as Ambassador to South America where people of his outlook could fit very well into local society. He worried endlessly about his clothes and his personal appearance. This was at a time when the utmost formality in dress was a requirement for diplomats. Father used to joke that Cousin Jonas spent hours in front of the mirror. Much later, when Father was fleeing the Soviet occupation, he happened to be at the Ministry of Foreign Affairs and was able to give him the documents needed to cross the border. Alas, his own fate was a tragic one. During the mass deportations perpetrated by the Soviets in 1941, Aukštuolis was taken to Siberia and perished there, far from his wife and family.

The National Theater was very much a part of the social whirl and a great place to meet people you knew or would like to meet. During intermission time, theatergoers would march around the circular foyer for just that purpose. Beside operatic and dramatic productions, there were also light operas, musical comedies or operettas. In the early 1920s there was a satirical theater that caused a sensation, presenting playlets (skits) that were the talk of the town. The name of this group was *Vilkolakis* (a kind of vampire). The performers, amateurs as well as professionals, wrote plays satirizing various individuals. They made the audience laugh, but they were so outspoken that some people were shocked. One scene in particular caused great indignation. Army officers in uniform shook with fear and crawled under the table at the sound of a rifle shot, which proved to have been nothing more than the popping of a champagne cork. The "vampire theater" was closed by the authorities after only a few years because it dared to mock the government and its military leaders.

Mamma and Aunt Aldona were also portrayed on the *Vilkolakis* stage. Two actresses appeared, one short and blonde, the other tall and chestnut-haired. They were dressed in what was considered outrageous American costume in loud colors, huge hats, and high button shoes. Swinging their long knee-length beads, they chased each other around the stage exclaiming, "In America they do thus and so" and contradicting what had just been said, "No, no, this is the way they really do things in America." Never let it be said that none of the Šliupas clan had a sense of humor. Mamma laughed heartily when relating this story and said that neither she nor our aunt had been at all offended at the time.

One of Father's favorite sayings was "I love people, no matter what their religion or nationality." He had Russian, Polish, Jewish, American, and British friends among others. He said that in his student days he increased his circle of acquaintances by organizing a balalaika and mandolin orchestra that gave several successful concerts. When he made friends, it was often for life. At

No. 4 on the Avenue, we were visited by two lifelong friends from abroad. Prof. J. Y. Simpson was there for our christening and was one of the godparents. This Scottish theologian and scientist was an envoy from Britain to old-time Russia. He and Father had become fast friends after meeting in St. Petersburg.

One of Mamma's fond memories was of a bright winter's day and her first glimpse of Professor Simpson. While out walking in the snow across one of St. Petersburg's innumerable bridges, she heard the jingle of approaching sleigh bells. She was startled when a sleigh stopped and two gentlemen, all bundled up in furs, offered her a ride. One of them turned out to be Father, highly amused that she had not recognized her own husband. The stranger in the tall fur hat sitting beside him was introduced as "my new friend, the Scottish professor." Later they were together again at the Paris Peace Conference in 1919, where Professor Simpson was a member of the British delegation. He was a staunch Presbyterian and developed a great interest not only in Lithuanian public affairs but in our Reformed Church as well.

A second lifelong friend was an American, Robert J. Caldwell, an industrialist from New York. He was a great talker, loved funny stories, and had strong ideas about applied psychology (the Dale Carnegie variety) as well as on making money. One plan, not practical in our local conditions, was to grow strawberries commercially in the winter in hothouses heated by electricity. Father and Mr. Caldwell had met by accident in the Adlon hotel in war-torn Berlin, Germany. Mr. Caldwell was there working with the Hoover Food Administration, distributing food and medicines in various countries of Europe. The two were greatly interested in each other's conversations. Father said that they had so much in common that they talked the whole night through, sitting on their suitcases in the unfurnished hotel lobby. Among the topics discussed, oddly enough, was spiritualism and possibilities of life in the Hereafter, according to the tale Father told us.

In those days, while Lithuania was getting back on its feet, Kaunas society was trying to get away from so-called foreign influences. Nobody would dance the Mazurka or the equally lovely Krakowiak because they considered them far too Polish. Political sentiment excluded Russian dances, although the dreamy and romantic Alexandrovsky waltz was still a favorite. There was some native folk dancing and the ancient *Suktinis* (Whirl about) was the proper way to start every public dance. However, nothing was quite as popular as the Viennese waltz.

If asked to direct the "Waltz with Figures," Father would be in his element. This probably had its origins in the ancient French contredanse and had some similarity to modern American country dancing. To the strains of Strauss's Blue Danube or other waltzes like the Merry Widow, the leader would get the dancers lined up and call, "advance...retire...couple to the left...couple to the right...join hands...form a circle...circle around and find your partner" and so on. Every so often, Father would call, *"Gyviau, Linksmiau"* (translated as "step lively"), which kept everybody laughing and dancing until they were ready to drop.

The "Waltz with Figures" ended with the command, always in French, *Chevaliers a genoux* (Gentlemen on your knees). The kneeling gentlemen would have their partners circle around them and then ask the ladies to let them kiss their dainty little hands in thanks for the dance. Perhaps this scene of happy dancers sailing around the ballroom with evening gowns billowing and swallow tails flying would be a good place to end this account of the social scene. The time was approaching when there would be no more balls and no more dancing. A long period of grief and mourning marked the death of our beloved Grandma and the breakup of the family circle.

Chapter Fourteen
Grandma Went Away

For several years after the purchase of our place in the country, it was used for family excursions. Grandma always enjoyed going there. It was just a few miles south of Kaunas. The place was in ruins with hardly a building left standing, owing to bombardments in World War I. It was not ready for occupancy or even for getting it back into shape for farming. Our parents went there on inspection trips to see how the work was coming along, sometimes taking us with them. Petrusia often came with us and made herself very useful. Sometimes she would go a day or two early to prepare for the family's coming. The gardener had to be told to trim the neglected bushes, cut the weeds, and sprinkle the garden paths with sand in order to make all things beautiful.

According to Father, Grandma's advice on agricultural matters was very valuable. After all, was she not the only real farmer among us? Brought up on a country estate, she retained a lifelong interest in the land and a love for all growing things. When transplanted to America, she was obliged to live in town, but part of her summers were spent on a farm in Pennsylvania's Allegheny country. She had persuaded Grandpa to buy the farm, although he much preferred living in town. He gladly visited the farm for short vacations but, as Mamma said, he just couldn't wait to catch the train back to Scranton and home.

Mamma said that her mother never ceased regretting the loss of her childhood home and often spoke with nostalgia about the estate in the country. Years later, I had a chance to see it for myself. This was the first visit for Mamma, Father and me. The estate, called *Ručeniai*, in the parish of Vaškai, was close enough to Biržai for her to have attended school there in her childhood. Though her time at the old home was short, Grandma loved the place deeply. When financial difficulties caused her brothers to sell the property later, they did so without a word to Liudvika (or Liuda), who was far away in the USA at the time.

Grandma was only ten years old when both her parents died. Guardians and a foster mother were appointed by the Court. They sent Liuda, the oldest child, and her five brothers and sisters to Latvia. Here there was a high school in the town of Mintauja, also known as Jelgava, much frequented by Lithuanians. It was in Mintauja that Liuda grew up and later met her future husband, Jonas Šliupas.

When I finally saw it, Grandma's old home was still standing and in good repair. It had been used as the village school for many years. Nothing was to be seen inside. The doors and windows were tightly closed. I tried to peer through the shutters. Was I looking for ghosts from the past? Had a coat of arms once hung on the wall? Grandma made fun of such aristocratic trappings. She met our questions by saying, "There was a black raven on the Malinauskas coat of arms. It had no eyes to see with and in fact was quite blind."

The farm buildings nearby looked too new to hold our interest. The orchard where Grandma must have walked was unkempt with weeds. There were a few apple trees, gnarled and mossy with age. They were not likely to ever bear fruit again. There was no hint of the lily pond or of the avenue of linden trees Grandma had talked about as such a romantic place. The parish priest was not available so there was no one to ask about church records, if any, of a family long gone. However, the church yard where my ancestors were buried deserved a visit. It was full of unusual and intricately carved wooden crosses. We found the grave of the mother Grandma had lost when only a child. A plain and very time-weathered wooden cross marked the spot. It bore the inscription "Karolina, pray for us." My great-grandmother had died in childbirth in her mid-thirties. Her husband, too, passed away soon afterwards. Grandma treasured the few memories she had of her mother and continued to miss her to the end of her days. Mamma told us that she had a recurrent dream about her mother calling to her to join her in the next world saying, "Liuda, come with me. Your life on earth will not be a happy one."

Though Grandma was in poor health, nobody suspected that we were about to lose her so soon. She died on Palm Sunday at age sixty-four, when I was eight years old. This was the first real disaster in my young life—the first experience of death for us children. We were totally unaware of funerals. At first we were not grief stricken like everyone around us because we believed what we were told, "Grandma has gone away for a while." In a sense she had gone away long before then, having been sick in the hospital for many months. It was only much later that I began to understand the depth of my loss and to have sincere regrets that I had perhaps been a disappointment to Grandma who had such great hopes and plans for me and my future.

Now I would never be able to show her I loved her by learning to be great at needlecraft like she was. Grandma had tried, with little success, to teach me embroidery and beadwork, but I was just not talented with the needle. It took a lot of patience on my part to work the one needlecraft project I remember: a pillow in grey with an appliqued felt donkey standing under a palm tree. The tree was green, but for some reason the donkey was a cheerful and very bright pink. Also, I had promised her many little stories and verses. Now my loving kind Grandma was gone, without having the satisfaction of reading any of the "masterpieces" that I had been too lazy to write.

Palm Sunday was an unusually beautiful day. It was warm, and the snows were gone. We children were not told about what had happened and were sent out for a ride in the carriage and pair. The coachman was told to take us for a ride to a valley outside of town. On the banks of a tiny rivulet, there was hope of finding some flowers. True enough, the twins and I succeeded in picking a few meager handfuls of blue hepaticas, some of the first flowers of spring. When we returned to our grandparents' residence, finding Grandma lying lifeless on a bier in the living room was a great shock. We were told to put our bouquets in her hands as a last present for Grandma. Later, when the funeral procession took place, it started from the home. Such things as funeral homes were unheard of. People made their own arrangements for getting the coffin as well as for transporting it to the cemetery.

Leaflets distributed in the streets or stuck on lamp posts announced the funeral rites of Liudvika Malinauskas Šliupas, described as a prominent name in literature. As was the custom, black horses caparisoned in black pulled the hearse while a brass band played the mournful Death March. The mourners followed on foot in a procession at least a block long. Riding in an automobile, even if you had one, would have been considered disrespectful. No matter how far, one went on foot to honor the memory of the deceased. The bereaved relatives wore black clothing during a mourning period of at least six months. Women family members were heavily veiled in black crepe, and men wore mourning bands of black material on their sleeves. At the grave site, there were many laudatory speeches about the dear departed. Then participants were invited to have a long funerary dinner at the home where tributes to the deceased were continued.

Grandma was buried in the Protestant cemetery. Much attention was paid to grave decoration no matter what the religion. Sometimes, I went with Mamma to tend the plants and flowers that Grandma had loved, planted where she now lay under a flat granite slab. Everything was kept plain and simple. There were no ornate statues of angels or huge mausoleums as some of our Roman Catholic friends had in their cemetery next door. In the summer the cemetery was a pleasant place with birds singing among the greenery. It was at its best in the fall, especially on All Souls Day when everyone remembered their dead. Graves were decorated with wreaths and flowers, and lighted candles were placed on the grave sites. To go to the cemetery on All Souls Day, walking among the rustling leaves of November and seeing the gleam of thousands of candles in the evening mist, was like a trip to a land of enchantment.

It was only a few short years until we lost other family members. We had few relatives and felt their loss keenly. Buried near Grandma were two of our beloved uncles who died comparatively young and within a year of each other. They were the professors Keistutis Šliupas and Father's older brother Jonas Yčas.

Grandma's death heralded changes in our family. Life was never quite the same after we lost her. For one, a *scandale mondial* arose because of the totally unexpected marriage of Grandfather Šliupas. Barely six months after Grandma died, he dared to marry again. This was not all. He dared to marry his housekeeper, Grasilda Grauslytė from Palanga, a woman considered to be unworthy of a man of his stature. Worst of all, she was the sister of our faithful Petrusia.

Grandpa had no intention of asking his children's consent as he well knew they would be dead set against it. Likely to be the chief objector was his daughter Hypatia who was much afraid of scandal and of what others might think. At a time when Mamma was away from home (maybe on a trip abroad), a date was chosen "accidentally on purpose" for the wedding. On her return, she was confronted with the problem of what to do with Petrusia. Should she stay on as our housekeeper after this sudden turn of events? Our father thought there should be no changes in Petrusia's status, and he was certainly right. Petrusia, when consulted, did not wish to give up her well-paid position and her security in the love of our family.

Grandpa explained that Grasilda was an exceptionally good cook and housekeeper who had taken care of him very well, especially while his own wife was too ill to do much. Of course, he wanted his new bride to be accepted, but Mamma would have none of it. She refused to invite them to the house saying, "Father can come but without Grasilda." Naturally Grandfather was outraged. The result was that we lost our one and only Grandpa whom we loved dearly. This rift was not healed in Grandpa's lifetime. He genuinely liked Father, his son-in-law, and the feeling was mutual.

Unbeknownst to Mamma, the two used to meet from time to time in a neutral place like a restaurant, always enjoying the exchange of ideas and the laughter. But Mamma, who had been her father's favorite daughter, refused to see him.

Years after Grandpa died as a refugee in West Germany, Mamma regretted her unforgiving attitude and tried to make amends. Grasilda and her young son Vytautas (born when his father was well over 65, which seemed such a great age to us at the time) were stranded in Austria, as refugees from the Soviet terror. They needed assistance in coming to the USA, and Mamma, as well as Aunt Aldona, helped them in every way possible.

Losing contact with our Grandpa, and the death of Grandma barely a few months before was a double blow to us children. Moreover, our trips to Palanga and the House by the Sea which we had made every summer ceased altogether, depriving us of those glorious summer there. This was because Grandpa and his new wife moved there to live, probably because it was Grasilda's hometown. Grandpa was totally fearless in expressing his antireligious views. This did not make him popular, and he was never given a suitable position. Finally, he was offered a post as mayor of this summer resort many miles away from the capital city.

Besides missing Grandpa, I missed Grasilda too. We knew each other well because she used to come visit her sister Petrusia before the famous marriage took place. Grasilda was fond of children and would play games with us. She was a great story teller and singer of songs. She taught me to sing out of a dog-eared copybook where she had written the words, but not the music, of a great many ballads and folk songs. Like many people throughout the country, she could carry a tune perfectly well without benefit of written music. Singing was a favorite pastime, and there were hundreds of folk songs in the collective memory of the people.

I was not to see Grasilda again for years, not until the early 1950s when she came to the USA. She was certainly an accomplished cook. Even today, I am still using the recipe for making *Barsčiai* (beet soup) that Grasilda gave me when we met again. As for Grandpa, when my brother and I were teenagers, we did see him a few times. Naturally we missed Grandpa's lessons in history and geography. This did not happen on a regular basis because he was away from home so much, but his stories were lively enough to whet our appetites for more. However heartless this may sound, not seeing Grandpa any more was less of a blow than the loss of our Palanga summers.

My brother and I were already in high school students when we had our first encounter in years with Grandpa, long unseen because of our Mamma's intransigent attitude toward his marriage. There was an art exhibit in Kaunas that my brother and I felt we had to see. On display were two watercolor portraits by the artist P. Kalpokas. The subjects were Martynas, Jr. and me—a boy in a bright blue sailor suit and a girl floating in clouds of light pink and blue. We were examining the portraits when Grandpa appeared out of nowhere. It was a joyful encounter. He said he missed his grandchildren, and we had of course, missed him too. I was a bit displeased because he paid more attention to my brother's portrait than he did to mine. Grandpa Šliupas went around the room telling everyone, "Come see the portrait of my grandson."

The only other time we saw Grandpa was at a much grander public event. This was in the *aula* (ceremonial hall) of the University in Kaunas where he was being awarded an honorary doctorate. I learned later that this was only one of three doctorates conferred on Grandpa at separate times. I remember little about the ceremony except the great applause following Grandpa's speech.

I still remember some of Grandpa's phrases that struck me as positively brilliant. In discussing the value of education, he said, "There are those who say that a nation of tillers of the soil, such as ours, does not need university training, and that overeducated people will not find jobs. With education, the nature of the work itself will change, and we will attain new heights not only in agriculture, but in every other field as well."

111

When the time came to leave Lithuania in the face of the Soviet Russian peril, there was one more encounter with Grandpa. This was not in person but by an exchange of letters between him and Mamma. In genuine concern for his safety, she wrote to him and received a none-too-cordial reply. He told his daughter curtly that there was no cause for worry as he could take care of himself. Grandpa died some years later, and we never saw him again.

We moved to our place in the country within six months after the death of Grandma. The farm was at no great distance so we came into town many times for shopping, for medical appointments, to visit friends or on other errands. After a few years, all of us children would be attending school in Kaunas Monday through Saturday, so it was not like parting with the city forever. However, No. 4 on the Avenue was never to be our home again. A new chapter in our lives was about to begin.

Part II

Tales of Turkey Lurk

Bringing Home the Hay

Chapter Fifteen
Moving to the Country

The odd name of our country home needs an explanation. Its real name was *Tirkeliškiai*, and it had nothing to do with turkeys. Friends of non-Lithuanian derivation, and particularly those who spoke English, found this name quite impossible to pronounce. It was Anne Crawford of Scotland, our teacher and family friend, who first dubbed the place "Turkey Lurk." She said it sounded like a good approximation. In her words, whether there actually were any turkeys there was not the point. The Yčas family estate should not conjure up a vision of grand and stately mansions. Whereas some of these still remained in Lithuania, ours was not one of them. Everything at Turkey Lurk, including the house we lived in, was very simple and plain. There were no towers, no sweeping staircases leading up to a columned veranda, no carefully laid out park with swans gliding in a lake and dark forest depths beyond. Turkey Lurk's sole claim to romance was an avenue of linden trees and a giant oak tree in an orchard of fruit trees, set in an area as large as a park. At the top of the oak was a wagon wheel where storks built their nests in the spring. On summer nights, nightingales with silvery voices sang among the bushes of flowering lilacs and jasmines.

Our property was really a working farm of close to 300 acres, which was what was left after the really big estates were divided up during the Land Reform in the early 1920s. Large estates were broken up almost at the start of national independence. When Lithuania arose, it was said that fewer than one hundred families owned all the land in this largely agricultural country. Many owners were absentee landlords, mostly non-Lithuanians with aristocratic titles who preferred to seek recreation in such glittering European capitals as Berlin, Paris, or St. Petersburg. Naturally, this landed gentry protested when they lost their estates even though some financial compensation was forthcoming. Dividing up the land was not exactly common practice in much of post-war Europe. Vast estates still remained in most countries. But Lithuania was an exception in this regard. Although not everybody approved of the Land Reform, many agreed later that further events proved that the Lithuanian government had been right. Small farms became the backbone of the country's economy and made it easier to recover from wartime devastation.

The environs of Kaunas suffered much damage because of fighting between warring armies during 1914–1918, including some ten Russian-built fortifications around the town for purposes of defense. In our day, the forts or earthworks with steep side walls were no longer in use. Inside were carefully constructed mounds that had been arsenals for munitions, cannons and other machines of war. Our fort made an exciting playground for those of us walking or riding by. The ditches and ravines made good exercise-grounds for practicing our horse jumps. It was exciting because it was forbidden territory. There was an off-chance that something buried deep in the ground might just blow up and blast us into "Kingdom Come."

Turkey Lurk, only a few miles south of town and on the edge of one of these forts, had been a prime wartime target. Hardly any of the farm buildings were standing when Father bought the place. There were masses of rubble where the living quarters, the horse stables, the cow shed, the granary and other buildings had once stood. A wooden barn of monumental size for storing straw and hay still stood intact. Its walls and roof were riddled with holes left by exploding shells and cannon balls. The alcohol distillery with an adjacent house for workers was in better condition than any, i.e., not quite ready to fall down. Out in the fields there were water holes large and small, left by explosions of one kind or another. Some were later ploughed over but others remained as marshes, favorite haunts for ducks and other wild birds. Storks often stood here on one leg waiting to catch an unwary frog. There were many of these majestic birds around. Indeed, there was a second stork's nest on another giant oak tree, even taller than the one in the orchard, at the edge of our property less than a mile to the south.

Strangely enough, few memories of our move to the country remain. Perhaps this is because it was an eventful year. There were momentous events in 1928 when our Grandma "went away." One of these was Grandfather's remarriage and the breakup of the family circle. For lack of motorized transportation, moving must have been difficult, with that immense Turkish rug, the Knabe grand piano, the mahogany dining room set and, in particular, our parents' really huge oversize double bed and two wardrobes each big enough to contain several children playing games of hide-and-seek. As Mamma said, there was no need to buy new furniture or get rid of the old. People in those times did not replace their furniture any more often than they had to. They tried to buy good quality, seemingly indestructible items, intended to last for the ages. There was so much furniture when we moved that there was hardly room for it all. Our modest dwelling in Turkey Lurk was much smaller than our house in town. For one thing, the Turkish rug was a tight squeeze, practically wall to wall, in our new living room.

Among my few memories of the move is the fact that it happened to be on a bright sunny day in the fall. There was joy in making new discoveries in the orchard, so much bigger than the one in town. During the Turkey Lurk years, the orchard was one of my favorite places, lovely at any season, even in the dead of winter. A picture remains in my mind's eye of the day we moved. Falling red and yellow maple leaves were rustling underfoot and berries of bright colors, edible and inedible, were sprinkled over the bushes. Since our family had made excursions to Turkey Lurk before, it was not entirely a strange place to me. Adjustment to the new life was not too difficult as there were so many things to explore. However, the new house to my way of thinking never really replaced Freedom Avenue No. 4. The Turkey Lurk house was merely a place to live in.

This ordinary wooden dwelling really did not deserve to be called a "manor," though some people used this name. It was across the cobblestoned road from the carriage house and stables and was of nondescript style. The house was new and quite carelessly constructed. It had "absolutely no frills" and was intended for use of the farm manager and staff. Our family never expected to live permanently at Turkey Lurk, so why build something fancy? When Father decided that we should move to our place in the country, improvements and renovations were a great deal of trouble and expense. So he must have had his regrets.

For example, that first winter we were there, the winds came whistling through the large cracks in the walls. No wonder the tall tile stoves and wood fires used for heating were ineffective. To keep the warmth in, double windows were always installed in the winter. They could not be opened, but there were tiny "windowlets" on top that could be used to let in some fresh air. The space between the windows was lined with white cotton wool. To our joy, we children were encouraged to decorate these spaces, either with everlasting (or straw) flowers or with Victorian-type cutout pictures popular at the time. Hearts and angels were my favorites.

The plumbing never worked very well. The huge metal tank in the attic for holding water sometimes overflowed and caused drips in the bedroom ceilings. The built-on addition to the house had nothing to recommend it. When finished, our home resembled two boxes of unequal height glued together. Rather surprisingly, we managed with only one bathroom. It was downstairs, and the bedrooms were upstairs. Mamma often remarked that the quality of the plumbing facilities, and particularly of the toilet paper, was much inferior to what was obtainable in America. The rest of us, of course, did not know the difference. One bathroom served the needs of the entire family and the domestics as well. This might have caused nocturnal problems, but there was a regular procession of chamber pots at set times of the day and night. The one and only bathroom had a tub and shower besides the usual amenities, but taking daily baths or showers was not a requirement for us nor, indeed, for anyone we knew (we later learned that most of the world's population does not believe in bathing every day, and that some 90% of those who make a fetish out of taking a daily shower live in the United States). As for our farm workers, could use bathing facilities with hot water supplied from our alcohol distillery, and there were outhouses directly behind that building.

Much rebuilding was required to get Turkey Lurk back into shape. Repairing the huge bullet-ridden barn standing off to one side of the farmyard was an endless job. It was silvery grey in color and had not been painted in years. As soon as one hole was patched, others would be likely to appear. The farm buildings surrounded a rectangle at least as large as a football field. The ruined horse stables (rebuilt in stucco) and the wooden cowshed (entirely new) stood opposite each other. Later, a second story with an outside staircase was built onto the cowshed to house Mamma's hordes of chickens. The winding road past the cowshed and the pond led uphill to some little houses, each with their own plot of garden, serving as living quarters for live-in farm laborers and their families.

A handsome new building of red brick, serving as the granary, stood near the dwelling house. It had several large storage rooms and was used for other items besides grain, like the great barrels of raw alcohol produced at the distillery and kept under lock and key. Nearby, there were at least eleven steamer trunks crammed with Mamma's "precious souvenirs." One of them contained her wedding dress, a souvenir which she valued highly. There were hundreds of loose photographs, postcards, baby clothes, albums and books from her young days in the USA and heaven knows what else. Nobody was supposed to open these trunks or to handle any of these treasures. Mamma seldom did so herself and most likely could not even remember what she had stored there. By one of the ironies of fate, those trunks and the keepsakes accumulated in them over the years had to be left exactly where they were when we left Turkey Lurk forever.

There was a washhouse, newly built of cement blocks, just across the yard, where house linens, sheets and towels were washed and sterilized in boilers heated by wood furnaces. In the washhouse was space for a garage which was used for this purpose when we finally purchased an automobile. Our green Chevrolet was bought just a couple of years before the Soviet invasion of 1940. It was promptly confiscated like all other private property and then, "Farewell, Turkey Lurk."

Water was one of the first priorities at Turkey Lurk. New wells had to be dug to replace those no longer in operation. Location of water in the earth was determined by the use of an ancient device called a "dowsing rod," a method still used in many parts of the world even today. People would walk around with forked twigs in their hands, waiting for vibrations to indicate where a well should be dug. There were many discussions about finding water close to our home. When dug, the well was a disappointment. It pumped up a liquid distinctly yellow at times. The high iron content made the water unpleasant to drink. Sometimes it ran so yellow that it was not even suitable for washing clothes. Because of this, rain water was saved whenever possible and stored in large barrels. It rained quite often as the skies in Lithuania were more often grey and overcast than blue and sunny. Not without reason was it said that the very name of Lithuania, *"Lietuva"* in the local language, might have come from the word *"lietus"* meaning rain, thus signifying a country of rain.

A wonderful source of water, crystal clear and very suitable for drinking, was at the edge of our property to the south. A tall oak tree was a landmark about a mile down the road. There were deep ditches several hundred yards in length near that tree. These were trenches used in the Great War that had ended not so very long before. Close by was a more pleasing memento of those events, a round pond forming an almost perfect circle. It seemed bottomless and no one had ever measured its depths. People from near and far came here to fill their water barrels. This was doubtless another bomb crater. The story was that an exploding bomb must have released the waters of an underground spring.

A full-time smith was employed for making horseshoes, repairing wheels and wagon parts, and for shoeing the horses. The smithy, where we sometimes went to see sparks fly amid the hammering and the clattering, was important for farming at Turkey Lurk. The land was worked by some thirty or forty horses, and there was very little in the way of farm machinery as we know it today. There were no harvesters or combines to reap and stack the grain at the same time. Much of this work was done by human hands. There was a tractor, but the farm hands never got used to it, preferring to use horses in the old-fashioned way. They complained about the foul smell of gasoline and difficulties of operation. The tractor was constantly breaking down for reasons nobody wanted to explain. It took some years before the laborers got used to this "fearsome monster." The giant threshing machine out in the barn, however, was a different matter and was much esteemed. It was a rarity in our district, and people came from all over the neighborhood to thresh their grain. After all these years, the peculiar hum of its electric motor rings in my ears as I write, bringing back the days of harvest in the fall.

At the end of summer, the Harvest Festival was celebrated with dance and song. There was a feast provided for everyone by the *Ponas* (landowner). A crown woven of ears of wheat, flowers and greenery was placed on his head amid general merriment and singing of folk songs. This would be done out in the fields, and then the landowner would lead the homeward parade of workers, marching with rakes and scythes over their shoulders. Father was honored with this Harvest Crown only a few times as I recall. Turkey Lurk was so close to town that many quaint old customs were dying out. However, the feasting at tables set with food and drink outdoors in the shade of the trees went on every year.

Chapter Sixteen
Horses, Horses Everywhere

Horses were needed not only for work but for everyday transportation as well. The carriage house by the stables had a choice of vehicles, an old-fashioned *charabanc* among them. This was a long, open vehicle designed for many travelers with seats running lengthwise. One carriage with wooden sides was designed for use on particularly muddy roads. There was also a two-wheeled *bėda* or dog cart designed for two travelers only. For longer trips, there was the *karieta* or victoria carriage for a pair of horses, big enough for the whole family. It had a folding roof overhead that could be raised in case of bad weather. For winter snows, there were elegantly curved sleighs for either one or two horses and bearskin rugs to keep you warm.

There was a coachman to drive us around, look after the horses, and make sure that the various conveyances were in good shape. To everyone's regret, Valiukas the white-bearded coachman was no longer with us. He would have enjoyed hitching up the two coal-black carriage horses that replaced Orlikas and Smigly of Kaunas days. These were almost identical and worked well together. They were named, *Žaibas* (Lightning) and *Perkūnas* (Thunder) and could be told apart mostly because Žaibas was the one with two white socks on his feet and a white star on his forehead.

There were great numbers of horses all over the country in those days. Indeed, there was a strange and almost mystical bond between the Lithuanian and his horse. Perhaps it was no accident that a horse is featured on the country's national emblem. The symbol represents a stylized horseman called *Vytis*. This knight on horseback was used on coins and heraldic shields since medieval times. In our day, the state flag of our country's President was a white *Vytis* on a wine background. Centuries ago, this same flag was the battle standard of Lithuanians when they were a warlike people with territories stretching far out to the shores of the Black

Sea. This attachment to horses can be traced back to prehistoric times. Excavations at ancient grave sites revealed that horses were buried next to their masters or even had separate cemeteries of their own. This curious custom of horse cemeteries was prevalent especially in the Lithuania's western area. Customs changed in later ages and horses joined their masters to be cremated with them on the funeral pyre. As late as the 16th century, Christian missionaries were complaining about these "disgusting pagan burial practices," which still survived among the people.

At Turkey Lurk there were plenty of animals (dogs, cats, sheep, piglets, etc.) for us to love, but horses were at the top of our list. It must be said that our brother did not share in the family passion for horses as having his nose in a book was his favorite pastime. Soon after moving to the farm, I learned some valuable lessons from riding a horse. When my pony, named Hector, took fright at some dogs yapping at his heels, he reared up and I landed on the cobblestone road near our house. As an old folk tale said, there must have been an angel there to put a pillow under my head. No bones or teeth were broken, but I had a mouthful of blood and gravel and was scared to death. For several months I was petted, spoiled and kept in bed as a precaution. Of course, I was afraid to mount a horse again, but Father insisted I do so. Soon I was riding merrily once more. If I had not gotten in the saddle again, I might have retained a lifelong fear of horses and who knows what else.

My younger sister, Evelyna, was so confident on horseback that she would ride standing up in the saddle like a circus trick rider. Nobody, however, loved horses like Evelyna's twin sister Violetta. Indeed she loved all animals and thought it would be great to be a veterinarian. Violetta was very fond of her own special pony, smoky white in color. She took care of grooming it herself. Father was always interested in the welfare of our horse population and would often go out to the stables. Even our totally unathletic Mamma was persuaded to try horseback riding for a time. Although he had occasionally gone out riding while we lived in Kaunas, by the

124

time we got to Turkey Lurk, Father was never again seen on horseback. Mamma's career as a rider did not last very long. One day she had a mishap while out riding near the forts. Somehow, she slipped from the saddle while trying to negotiate a ditch. A great surprise to her was that her mount, a gentle mare, stood stock still and waited for her to get on again. No harm resulted, but Mamma got such a scare that she went riding no more.

Once in a while, Father would take us to a horse fair, an event to look forward to. Here you had to watch out for people trying to sell you an animal under false pretenses. Gypsies were especially adept at this game, fixing up injured horses so nobody would know the difference. They might do a clever paint job to change the color, hoping that a stolen animal would not be recognized. Besides those of nondescript ancestry, one might see a native breed of small and sturdy horses at the fairs. They were called *Žemaitukai* from the Lithuanian word *Žemaitija*, the name of the province of Samogitia where they originated. They had great strength and endurance and were much in demand for heavy hauling jobs and for farm work.

A trip made by a young man on horseback made headlines in the newspapers one summer. He aimed to traverse the entire country from one end to the other by this means of transportation. He was photographed and made much of wherever he went. There were radio interviews and long newspaper articles about his adventures. I caught a glimpse of him in Biržai when I was there visiting relatives. I cannot remember how he looked, but I do recall that he was mounted on a big golden colored horse with a white mane, somewhat like a California Palomino.

Some of the most popular public events were those involving horses. At the agricultural fairs, the exhibits of horse breeders and demonstrations of dressage were likely to draw the biggest crowds. There were splendid and very accomplished riders in the Lithuanian Army. When the Hussars put on a public show of jumping, trick riding and racing, practically everyone we knew would try to attend.

125

I recall a breathtaking performance by a champion rider, Col. A. Valušis. He was an adjutant to President Smetona. Later, he married the boss's daughter and became the President's son-in-law.

For some at Turkey Lurk, fond memories are associated with the "Summer of the Horses," when an entire cavalry detachment, a squadron of Hussars, was stationed on the premises. The Lithuanian Army usually sent its cavalry regiments out to the country to pasture the horses in the summer. Beside the Hussars, who wore red trousers, there were also the Uhlans in blue. Cavalry mounts were usually of the Trakehner breed, originating from a place called Trakehnen (*Trakėnai*) in East Prussia. These were Quarter Arabs, small-boned, light footed and very swift in action. Horse breeding farms had been initiated in East Prussia in the 18th century by King Frederick the Great. Ever since then, Trakehners had been in great demand throughout much of Europe. In some countries, horses remained an important part of the military forces right up to World War II. As late as the fall of 1939, the Polish Army used cavalry in a vain attempt to repel the German invasion but were outclassed by tanks and other machines of war. Alas, the horses and their riders were no match for mechanized equipment and were slaughtered in no time. I remember shedding tears when I heard the pitiful news.

There was a jingling of spurs and the tramp of many feet when the cavalry detachment rode into Turkey Lurk one day. A squadron in those days meant around 150 to 200 horses and men with a captain in command. Our huge grey barn was the scene of unusual activity as the Hussars bedded down in the hay. They had portable metal kitchens on wheels where they cooked their food. In the mornings and evenings there would be bugle calls when it was time to get up or to go to bed. The presence of so many uniformed men caused a great stir for miles around, especially among the country girls in the vicinity. I was so young and naive that I did not understand what the excitement was about. The new inhabitants of the barn began to have company. It appears that there were entirely too many visiting females who interrupted their sleep at night. The joke was going around that the Hussars complained to their officers, asking them to do something about this problem.

Naturally the officers did not sleep in the barn but found their quarters and their meals with us. They were good-looking men, doubly attractive because of their splendid uniforms. In later years, I heard the saying "It is the uniform that takes the girls by storm." The officers were friendly and very nice to us. Although too young by far, we three girls almost fell in love with our house guests. After all this time, I still remember the names and the charm of the dark-haired Captain Gecevičius and the blond Lieutenant Gasiūnas.

There were also visiting cadets from the Kaunas Military Academy to admire. A white belt was part of their distinctive uniform, and the social graces were also part of their training. Perhaps a dozen of these young men would gather in the orchard in the evening twilight. Sitting on benches in the arbor on Lilac Hill, they would sing songs both military and romantic, all in exquisite harmony. Some of these songs keep drifting back to me over the years, like *Šėriau žirgelį* (I fed my steed). This is a conversation between a rider and his horse. In an approximate English translation it would be: "Oh steed, my steed, would you carry me a hundred miles in a few short hours?" The horse replies: "If you gave me oats and plenty of water to drink, I certainly would." Equally striking was *Geležinio vilko maršas* (March of the Iron Wolf), which translates as: "Oh horses, raise your heads high. Tomorrow we ride out to battle. Farewell, our sisters, farewell."

There was much singing among the military. Indeed it was a part of their life, if not of their discipline. Soldiers on the march often accompanied their steps with song. These cadets, being horsemen, could not refrain from songs about riding out to battle on their noble steeds, bidding a fond farewell to the girls they left behind. We might mention that military service was compulsory for all young men between the ages of 18 and 21. Those who had the qualifications, including a high school diploma, might be eligible for Officers Training at the Lithuanian Military Academy.

That summer we had the honor of being taught proper riding by the squadron's chief riding master, a bluff old gentleman with a handlebar mustache. Among the thrills was the chance to ride some outstanding horses including two huge black steeds assigned for the use of the President of Lithuania. They were so gigantic that I was quite petrified with fright. Totally forgetting my lessons about putting the foot into the stirrup, I had to be lifted into the saddle and did not stay on very long. Mr. Pivorius, the riding master, was a good-natured and very patient teacher. He found an even-tempered sorrel mare called Ruta and persuaded my parents to buy her for me. She was a true lady of excellent disposition. Her ankles were unusually small, even for a Trakehner. Once when I was leading Ruta back to the stable, she happened to step on my foot. Her tread was so light that no harm resulted. Ruta stopped short immediately and gazed at me. There was such a sad look in her eyes that I was sure she was telling me how sorry she was.

One of the hazards of that summer was the many flies buzzing around. With so many horses, the "natural fertilizer" caused the flies to increase. Extra precautions had to be taken with screens on doors and windows and with sticky flypaper hanging from the ceilings. Flies were a real nuisance but at least we had no other pests like mosquitoes.

Petrusia, however, was not complaining. That summer she found love and true romance. She struck up a friendship with a red-trousered warrant officer of the Hussars. He wooed her with music and song. We were told about the midnight serenades she heard under her window. Such a romantic thing had never happened to her before. Father was delighted to arrange the wedding, but the story did not have a happy ending. Petrusia married her dashing military man, and at first all was well. Later on, during the Soviet occupation, she and her young son and her husband were deported to the depths of Siberia. He soon died, and some ten years later his widow and son were allowed to return to their homeland. By this time their health was broken and they too did not live long. If Father had known of these events, happening years after his death, he would have been deeply grieved to think that he had arranged this marriage with the best of intentions.

Chapter Seventeen
Managing the Farm

Running the farm was in the hands of a farm manager. Father was no farmer since his mind was on other matters. Active in government affairs for a time, he soon retired from politics but still spent a great deal of time with his former associates. His avocations included writing, business and human relations in general, and he liked to spend more time in town than in the country. Father had a law degree but seldom practiced his profession. Occasionally he did consulting work advising people on their property rights and various personal problems. This is not to say that he did not enjoy being the owner of Turkey Lurk. Like most Lithuanians, he had a great love for the land. Everyone we knew, rich or poor, educated or not, wanted to own a piece of the earth, seen as mother of all growing things.

Father liked to take long walks around the marches of the property early in the morning, before leaving for his trips to Kaunas. Sometimes he would take me along in the springtime. It was a delight to share in his enthusiasm for the first signs of the green blades of rye, oats or wheat coming up through the earth or to hear his stories of the various birds and their songs. Father would say, "Do you see that bird rising up straight into the sky, singing as he goes? That is the lark telling the world that spring is really coming." It was about this time that the swallows appeared. And when the long-legged storks came, as Father said, one knew for certain that warm weather had come to stay. It was too cold here for most of the birds so they wintered somewhere in the South, perhaps as far away as Egypt. As for the cuckoo and the nightingale, we were not to expect them until late in May when the fruit trees were in bloom. "When you hear the call of the cuckoo for the first time," Father said, "make a wish, and it will be sure to come true."

The nightingale was the queen of the songsters, and her voice was like the music of a bubbling fountain. From Father, I learned some of the folk songs and rhymes about her, like a verbal

131

approximation of her song. Starting quietly, then rapidly mounting to a crescendo, her voice would slowly sink down again before she repeated her trill, *"Jurgiúk, Jurgiúk- kinkýk, kinkýk - paplák, paplák, nu-va-žiuok..."* A rough English translation of this nonsense verse would be: "Georgie, Georgie, harness your horses, crack your whip and drive on..." The nightingale does not exist on the American continent, but the Southern mockingbird gives a fairly good imitation of her incomparable song.

Sparrows would remind Father of his native village. They had been just as plentiful there as they were with us (this hardy bird seems to thrive almost anywhere in the world, whether in the chilliest winter or the hottest summer weather). By the village stream was an elm tree, always alive with the chirp and chatter of hundreds of sparrows and the constant whirr of their wings. There was a popular saying among the young men eligible for military service in the old Czarist Russian days, "Go, catch a sparrow in our elm tree. This would be easier than to get me to serve in the Russian Army." Conscription was a dreaded experience and for good reason. At that time, military service could last as long as twenty years.

One memory of Father's childhood would lead to another. Every youngster had to take smaller animals, like sheep and goats as well as geese and other farm birds, out to pasture at sunrise. At sundown, they would bring them home again. When children got bigger, larger animals, like horses, would be entrusted to their care. Then they might have the thrilling experience of camping out on summer nights. They would build fires and roast potatoes in the embers. For entertainment, they would tell stories about the marvels of the starry heavens. One was about the luminous pathway formed by the countless stars of the Milky Way. In Lithuanian, it was called *Paukščių Takas* (Path of the Birds) and was the road to the next world. Spirits of the departed traveled this way to Paradise on the wings of bird-like messengers from the sky. Such childhood tales sounded so entrancing that I would ask, "Father, when are you going to write them down?" He fully intended to write about his childhood days but never got around to it because other and more important tasks got in his way.

Practical questions about running the farm interested Father much less than a host of other things. He may have enjoyed being a "gentleman farmer," but the farm enterprise never became a paying proposition. No farm manager (and there were several) seemed able to make Turkey Lurk a financial success. The alcohol distillery was the only thing on the farm that was profitable. Father was not too interested, or maybe he was too lenient and did not demand enough from his farm managers. One of the earliest such managers was a vigorous young man in high boots who made his daily rounds on horseback. This was Stasys Neimanas, who had cavalry experience in the Czarist armies of General Denikin during the Russian Revolution. He liked people and gave parties for his friends at the house where we moved later. Assisting him in keeping the accounts was a pretty young bookkeeper who later became his wife. Stasys Neimanas was a student of theology, graduating from the University in Kaunas. In later years, he became a much loved minister of our Reformed Church.

Another rather remarkable farm manager was named Jaroševičius who left his imprint on life at the farm. He never learned to speak proper Lithuanian. To hear him "murder the language" in a peculiar combination of West Country dialect and Polish phraseology was a joke to all who heard him. Mr. J took pride in having formerly served under aristocratic masters at a baronial estate. He wanted to give an air of elegance to Turkey Lurk by introducing peacocks just like on the estate and saw to it that this was accomplished. Before they had their wings clipped, the peacocks used to sit high in the tree tops screeching their hearts out in a peculiar cry that once heard is hard to forget. To some of our people the voice of the peacock was like the anguished cry of a soul tortured in Purgatory. In any case, the peacocks were a nuisance. They would strut around fanning out their tails and looking decorative, and then the dogs would get after them. Often Mr. J would come running to one or the other of us with the complaint, "*Pani, Pani,* the dogs have ruined the beautiful tail of the Paulina." He never did learn that the word for peacock in Lithuanian was *Povas.*

Still another farm manager is memorable for quite different reasons. Our parents said that he really knew his business, so it is unfair to his memory that his name has been forgotten. Unlike some of the others, this man had the healthy respect of his lead man, or head laborer, and those who worked under him. Everyone respected this farm manager even more when he survived a near-fatal accident. There was a violent thunderstorm one day when he happened to be near the old oak tree in the orchard. For some reason, although he knew it was dangerous, he took shelter under it. The tree was struck by a bolt of lightning. The farm manager related afterwards that he fell to the ground and lay there for quite a while. Though severely shaken, he was able to get up none the worse for the experience. The lightning bolt left a wide swath of charcoal black, stripping the bark from the treetop down to the very roots. The oak, a hardened veteran of many centuries, withstood the blow and continued to flourish for a good many years to come.

As for everyday tasks at Turkey Lurk, there were dozens of laborers who kept the place going. Besides live-ins, there were outside workers hired seasonally by the day, week or month, like the women hired to dig potatoes in the fall. Sometimes housing and food were part of their pay. There were many hungry mouths to feed. Farm workers had their meals in a very large kitchen in the ancient building adjoining the distillery. Some brought their own food or else shared in the meals cooked by a special cook, all according to the contract. On fine summer days the workers might sit on benches under the immense white lilac bush in the middle of the yard.

Vast quantities of black rye bread were baked in the ashes of a brick oven (not unlike the *horno* ovens of the American

Southwest). For us children to be allowed to come into the kitchen was a special treat. If we were lucky, we might see the dough rising and the loaves made ready for baking. These would be placed on a sort of wooden paddle with a long handle and then thrust into the well-heated oven.

The full-time cook for the farm hands was rather short-tempered as she had much to attend to. Not everyone wanted to eat at the same time or to sit at the same table. There were social distinctions to be observed. Educated people (even those with a smattering of education) could not be expected to sit with the unlettered workers. The farm manager, his assistant and the gardener (mostly single men without families) formed the core of the so-called "Table for the Intelligentsia." They were not satisfied with the regular menu and demanded special dishes, which must have tasted very good. One of our tutors, named Lieponis, who was preparing us for high school examinations, preferred to dine with this "Intelligent Crowd," although he was perfectly welcome to eat with us at the Big House.

As mentioned before, farming at Turkey Lurk was not exactly a financial success. Mamma tried to make a contribution, but she was even less commercially minded than Father was. She liked poultry and thought she would try her hand at chicken farming. Being familiar with things American, she finally decided to breed Rhode Island Reds. According to her, they were great for egg laying and also for the meat. Her chickens, numbering several hundred, were kept from freezing in winter because they lived in their second-floor palace above the cowshed. Warmth emanated from the black and white dairy cows (the Holland, or Friesian, breed was very popular then), and from the pigs in their sties below. Keeping chickens was an expensive proposition. There was special feed and even electric lighting for them at night (an unusual luxury at the time). There was also that wonderful machine, the incubator (imported, of course), for hatching chicks. All this despite the high cost of electricity. Nobody we knew had an incubator, and most people had never heard of one. It was great fun for all of us to show it off to the guests, including agricultural agents sent by the government. Those of us who knew English thought it amusing that one of the agents interested in our chickens was named Mr. Chikota.. The incubator had a glass front so you could see what was going on. Adults as well as children were amazed to see chicks coming out of the shell.

Mamma had expensive tastes and was always buying costly items. In her chicken-farming days, there was a magnificent red rooster shipped all the way from England, which she named Tom Barron after the name of the exporter. Two of our favorite dogs might have been imported as well. These were English breeds, an Airedale terrier named Teddy and a Springer spaniel named Tubby. By the way, nobody thought of dog food specially prepared for animals as there was none available. Dogs were fed table scraps and were always foraging around for garbage. When they got older, both Teddy and Tubby got immensely fat.

None of the farm produce seemed to make a profit. This included fields of home-style cabbages and cucumbers and exotic vegetables in which Mother took such great interest. But then, standard crops such as rye, wheat, barley, oats and clover did not pay either. There were quantities of milk, hand-operated churns for making butter and presses for cheese, but there was no profit there at all. Some money was coming in, though not much, from the fruit crop in the orchard. There were pears, plums, cherries and several kinds of berries, but only the apples were considered saleable. Early in the year, merchants would come to bid for the apple crop. It was usually a Jewish merchant, known as the Apple Man, who would get the contract. He would arrange for the picking, storage and merchandising of the fruit. When the apples were ripe, he kept a close watch over his domain to see that none were stolen (stealing apples was a favorite game of neighborhood kids). The Apple Man brought his own watchmen and even fierce guard dogs to scare marauders away at apple picking time.

One summer, my sisters and I thought we had a brilliant idea on how to make money. Our parents said, "Go to it, and keep the profits." One of the Twins got this idea because we had a great supply of linden blossoms. Natural teas made of dried leaves and flowers were popular home remedies, and Linden Tea was one of the best for fighting fevers and headaches. Linden blossoms were very expensive in the pharmacies. We spent a great deal of time that July, perched like birds in the trees of Linden Walk plucking the flowers. There were several baskets full when we were through, but when they dried, they shriveled up to practically nothing. So where were the profits? However, the pleasure of our expeditions and the exquisite perfume of the linden blossoms lingers with me still.

The alcohol distillery, however, was really profitable. Alcohol was made from potatoes but our own crop was never sufficient. Besides, our soil was too rich and much more suited to growing the grain which constituted the major crop on the farm. Potatoes were brought in by the carload to the nearest railway station. It was not the fresh, but the frostbitten and slightly deteriorating potatoes that were needed for making alcohol. The excess left over from the process of making alcohol was a foul-smelling mass called *broga* and made excellent fertilizer for the fields. It was a good thing that the distillery was at some distance from our house. The building had been there much longer than anyone could remember. It dated back to the mid-19th century and was probably built by owners previous to the Frenkelis family.

Lest anyone should think we made illegal moonshine—well, they can think again. Alcohol was a tightly controlled monopoly and the government guaranteed to buy all that was produced. In our day, alcohol production brought excitement to people for miles around. There were always witless oafs who wanted to steal the unrefined (methyl) alcohol and drink it despite dire warnings about the terrible consequences to their eyesight, not to mention severe punishment by government excisemen or inspectors. Seals with the government emblem were put on the alcohol barrels stored in the red brick granary and kept under lock and key at all times.

One such exciseman who enjoyed throwing his weight around bore the improbable and awe-inspiring name of Mitalas. He checked every single seal on each barrel to make sure there was no cheating or monkey business. A visit from this exciseman, a true bureaucrat, was a terrifying event for anyone even remotely involved. He had the power to impose heavy fines and to threaten miscreants with prosecution. Favorite foods and special dinners were prepared for this Mr. Mitalas, including French wines if he so desired, to make sure he would have no complaints.

Alcohol production was a closely-watched operation and was no simple matter. Finding a reliable distillery manager, and also the right people to run the machines, was not that easy. The manager, usually a man with a family, was entitled to his own apartment and had all sorts of privileges. He, too, had to make sure that none of this "precious product" would be siphoned off into the wrong hands, in which case the manager and of course the owner of the distillery would be held responsible. Distillery owners throughout Lithuania banded together to protect their interests in an association with headquarters in Kaunas. There Father was entitled to a desk where he could do his paperwork. It must be noted that despite repeated warnings, our housekeeper Petrusia found a way to outwit the stringent regulations. She was a trickster at heart and would manage to swipe methyl alcohol by the pailful, which she said was so excellent for washing windows.

Chapter Eighteen
Invited Guests and Unexpected Visitors

Turkey Lurk had plenty of visitors in our first years in the country. A few were invited guests, while others just wandered in. Some images come to mind, but not necessarily in the right chronological order. The following incident must have happened soon after we moved. One day, I was exploring a neglected and much overgrown path that I called "the jungle." It was at the end of the orchard. There was Father, sitting on a garden bench, talking to a man I did not know. A black-robed gentleman with silvery hair was sitting beside him under the lilacs. The robe was long and went down to his ankles. This was a *soutane*, the traditional garb of a priest of the Roman Catholic church. I was invited to approach and be introduced to Father J. Maironis, one of the greatest poets of modern Lithuania.

His stirring patriotic verses were so popular that many people, Father included, would often recite them from memory. His poems had powerful appeal because of their rhyme and rhythm, and many were set to music. Even today, his songs are sung wherever Lithuanians gather. I was terribly embarrassed when Father Maironis invited me to recite a poem—any poem would do (even very young children were supposed to entertain guests in this way). I stood completely tongue-tied, unable to say a word. My usual courage left me, and I ran away, which amused the two grownups very much. As it turned out, Maironis died a year or two afterwards, and we never met again. People thought so much of him that his house in Kaunas became a sort of national shrine, and his statue was placed in front of it.

Father had several priests among his friends. They felt free to discuss any subject with him in a way they could not always do with their coreligionists. One of them was the remarkably broad-minded Canon P. Dogelis. He liked to come to our home for a hearty country meal, accompanied by quality red wine. More often than not, this was wine he had provided himself. The Canon's duties included the importing of sacramental wine for the use of churches in the area. Nothing but the best would do, like Chateau LaFitte from France. He would let Father know when there was a new shipment and was always willing to part with some bottles. One day, we drove to the Cathedral in Old Town, where the Canon was the clergyman in charge, to get some of this wine. This is where I saw a remarkable sight. Crawling around the church floor on her knees was a little old woman. She was barefoot and had a peasant-type kerchief on her head. In answer to Father's remark that this seemed a little strange, Canon Dogelis said that this *davatka* (devotee) thought she could expiate her sins by humbling herself in this way. He added that he himself did not believe in this sort of thing and deplored such cases of ignorance and misguided piety.

I do not remember being overly excited when the President of Lithuania and his wife came to dinner. It was not really surprising to have Antanas Smetona as a guest because Father was an associate of his in the olden days. He was on excellent terms with the President as well as with other leading personalities and Cabinet members, including several Prime Ministers past and present. Mr. Smetona, very approachable and quite unassuming, was a scholarly individual who liked to read the works of Plato and other Greek philosophers. He did not overawe any of us, but his wife, an outspoken chatterbox, was something else. If the First Lady disliked somebody or something, she would be sure to say so. It could be the food, the wine, the hairdos or the apparel of the hostess and/or guests that she objected to. Some people found Mrs. Smetona's cutting remarks hard to forget.

For years, Mamma remembered her saying when they first met long ago in Vilnius, "You could be a good-looking woman, but WHY do you always wear low-heeled shoes?" An avid card player, she seemed to judge people on the basis of how good they were at playing *Preferance*, an old but still popular game dating back to Russian Czarist times. Without going into political matters, it must be mentioned that Mr. Smetona did great things for the postwar reconstruction of the country. He stayed in power for so many years that younger people could not remember any other President. Some said he was around too long and thus much of the good he had done was forgotten. It seems that the scepter of power, once taken up, is hard to put down. Indeed, there have been statesmen in other countries of the world besides Mr. Smetona who were unable to step down when the time came.

Col. A. Merkys, a former Minister of Defense and career Army Officer, was also a memorable visitor. He was a really good looking man with eyes of sparkling sapphire blue. Our English governess Miss Saunders had given him the epithet of "the handsomest man in Lithuania," and she was not far wrong. Colonel Merkys talked to me, a mere school girl, just as if we were old acquaintances. He brought a briefcase stuffed with papers and explained that he was at Turkey Lurk at the behest of President Smetona. He wished to get Father's informal opinion on the new Constitution of Lithuania which was about to be promulgated. Colonel Merkys, like Father, possessed a degree in law and had been asked to help with the document as a legal authority.

Like others of the older generation, Colonel Merkys had a fondness for the Latin language. He quizzed me on fine points of grammar as well as my knowledge of poetic quotations. He himself could recite reams of hexameter from the Metamorphoses of Ovid. When serious talk started, I was not asked to leave the room provided I could remain quiet and not interrupt. I remember a lot of laughter amid the legal technicalities which, of course, were over my head.

Father and his guest were highly amused that the President wanted to start the text of the Constitution with the words, "Every citizen of Lithuania should be happy, healthy and prosperous." Colonel Merkys, a charming man of considerable charisma, had no trouble in getting to the top. He later became Prime Minister and was in office at the time of the Soviet occupation. He was left in charge of the government, being invested with presidential powers when President Smetona fled the country. In June 1940 there was a wave of arrests. Colonel Merkys was captured at the airport while trying to escape. The Soviets deported him and his teenage son to the Russian interior. The son eventually made his way back to Lithuania, but his father died in exile.

Among other memorable visitors was the Minister of the USA, a diplomat who became a personal friend. Mr. Kuykendall was born in a tiny town in Pennsylvania as was our Mamma. He was a reader, like she was, and lent her American novels from his personal library...It is too bad that he did not advise her on how to retain her US citizenship. Due to her years of living abroad, Mamma was no longer a citizen according to the laws of that time. This caused many complications later during our flight to the United States as refugees.

Visitors like these were long remembered, but the day when Russian Prince Ilarion S. Vasilchikoff came calling was even more of a red-letter day. This old friend of our Father's (from the Russian Duma days where they had both served prior to the Great Revolution) decided to come without telephoning first. We had a telephone, but people visited back and forth quite often without thinking of using it. My parents were not home, and I thought it was up to me to play the hostess. This exceptionally tall man let this small girl take him by the hand and show him the local attractions. Vividly remembered is the trip to the smithy to watch the sparks fly, to the horse stables and to the orchard. The Prince admired everything and complimented me on my knowledge of English. What we ate I do not remember, but years later he still talked about the royal reception he got that day.

The Prince came to Lithuania after the Russian Revolution because it was here, near the river town of Jurbarkas, that he owned vast estates and forest land. Most of it was lost during the Land Reform. His Highness, an addict of the gaming tables, spent much time playing roulette, baccarat and other games of chance in places such as Monte Carlo. He appealed to Father for help in his financial difficulties. On Father's suggestion, the designated Land Reform compensation was not paid out to him by the Government in one lump sum, as was the rule. It was issued, instead, in partial payments over a longer period of time which kept the Prince from squandering his money all at once. Acting as legal consultant to people in trouble and finding ingenious solutions was something Father really enjoyed doing.

Like many of his peers, the Prince was a widely traveled man of broad cultural viewpoint. He spoke many languages, but Lithuanian was not one of them. Perhaps this was because so many Lithuanians were accomplished linguists. Our people spoke such a variety of tongues that he did not feel it necessary to learn our language. It may be of interest to mention here that aristocrats of princely title seldom marry outside their class. Prince Ilarion's daughter Tatiana, for example, married Prince Metternich of famous Viennese ancestry. Later, she lived with her husband among their vineyards in Germany's Rhineland, helping the family fortunes by making some of that fine Johannisberg Riesling wine.

All this time, we were being tutored at home and did not have many children to play with. True, there were the children of our farm laborers, but we never seemed to get on an equal footing with them. They acted shy and perhaps our ways were too strange to them and vice versa. Once in a while real playmates would come for a visit. Two boys, the mischievous Algimantas Siemaška and his cousin and loyal follower Gediminas, might spend some of their school holidays with us. They taught us skills such as constructing (and flying) our own kites made from ordinary wrapping paper and string. Algimantas loved to annoy people with his tricks. Every day was April Fool's Day as far as he was concerned. He liked to get up at dawn to enjoy the forbidden pleasures of the blacksmith's shop, trying to start the fire and to hammer on the anvil. Later on, while attending the Jesuit High School in Kaunas, Algimantas was expelled by the Reverend Fathers for putting ink into the fonts of holy water.

Visitors sometimes included people whom we did not know. Hard to forget were a lady and her daughter, two strangers who stayed in our home for a time. Mrs. Yazikoff, a refugee from the Russian Revolution, was our guest until she could figure out what to do next. Our American friend Robert J. Caldwell, a philanthropist who helped many people in distress, sent Mrs. Y and her young daughter Mara to us. I have no idea who they were and what their experiences had been, but they must have been persons of some consequence. Mr. Caldwell, for all his generosity, favored rescuing people who had aristocratic titles or had other claims to fame. No criticism is intended here. In fact, Mr. Caldwell's little vanities made him all the more human. Mrs. Yazikoff, a subdued and mournful woman, tried to make herself useful in the household, but there was nothing much she knew how to do except give us Russian lessons. We did not take too kindly to her efforts; in fact, we laughed entirely too much. As for Mara, a spoiled brat of the age of Martynas, Jr., we teased her unmercifully. One time on the skating rink on our frozen pond, I remember my brother pulling her by her long braids. Mara, a crybaby and a tattletale, burst into tears and ran to her mother. Eventually, the Yazikoffs went away and settled somewhere in Yugoslavia. In time we came to regret our unfeeling and rather cruel behavior.

The Yazikoff visit happened during one exceptionally cold winter. The year was probably 1929, when there were unexpected blizzards all over Europe. Snow fell even in southern Italy, and some trains were unable to get through. In the Baltic Sea, which normally does not freeze over, there were masses of floating ice. Turkey Lurk was snowed under, and spring was unusually late in coming. Snowdrifts five or six feet high were backed up against the orchard fence. They made ideal places for us to dig tunnels and construct make-believe igloos. The grownups did not think this was a good idea and were seriously worried that these "snow mountains" might collapse and bury us alive. Sometimes an ominous crackling sound was heard in the orchard. People said this meant the frost was hitting especially hard and that the younger trees might not survive. Among those that perished that winter were some dozen imported cherry trees, the "Queen Anne" variety, planted by Father. They were supposed to have yellow fruit with a pink blush, but alas, we never saw any. These delicate trees froze and never revived.

Among the memorable visitors who came without warning was a peddler in his one-horse cart selling ribbons, laces, buttons and yard goods. He was an old man with long gray hair and beard, dressed in the distinctive garb of an Orthodox Jew. The peddler said his wares were cheaper and prettier than the ones you could get in the stores. He had considerable success with customers who could not manage to shop in town. We also looked forward to the coming of the wandering musician with his hurdy-gurdy. He generally had some small animal in a cage, a guinea pig or a monkey. These were trained to pull out an envelope containing a card outlining your fortune and a shiny trinket, like a brooch or a ring, at a cost of a few pennies. To perform this task, the guinea pig would use its teeth and the monkey its tiny hands.

When the organ-grinder turned the handle of his instrument, the music was so lively that everyone within earshot would want to get up and dance the polka or the waltz. Other guests, welcomed by everyone, were the "Three Kings" dressed in costume, often riding horses with their suite of servants, shepherds and dogs. On January 6, the official ending of the Christmas season, they went from house to house, in the towns as well as in the country.

One summer, a band of Gypsies established their camp on the forts at the edge of our property. In the evenings, sounds of accordion music would drift over to our home and occasionally we might see the flickering of camp fires. Camping on the fort grounds was officially forbidden. Soon the Gypsy chieftain came to ask Father's permission to camp in the fields of Turkey Lurk. If this were allowed, he said, he would guarantee that none of his people would ever steal anything from us. And he was as good as his word: none of them stole a thing while they stayed on our land.

In the following weeks we learned something of the ways of the Gypsies. Often, some of their women, in distinctive, long, finely pleated skirts and strings of bright beads, would come to the kitchen door asking for "just a few eggs, onions, or potatoes..." In return they offered to tell our fortunes, always having a deck of cards handy. Most of these people spoke our language but also used another, quite incomprehensible, *Romany* tongue. Gypsies said they came from "somewhere far away." If asked about their nationality, they evaded the question and often responded, "We are all Roman Catholics here." This was quite a joke as they did not appear to be religious in the least and had no dealings with priests or churches.

Gypsies, just like the stories say, had no permanent home and thought of themselves as being wild and free. The main occupation of those we met was horse-trading at the fairs. Working at any steady job was not for them. Gypsies resisted all government restrictions, simply disappearing from view, traveling elsewhere in their covered wagons and going into hiding. They seemed to travel at will to other countries without papers or passports, just as if national borders did not exist.

Part of the ambience of Old Russia that was still with us was a fondness for Gypsy orchestra music and particularly the ballads known as "Gypsy romances." None of the Gypsies we met in those days were musical performers beyond playing a few tunes on an accordion. We never saw them decked out in fancy clothes. They lived a hand-to-mouth existence and said that they were poor people. We were told to avoid close contacts with the Gypsies. It was said that they had their ways of kidnaping boys and girls and that some children had been persuaded by their sweet talk to run away from home, never to see their families again. The Gypsy way of life was considered romantic by some, but it did not tempt me at all.

Chapter Nineteen
Pleasures and Pastimes

Mamma was hardly aware of money as such and was what one might call a compulsive shopper. Father, whose policy was one of "live and let live," seldom told her to watch her pennies. She liked to buy household things in quantity, never purchasing just one broom, for example, but five or six at a time. If she found a good grade of toilet paper, she would buy many dozens of rolls, but who could blame her? What was obtainable in the stores was of poor quality compared to the velvet-smooth tissue she had been used to in the USA. Mamma also indulged in luxuries which must have cost plenty. Father loved his peace and did not like any kind of argument. If he did reproach her for being extravagant, Mamma firmly stood her ground. Like a true Šliupas, she would not give an inch if she thought she was right. So she went on sending away for foreign catalogs and ordering table linens from Ireland and Liberty fabrics from London. She was fond of books, particularly those in English, and frequently ordered them from abroad.

By this time, there was a large selection of dress materials of every kind in the Kaunas shops. However, the sample swatches obtained from the Liberty Company in London, England, showed that these exquisite floral prints, in the manner of old English gardens, were far superior. There was plenty for our live-in seamstress to do, making clothes for us girls and everyday dresses for Mamma as well. Our nurse Elena who used to do this work was no longer with us. We girls were too big to need a nurse, and brother Martynas, Jr. was more than ten years old by now.

Through her Russian connections, Elena settled in Paris, France. After we reached the USA, in the 1940s, Martynas, Jr. sought and found her. They corresponded until she died some time in the 1960s. Elena, who was such a good seamstress, succeeded in getting happily married. Her husband was also a refugee, a Russian Cossack named Fedoroff. She found a good position sewing and designing clothes in some Parisian atelier or dressmaking establishment. From Elena we learned the fate of Liuda, another one of our maids. We remembered her as a pretty girl with red cheeks who had been my twin sisters' nurse from the time of their birth. The two had always been friendly, and Liuda followed Elena to Paris, also becoming proficient in sewing. She later married and had a child. There must have been some deep unhappiness in her life. The last we heard was that Liuda had committed suicide in France by jumping in front of an onrushing train. No one could explain the reason why.

A seamstress named Otilija would come toward the end of winter to stay with us. The rattle of her sewing machine was a sure sign that spring was coming soon. Her nimble fingers and feet (it was a Singer treadle machine) turned out some beautiful creations without benefit of ready-made patterns. Very few people had store-bought clothes because they were not ordinarily available. Seamstresses who went from house to house were not at all unusual. There was one named Antosia who caught the fancy of our chauffeur Ladyga. This was, of course, years later when we finally had a car. Father would have liked to do the driving himself but had no talent for it. Evidently his reactions were too slow. Driving came so hard to him that he soon hired a chauffeur. When the pair married and set up housekeeping in Kaunas, Antosia still remained our seamstress and we went to her home to have our clothes made.

Mamma's everyday clothes made by a seamstress were all very well, but when it came to dressing up she did what some other ladies were doing. She had gowns made by a designer in town. The leading atelier of the day was operated by the famous Trejiene (Mrs. Trejus). Her creations were much admired. It was said that she had been trained abroad, perhaps in France or Germany. To have a dress made in her atelier was to be assured of social success. Ordering dresses from Mme.T was not the least of Mamma's extravagances. She discovered a lady who did exquisite embroidery and delighted in having her decorate pillow cases, tea towels, tablecloths and blouses, as well as other garments. Evelyna and

Violetta had white batiste dresses with strawberries embroidered all over, while mine was also hand embroidered and decorated with green gooseberries. As for clothing worn by the men, there were many fine tailors in Kaunas. I do not remember Father ever getting a ready-made suit. He went to Mr. Rimša or Mr. Kuosaitis, the leading establishments in town. Years later, when people fled the country due to the Soviet invasion, Mr. Rimša turned up in South America, still successfully plying his trade, and there were rumors that Mme. T also found success there and opened an atelier in Colombia.

One of Mamma's great pleasures was maintaining her extensive garden of flowers and vegetables. She spent many hours perusing her gardening books and encyclopedias. From Mamma I learned that the jasmine bushes that bloomed white and fragrant all over the orchard were only one species called by this name. The jasmine, celebrated by poets of the Orient, was not necessarily of the same variety in Lithuania as grown in the USA, where it is sometimes called "sweet mock orange."

Women were sometimes hired by the day to help in the planting, weeding and cultivating of Mamma's peonies, tall blue delphiniums and her favorite black tulips imported from Holland. Not to be forgotten were her roses, particularly one with large white blooms called "Frau Karl Druschki." Mamma said, "I love it because it was my Mother's favorite rose." Cherished by Mamma throughout her lifetime, it was found in her garden wherever she happened to live. She would tell how this rose (still existing in the 1990s) just missed being named for the Prussian Chancellor Bismarck, but the wife of the Rose Growers' Association got the honor instead. As for me, I preferred a briar rose with exquisite tiny pink blossoms growing in a dense thicket at the bottom of the orchard. In my imagination, it was this briar rose that covered the castle of the Sleeping Beauty of the fairy tales, where she waited one hundred years for the coming of her Prince.

Mamma also grew unusual vegetables like American-style corn, sweet Spanish onions almost as big as your fist, artichokes, eggplant, root celery and asparagus, to name only a few. All these grew amazingly well in this near-black rich soil, generally with help from Burpee's (American) and Sutton's (British) seed catalogs. Organic fertilizers were plentifully provided by our farm animals. Chemical fertilizers were not much used and were considered too expensive as most of them had to be imported from abroad. Many vegetables grown by Mamma were new to our country. It took a long time for local tastes to become sufficiently educated for people to eat spinach, artichokes, celery, or even tomatoes. Later, our farm workers learned to like them, but in the early years I can remember them throwing tomatoes at the walls and muttering that they would certainly not eat "those poisonous looking apples." Right up to the end of our life in Lithuania, people would not eat corn on the cob considered by them to be "fodder for cattle."

Food produced on the farm, though not a profit-making enterprise, always came in handy, considering that there were so many people to feed. Great barrels of sauerkraut were made by using a special chopper, somewhat like a French guillotine with a razor-sharp blade for shredding the cabbage heads very fine. Also salted away for the winter were cucumber pickles flavored with dill, everybody's favorite seasoning. These were kept in the cellar and lasted many months. Quantities of meat were salted away in preparation for smoking. The air in the farmyard smelled enticing when the aroma of hams, sausages and sides of bacon arose from the smokehouse.

Father loved history and instilled an interest in the subject in his two older children. He told us that there was historical interest in the place where we lived. Before we got there, Turkey Lurk had been part of a large complex of estates, owned by a Jewish family named Frenkelis. All they had left now was one farm on the banks of a nearby river, not far from Kaunas. This was an unusual family, which included some amusing eccentrics.

The trenches, still standing intact, were reminders of the World War. Our history-minded Father was interested in preserving monuments left from the past. He would not allow anyone to plough the trenches over, though some of his friends urged him to do so. It was only in 1938 that he gave in and agreed to have the trenches destroyed. Ironically enough, another World War was to break out just a year later. Another "monument," a pile of brick and stone and some ancient foundations at the south end of the farmyard, however, had to remain undisturbed. Even the oldest inhabitants (and there were some resident workers who had been born at Turkey Lurk) could not remember what the ruined building had been.

One of these old-timers, named J. Pažėra, had spent his entire lifetime at the place and, as he said, had seen masters come and go. This grizzled old laborer was totally dependable and was often chosen for special jobs. He told me once, while clipping an oversized lilac hedge, that the manor had formerly stood by the avenue of linden trees near the Green Pond. While ploughing the space for planting Mamma's special Spanish onions, he had uncovered bricks and tiles as proof. Pažėra could have told me a lot more about the olden days, but at that time, I was only casually interested in what he had to say. Not only Pažėra but his father and grandfather had always lived on the estate. The grownups said that they had been serfs, a word I did not understand then. I learned later that serfdom, now long abolished, was a Russian institution somewhat comparable to slavery in America. In old-time Russia, serfs were bound to their masters' land and could be bought or sold when the property changed hands.

Among remnants of olden days, which Father thought worth saving, was the wayside shrine by the road near our house. Father respected the beliefs of other religions, and considered the Roman Catholic wayside shrines and crosses to be of interest. Nailed to a maple tree was a crucifix on a sky-blue background, all under a tiny roof. Father saw to it that it got a new coat of paint every so often.

151

The story was that local "true believers" had put it up years ago to "purify the place from infidels," and also to annoy the Jewish owners. What the Frenkelis family thought of this, nobody knows, but in any case they allowed the shrine to stand undisturbed. .

Father had remarkable powers of persuasion, and his enthusiasm was contagious. Soon my brother also caught the historical bug. He discovered a "genuine monument" on the window ledge of an attic. In the house next to the distillery, he noticed a small metal flag crumbling away in the rust. However, one could almost make out the date, which looked like 1812, the very year that Napoleon Bonaparte marched through Lithuania on his way to conquer Russia. True enough, Napoleon had actually stopped in Kaunas, not too far away, and watched his troops being ferried across the river Nemunas. According to local legend, Napoleon had buried his gold in one of our bigger ponds. My brother believed that Napoleon might have indeed come to Turkey Lurk, leaving his treasures behind. Martynas, Jr. decided to dig in the slimy waters where there were masses of nasty bloodsucking leeches. He spent hours on this project, floating around on a makeshift raft, while I observed events from a safe place on shore. However, there was never so much as one speck of gold to be found.

The pond was also the scene of other scholarly pursuits, such as finding out which kinds of birds and animals could swim the best when tossed overboard. It was discovered that pigs were champion swimmers, that cats could swim and that chickens, also, did rather well "when properly terrified." My brother searched endlessly for caterpillars and various insects and collected frogs' eggs to put in glass jars and watch them hatch. He wrote an article when he was about ten or eleven on "hunting wolves in Lithuania," which was printed in something called *The Children's Newspaper* of London, England. Incidentally, British publications such as *Punch Magazine* and *The London Times* regularly came to our home. Mamma was fond of *The Literary Digest*, an American publication, alas now long defunct.

Shortly after Martynas, Jr. found that historic flag on the window ledge of the attic, I made a discovery of my own. A spinning wheel of former days was unearthed in the incredible debris under the eaves. I had never seen one before and thought it fascinating. We lived too close to town for anyone to use such "countrified" equipment, though spinning wheels were still in use in the outlying provinces where flax was grown. Many country folk still used looms to make linen sheets, bedspreads, towels and woolen clothing materials. Another curiosity was a small black steam engine standing in the barn, probably going back to the days when there was no electricity. Nobody remembered why it was there. The engine was of no use to anybody, but was considered a museum piece and was never discarded.

Not to be forgotten was the discovery of a sidesaddle dating back to the times when ladies in long riding habits gracefully draped themselves over their horses. It was found by Anne Crawford in some musty corner of the stable. She not only found it, but actually used it to the amusement of all who saw her. This "city gal" became a horse rider *extraordinaire*. As she said then, she did not care if people thought she made a spectacle of herself riding around on that reminder of Victorian days. The last, and surely the most remarkable of our several tutors and governesses, was this vivacious Scottish redhead named Anne Crawford.

Other historical monuments were discovered during a walk around the property. In general, wandering around alone was not my habit, but this time nobody wanted to come with me, so I went by myself. We knew the grounds of the forts on the borders of Turkey Lurk very well, as we liked to walk or ride horseback there. The main highway running south from Kaunas was next to the forts, but I had never seen what was on the other side of the road. It was a gray autumn day as I set out accompanied by my faithful companion Pinky, the Doberman Pinscher. Despite the ferocious reputation of this breed, Pinky was the nicest and most lovable dog you could hope to meet. When he was a tiny puppy, I fed him milk from a baby's bottle as he sat on my lap. He had been brought up entirely on love and tender affection. Nobody taught him to be a guard dog or a killer. He wore a collar but never needed to be on a leash. Of all the dogs we ever had, Pinky was my favorite, and he knew it.

In all his life, Pinky did only one really wrong thing. He tore the mailman's trousers, but maybe one should not blame him too much. No dog really likes strange folks riding a bicycle. After some years of picking up our mail at the post office, well over a mile away, we had mail delivered right to our home and felt it was a great improvement. Pinky, however, could never get used to it and would have to be held back at the approach of the mailman's flashing bicycle wheels. One day, when nobody was watching, Pinky made a dive for the "invader." Naturally, the mailman was very angry as his trousers were torn beyond repair. Father had to give him a considerable sum of money for the purchase of a new pair of trousers.

Walking through fields and woods I had never seen before, on this grey and gloomy day, I did not encounter a single human being. This gave me a strange and eerie feeling, as if I were completely alone in the world. All of a sudden, there was a hillock thickly covered with pine trees. Something impelled me to climb to the top, and here was a surprise. Rows of wooden crosses, weatherbeaten and unpainted for years, had German names like Heinz, Max or Dieter and dates from the period of 1914–1918. I had wandered into an abandoned cemetery, the last resting place for German soldiers who fell in battle during that time. Nobody had ever told me that Germans and Russians had fought so close to where we lived. I was quite overcome by the idea of all these men, far from their homeland, who had fought and died—and for what? This was a gloomy and forbidding place full of secrets. The pine branches sighed in the wind. They met overhead so that not even a patch of sky was to be seen. Gripped by unreasoning fear, I did not linger. If I had stayed any longer, I might have seen ghosts of the departed warriors among the shadows.

Strange to relate, a place that stays with me is one that I never saw. In our neighborhood were farms, or remnants of estates, where we sometimes visited friends or acquaintances. But there was one where we were never invited. The owner was not home to invite us as he resided permanently in Kaunas. He was a white-haired attorney by the name of Zabielskis. His son George sometimes stopped at Turkey Lurk on his way to *Alšeniškiai*, riding his motorcycle to see how things were going at the farm. Mr. Zabielskis, Sr. could not bear to go there. Just before the year 1914, he had planted what was said to be a magnificent orchard. Besides exotic cherries, he had all kinds of fruit trees, which he loved. The bombs of World War I totally destroyed the orchard, and he did not have the heart to ever go there any more. For me it remained a place of broken dreams, all the more real because I saw it only in my imagination. And now with the lapse of years, I can actually feel the pain of the owner in his loss. Today, nothing remains of our orchard at Turkey Lurk. It was completely ruined and is no more. I have no desire to ever go there again.

Chapter Twenty
Synods of Yesteryear

Going to the Synod of the Evangelical Reformed Church was a very special summer outing that left vivid memories. Father was deeply attached to the Biržai district where the Yčas family had its roots, and he also loved his Church. In our time the annual meeting always took place in the same little country town in the North. Brother Martynas, Jr., the oldest, went to the Biržai meetings with Father at an earlier age than I did. The Twins, too, went when they got to be old enough. Mamma went along, but she did not enjoy the trip like the rest of us. We loved our relatives dearly, but Mama was never close to them. Truly, the Yčas clan so numerous in Biržai, could have been too much for her. Most Reformed families of the area were related since they did not want to marry outside their own religious circle. Father jokingly said that there were only two families left which were not related to ours. He said, "Our cousin Danutė had to spoil it all by marrying into one, which left only one family not related to us."

It was around 1930 when I first went on this Synod outing. The word "Synod" is likely to evoke visions of dull meetings of church dignitaries arguing about theological questions. Not so with us, where lay people had an important role and discussions were really down to earth, all within the framework of parliamentary rules. Our particular type of Calvinism was somewhat like the democratic system introduced by J. Calvin himself in Geneva, Switzerland. In our Synods, you could express yourself freely, even contradicting powerful officials if you liked. Our ministers were regarded not as supreme authorities, but as learned teachers better able to explain the Bible and religious matters than we were. They were university-educated men who also had human frailties. At the Synods, the opinions of our ministers were heard with proper respect, but were not always final.

Synods were a popular part of our church life. They were occasions for happy meetings, good fellowship and much rejoicing.

People gathered not merely out of concern for church affairs. Meeting friends and family members was also something to look forward to. The traditional time for the gathering was around Midsummer Eve, known throughout the country as the Feast of St. John. Going to the Synod was an event for young people as well as adults. We were not invited to take part in the meetings, but there were plenty of other things for us to enjoy, such as parties and excursions.

Family members of whatever age were likely to share some of the same traditions and interests. That noxious term "teenager" had not yet been invented and still has no equivalent in the language. The old and the young did not regard each other with distrust or hostility because the so-called generation gap did not exist. One became an adult only on reaching majority at the age of 21. A comical saying often quoted was *"vaikai ir žuvys neturi balso"* (children and fish have no voice).

In our family, being left out of a Synod trip was generally a keen disappointment. For one thing, it meant missing a train ride, which was such a rare pleasure. If you were going from a larger town, like Kaunas, Šiauliai or Panevėžys, trains or buses were the preferred mode of travel. Automobiles were few and not many people used them. Many country roads were unpaved and motorists could meet travelers in horse drawn carts. The horses would rear up in fright and might even cause an accident. Cars were such an unaccustomed sight that the drivers could be as scared as their horses.

Biržai was then a quiet little town of perhaps a few thousand inhabitants, almost untouched by modern progress. None of the big trains went there. When you got to Šiauliai, where a lot of railway lines converged, you got off to catch a smaller train, a tiny narrow-gauge engine pulling teeny-tiny cars. It went very slowly and stopped many times, so it was likely to be very late when you finally reached where you were going. By modern Jet Age standards, the distance was hardly great. From one end of Lithuania to the other was only a few hundred miles. However, the time it took to get from here to there was another matter. People did not mind doing everything at a really slow pace. One reason for enjoying travel was the scenery you could take in on the way. You could just sit and collect your thoughts during the trip, besides getting your reading, writing or knitting done. You could always meet an interesting person among your travel companions. You might find out something new or perhaps even trade your lunch or your sandwiches with a new friend. No food was sold on trains, and you had to bring your own. In no time at all everybody was looking in the picnic basket. Hard-boiled eggs, tomatoes, salted cucumbers, ham or salami sandwiches and the rest of the goodies soon disappeared.

When we got to Šiauliai, the little "choo-choo train" was waiting for us. This was a real "milk train." On board were tall metal milk containers and baskets of farm produce, as well as live geese, ducks and chickens. The cackle, the quacking and honking of the frightened birds, the clatter of milk cans, and the chatter of the human passengers made it a noisy ride. The train wheels went clackety-clack and the engine also made a racket, merrily blowing its horn before and after every whistle stop. It was no use asking exactly when the train would arrive at our destination, but "better late than never" was the general feeling. Questions about time were less important than the chance of meeting people on board who were also Synod-bound. One such memorable travel companion was a genial white-haired gentleman. His stories and jokes kept us laughing so hard that no one noticed the hours slipping by. He had a leather satchel with several oranges inside—a rare delicacy—which he shared with us. Our new friend had a way with young people and we quite forgot we were dealing with the Rev. K. Kurnatauskas, one of the highest officers of our Church.

Sometimes the stars were already out when the Biržai railroad station finally rose up out of the darkness. Everybody got out and walked as there were no taxis in town, horse-drawn or otherwise. Walking was a good way of relieving your aching bones after hours of sitting on a hard train bench. The road, paved in cobblestones, had no sidewalks and few street lights. It led past the town hospital to the street near the lake shore where our parsonages were. First one passed the twin-towered Roman Catholic church gleaming white like a ghost in the moonlight, then on to the market square with its statues of local celebrities. Some of them were of the Reformed faith, one a Radvila nobleman, the other S. Dagilis, a local poet of renown. In the administrative district of Biržai, over half of the population was Protestant. Then one went onwards past the Castle Park to the so-called "old" wooden parsonage where Synod meetings were held in a hall of ample size.

There was a second or "new" parsonage, built entirely of brick, with several ministers serving this large area. The parish extended into villages and farming communities to which ministers, like Rev. F. Barnelis, traveled by horse or on their bicycles. Only in later years did one hear of a younger, more adventurous, pastor who rode a motorcycle on his parish rounds. The new parsonage, no less hospitable to guests than the old one, was the residence of the head of the Church, General Superintendent Rev. Prof. P. Jakubėnas (the title of Bishop was not used in our church). At about equal distance between the two parsonages was the red brick Reformed Church with its high Gothic tower. In front of the walls around the churchyard were wooden hitching-posts with metal rings for the use of people coming in from the country by horse.

Church membership was composed more of rural folk than of town dwellers. They came in large numbers for Sunday services or religious gatherings and special events like the weekly Market Days. One would hear the clop-clop of horses' feet as the wagons came into town. The men were likely to be wearing visor caps and long boots. Some of them had beards and long mustaches turned either upwards or else down in the so-called Tartar style. Caps or hats were seldom worn by the women who preferred to wear brightly colored kerchiefs on their heads. A square scarf, like a bandanna, would be folded in a triangle and tied under the chin.

Most women wore long full skirts, usually dark in color and topped by aprons either embroidered or handwoven in striking colors.

Country folk excelled at weaving, often spinning their own home-grown wool and flax. Many cottages had spinning-wheels and looms, and the housewives made good use of them. They did needlework as well but, on the whole, preferred to weave and turned out some amazingly intricate designs. City dwellers were just beginning to appreciate their handiwork. Bedspreads, tablecloths and even window draperies, all woven by hand, were quite in vogue in Kaunas and elsewhere. The outdoor Biržai markets often displayed dishes, pitchers and bowls, all made of wood or clay, and were produced using few modern implements.

Country people were often more devout than some of the more sophisticated town dwellers. Prayer meetings were held in village homes. People would be summoned for periodic Bible readings by a messenger who went from house to house. These Reformed people had definite ideas about how their faith differed from that of the Roman Catholics. There was no veneration of saints or of the Virgin Mary. In the Biržai church, everything was starkly simple. There were no pictures or statues and, of course, no crucifixes, no stained-glass windows and no altar. One was supposed to worship in surroundings of utmost Calvinist simplicity. There was just a plain Communion Table, called Table of the Lord. Above it was a wall with the Latin motto *Soli Deo Gloria,* (To God alone the Glory), emblazoned in gold letters. The Huguenot Cross was widely used as an age-old symbol of the Reformed Church, and there was a large one above the Communion Table.

One of the favorite days in the church calendar was Reformation Day in late October, and Martin Luther's *A Mighty Fortress* was a hymn sung with the greatest enthusiasm. Reformed people enjoyed some splendid church music during the Synods. Sometimes, performers included singers of the Kaunas opera like the famed Kipras Petrauskas. Once in a while, there would be guests from abroad, like Prof. James Y. Simpson of Edinburgh, Scotland.

Our Church kept in touch with leaders of the world ecumenical movement and regularly sent delegates to conferences of organizations such as to the World Alliance for Friendship through the Churches.

At Synod-time there would be wreaths of greenery and bunches of roses, phlox, dahlias, and blossoms of the peony in white, pink and red. There was no ban against flowers in church, and country folk liked to bring them in from their gardens. Simple people who had never heard of flower arranging would assemble gorgeous bouquets in a rare harmony of colors. Often they included green branches of the *Ruta* (rue), an aromatic herb found in most Lithuanian gardens. Among other uses, wreaths fashioned from sprigs of rue were worn by brides at weddings instead of the orange blossoms traditionally used elsewhere in the world.

Country folk had respect for the proper keeping of the Sabbath. They would rest, meditate and read the Bible. There was to be no work and no unseemly recreation. This seemed strange to us who lived in town. We did things on Sundays of which our country cousins would have strongly disapproved. Opportunities for recreation for farming folk were very limited. Movie houses existed only in the larger towns. Family festivals, dances, picnics, trips to town on market days, church gatherings and similar outings made a welcome break in the monotony of farm chores. Turning on the radio was becoming a popular pastime, that is, if you were lucky enough to have one.

Hotels rarely existed, and Biržai had none at this time. People coming from a distance were often lodged with friends and relatives or else at a minister's home. Synod participants were often invited to stay in private homes (in our case always at the Old Parsonage). We were packed several to a room, sleeping on floor mattresses, on sofas or whatever was handy. Nobody complained about discomfort or lack of privacy since this could be a chance to be with people long unseen. Synod participants had their meals outdoors at the Old Parsonage, sitting on the back veranda looking out on the rushes growing in the lake. Another long veranda in front of the house had steps that were strategic spots from which to see what was going on. All Synod people, whether coming and going, had to pass this way, and often the curious children sitting on the parsonage steps had to be shooed off. We would sit there late into the evening, watching the dance of the fireflies (called *St. John's bugs* in Lithuanian). Their flashing lights seemed to rival the gleam of the stars in the sky. Trying to catch the elusive fireflies was a great game. Sometimes, we captured a few and put them into a glass jar for observation. However, we never found out exactly how they switched their lights on and off.

At meal times, and particularly at the traditional dinner marking the end of the Synod, the pastor's wife, Mrs. Birutė Barnelis, was in her glory. She exhibited her prowess as chief cook and organizer of many willing helpers, serving repasts which brought the Biblical Feeding of the Five Thousand to mind. The aroma of roast chicken, ham, *kugelis* (potato pudding) and freshly caught fish sizzling in the pan still float in the imagination. A special treat in warm weather was the cold *barščiai* (borscht), a soup served cold with freshly boiled potatoes on the side. This could be either pink in color, if made with beets, or green, if made with sliced cucumbers and plenty of chopped green dill. Especially outstanding was the ice cream coming afterwards, made in the olden way in a bucket cranked by hand. This was colored a luscious pink and tasted of real strawberries. It was loaded with rich cream, eggs and sugar. There no calorie counting or fear of high cholesterol to bother anyone then. As for using alcohol or tobacco, our Church had no Puritanical restrictions. One refrained, however, from drinking or smoking at Synod dinners.

At the table there was much laughter and good humor. Serious notions and disagreements had been left behind in the meeting hall. There were plenty of funny stories to tell. Single people were subjected to the age-old game of matchmaking and "who had been seen stepping out with whom." One bachelor minister, Rev. A. Balčiauskas, was a frequent target. The senior pastor's wife had a sister, still unmarried, a professional woman and not a bit bad-looking, so what was he waiting for? There was much singing of the folk-songs everyone loved. The Biržai district was justly famous for its numerous ancient songs in the typical local dialect, and singing contests by people from the different areas of Lithuania was a favorite form of after-dinner entertainment. The Biržai contingent was usually the winner, if only for the overwhelming loudness of the voices.

The Synod director, or chairman, did not have an easy job. Father was sometimes elected to fill the position. He said that one had to have a sense of humor and also much patience in order to keep the peace. All participants had the right to express their opinion. At times we would hear loud voices raised in argument in the meeting hall and felt we just had to peep through a crack in the door. But young people had better things to do than to snoop around these meetings. There were rowboats waiting on the shore for delightful trips around the lake. Those who were really bold could dive off the edge of the boat for a swim. One could float around and catch fish or try to pluck water lilies, an unbelievably hard and slippery task.

A palace called *Astrava*, now in ruins, was across the water. This former estate of a local nobleman was well worth a visit. The building was deserted and falling into disrepair, but two majestic lions in stone continued to guard the front steps. The once splendid park was now a jungle of weeds. In the town itself, not far from the Reformed Church, was another building in ruins and of far more interest. Set on a hill was the castle of the Dukes Radvila. Little had been done to restore it except for casual attempts to prop up the red brick walls of this roofless three-story building. The park surrounding the castle, however, was renovated and had attractive rose gardens, tennis courts and croquet lawns along the winding paths. It was a romantic place for evening strolls and for dreams of long ago.

The Radvila family dated from the 16th century and held sway over many generations. This princely family was largely responsible for the introduction of the Reformed religion into Lithuania. The Protestant branch of the family died out after a few centuries whereupon Roman Catholic relatives took over their lands and castles. In Biržai, some of the new heirs were wastrels who squandered the family fortune. In order to raise money, they sold their properties, (including the castle, the town and the entire district) to the highest bidder.

North of Biržai was an evergreen forest, one of the country's largest, with swamp lands, which were a good source for peat, then widely used as fuel. The Biržai district, as some other places in Lithuania, had several *piliakalniai* (tumuli or castle mounds) of unexplained origin. According to archeologists, these man-made hills were used in prehistoric times for purposes of defense, for religious rites or for burial grounds. Of more interest to us were the scary tales that the mounds were reputed to be haunted by sorcerers and evil spirits. Folk names for these places were Devil's Castle, Witches' Mountain, Demons' Cemetery and the like.

We were always reluctant to leave Biržai, where the days were always too short. There were unusual excursions to make and well-loved relatives to visit. We always looked forward to a trip to our Father's native village, named Šimpeliškiai. In the nearby cemetery of Kilučiai, our Yčas forefathers had been laid to rest. In June, the gravestones were surrounded by clumps of wild flowers, such as white daisies and cornflowers as blue as the sky. The house where Father was born was still standing. In the living room was a large and marvelously lifelike photo of the grandfather we never knew, also named Martynas Yčas. He had left his young family in America to seek his fortune and had never returned. There was a stream with a plentiful supply of crayfish. Sometimes we went there with our Yčas cousins to catch crayfish in a net, always in the dark of evening by the light of a lantern.

The tiny crayfish was considered a great delicacy, although getting the meat out of the shell was quite a task. People said it was far superior in taste to its giant cousin the lobster. No one enjoyed eating crayfish more than Father, with the possible exception of his cousin and great friend, Dr. J. Mikelėnas, chief physician of the town's hospital. Seated on the veranda at the Old Parsonage, they would hold contests to see who could consume more crayfish in a given period of time. I can still hear their laughter as the mound of empty shells in front of them grew into a great mountain of bright red.

The two cousins loved to sing and were fond of the romantic ditties of their student days. They would reminisce about the time when they studied at the University of Tomsk in far away Siberia, behind the Ural Mountains. Dr. Mikelėnas was a great raconteur, just like Father. I cherish the memory of their tales of bygone days, including the great adventure of going home for the holidays. Even in good weather, the train trip could last as long as ten days. In winter, it might last longer as the train would have to chug its way through the snowdrifts. At the railroad stations, there would be urns like giant samovars filled with steaming hot water. The passengers could have tea and could heat the frozen *koldūnai* (meat dumplings) that were part of their provisions for the journey.

My last time in Biržai was, perhaps, when I was confirmed. There would generally be a whole flock of budding church members during Synod time, the girls dressed in white gowns and the boys in dark suits. We were then in high school, having supposedly reached the so-called age of discretion. I remember more about the gaiety and the parties held to mark these events than I do about the pre-confirmation classes conducted by our ministers. Some of what they communicated to us, however, remains to this day. This was a strong feeling that it is a privilege to be a Protestant as the Great Reformers left us a rich heritage, urging us onwards in the constant search for enlightenment. We were told that our Reformed people were a living example of how a tiny religious minority could be strong in spirit though few in actual numbers.

Of all the attractions of Biržai, best of all was the village where tales about Father's "thatched roof days" came to life. The thatched roofs were long gone, but most of the buildings at the old home place were still intact when I visited there in the 1990s. By some miracle, the village had not been destroyed to make way for Soviet-type collective farms, as had happened to thousands of villages throughout the country. However, the family home was much changed. It had become two separate structures instead of one. It was no longer possible to go to the attic, the scene of one of Father's most poignant memories.

Just before he left for America our grandfather, also Martynas, took Father to the attic to show him something hidden under the eaves. Father was perhaps four years old at the time and still unable to read. When told, "Little Martynas, put your hand into this hole," he pulled out a bundle of tightly-rolled newspapers. Grandfather explained, "The printed word is of more value than all the treasures on earth." These were words that Father did not understand at the time. He was too young to know that the old home place was being used as a storehouse for forbidden publications and that the threat of arrest by Czarist Russian police was hanging over the household.

Chapter Twenty-One
Family Excursions

Here are some memories about a few family trips around the countryside: It was Father who led these expeditions, often made by horse and carriage, to points of interest if they were not too far from our home. For years we had no car, but sometimes it was possible to ride in a borrowed or rented automobile or even to take other transportation.

Down the River to Klaipėda. Of the several rivers in and around Kaunas, the Nemunas was the mightiest of them all. One of the most memorable excursions was a trip down the river in a steamboat. The Nemunas, subject of many a song and story, was known as "Father of all rivers." It flowed majestically through the entire country from its beginnings in the Byelorussian Marshes down to the Baltic Sea. Not all was navigable. In fact, rapids and blockages like the rocky Devil's Bridge began just north of Kaunas. The Nemunas is not one of the major rivers of the world, being less than one thousand kilometers (about six hundred miles) from beginning to end. However, it is as well loved by its people as the Mississippi, the Rhine or the Danube is elsewhere.

We embarked from the pier, which was adjacent to the church of Vytautas the Great founded by the Grand Duke himself in the late 14th century. Our paddle-wheeler was named the Keistutis. Mamma said that Grandma had traveled on a ship of this same name when she was here several decades ago, returning from the USA to look into her family inheritance. Some said that the steamer had been sunk in the battles of World War I. Was this the same ship? Be that as it may, it was my first such voyage, and it was a thrill when the paddle-wheel started to go around amid the churning waters and the gangplank was raised. Sights along the way were castles, historic castle mounds (man-made tumuli), farmsteads and stately manors perched on the waterfront. Church towers, sand bars and mysterious forests seemed to glide by with remarkable speed. Very impressive was the ancient church of Zapyškis with a facade of odd triangular shape, founded in early Christian times. It was so close to the water's edge that it was flooded nearly every spring.

One of the islands, opposite the resort town of Kulautuva, was the spot chosen for the signing of a "final" peace treaty between Duke Vytautas and the Teutonic Knights of the Cross. This treaty was one of many which was made only to be broken. The fierce Knights conquered East Prussia, slaughtered the original inhabitants and then tried to spread Christianity among pagan Lithuanians by fire and sword. Further on were other reminders of the Knights, like *Raudone Castle* with its red brick tower. Then came the estates of *Raudondvaris* and of *Gelgaudiškis*, the former sites of medieval castles. The latter was a showplace with an extensive park. Here were the roots of the Gelgaudas family, spelled "Gielgud" by English descendants like Sir John Gielgud, the famed British actor. According to local legend, Palemonas, a Roman of the first century AD (probably an imaginary character), had settled near here when he came from Italy. Whether the story was true or not, more than 50 ancient Roman coins (a rarity in Lithuania) were found in a tumulus in the vicinity.

The town of Jurbarkas and the forests around it held interest because the entire area had formerly belonged to a friend, the Russian Prince Vasilchikoff. Everyone on board had brought quantities of good things to eat. There was constant picnicking as there is nothing like fresh breezes blowing to increase the appetite. We were having our supper as we passed the Sacred Mount Rambynas. Here the pagans had worshiped their gods and tended their sacred fires. In our time, people gathered at Rambynas on the Feast of St. John to light bonfires and practice special ceremonies connected with Midsummer Eve.

On the opposite bank was East Prussia and the town of Tilžė (Tilsit), which had associations with more recent history. It was the center for clandestine publications when printing in the Lithuanian language had been forbidden by the Russian occupants. Our own Grandpa Šliupas had participated in these activities. By this time, I was too sleepy to take in any more stories and hardly noticed it when the magnificent scenery of the Nemunas Delta came to view. Before getting to the Baltic sea, the Nemunas breaks up into a mass of rivulets dotted with marshy islands. We were approaching the end of a long day. And so, at nightfall, we finally reached our journey's end.

The Village of Old Believers. With the first signs of Fall, Father went on an expedition to find workers for the potato digging season. Potatoes were harvested by women hired by the day. They would do the job by hand, throwing the potatoes into baskets as they went. The best workers for harvesting were Russians who lived in their own village in a place called Ibianai, north of Kaunas. Russian colonists had been settled here in the 1860s. They had their own church and school to serve the needs of about one hundred homesteads scattered roundabout. These people were known as Old Believers, differing somewhat from the Orthodox faith. They did not want to conform, being rigid in their ideas, and the Lithuanian government left them alone to live in the lifestyle to which they were accustomed.

The Old Believers seemed to have an aversion to modern progress. From my several trips to the village with Father, by horse and carriage, vivid impressions remain of another world. Lined up on an unpaved and muddy street was a row of dilapidated cottages. Chickens, ducks, and animals like sheep and goats, lived in the same quarters as their human owners. The people we saw were dressed in typical Russian costume, like we had seen in picture books. The men had long beards and wore high boots. Their shirts, worn outside their pants, were belted around the middle. The work contract was made not with individual workers, but with the head man of the village. It seemed that he was the only one there who spoke Lithuanian, otherwise communication had to be in the Russian language.

Food, lodging and transportation for the "potato women" were provided by the employer, as spelled out in the contract. At the appointed time, a long hay cart and pair were sent to the village to fetch the workers to Turkey Lurk. These were some twenty sturdy young women. They were great singers and their voices carried for miles. They sang folk songs as loud as they could at the top of their voices, and how they loved to sing. You could tell that they were coming long before you saw the approaching wagon or the passengers. Although those particular Russians were said to be a rowdy bunch, prone to robberies and other crimes within the village itself, these women workers behaved in a disciplined and orderly fashion and performed their duties with great exactitude. After the job was completed, the horses were harnessed again, and the potato harvesters went home blithely singing Russian songs just the way that they had come.

Waiting for Darius and Girėnas. A great event in mid-July 1933 was the expected arrival of two courageous aviators from the USA flying their own plane from New York City over the ocean to Kaunas. Inspired by the recent exploit of Charles A. Lindbergh's New York to Paris flight, two Lithuanian Americans were to make a similar attempt. The news that Captain S. Darius, formerly of the US Army Air Force and his companion S. Girėnas, a civilian pilot, had such a plan, caused great elation and excitement throughout the country. Every detail of the preparations for this flight was followed over the radio and by the press. The two flyers purchased a 27-foot plane with their own money and named it the "Lituanica." It was said to be technically well equipped for the trip, but for some reason carried neither a radio nor a parachute.

In this era, well before jet travel became common, Darius and Girėnas were already heroes in the public imagination. Practically everyone we knew was planning to be at the Kaunas airport to cheer the daring aviators on their arrival. Our parents seldom took us to places where great crowds gathered, but they did not want us to miss this special occasion. The Kaunas airfield was small, and the military and civilian planes using it were few. The airfield was near the suburb of Aleksotas. We got there early in the morning and found crowds milling about. We sat on the grass or remained standing as there was no seating available. There were many women and children bearing bouquets of flowers. Most people brought their picnic baskets, and we had one too. This was fortunate as it was to be a long, long wait.

We waited and waited for hours. Late in the day, word got through that Darius and Girėnas were not coming after all. Both they and their plane had met with disaster. Everyone was deeply grieved to hear the tragic news. The Lituanica had crashed in the forest of Soldin, Germany, on July 17th, east of Berlin, and the pilots were killed instantly. They were only four hundred miles from their destination. An investigative commission later established that the disaster was due to atmospheric conditions and was not because of foul play, as some people had been only too ready to believe.

The remains of the two pilots were brought back to Kaunas together with the wreckage of their plane which was placed in the National Museum. Darius and Girėnas were given a magnificent state funeral. A monument inscribed in several languages was erected at the tragic spot in Soldin. This was just the beginning of their rise to fame as national heroes. Many monuments were built in their honor, not only in Lithuania but in the USA as well. Streets were named after them and commemorative postage stamps were issued featuring a double portrait. Literary works, poems and songs about them were composed. The two flyers received the ultimate accolade by becoming part of the country's folklore in ballads widely sung by the people.

Tombs of the Radvilas. It was Father's great pleasure to take us to places with historical associations, particularly if they were connected with the Reformed faith or with our family's ancestry. One such place was Kėdainiai, associated with the Dukes Radvila, the Calvinist magnates of Biržai. Their vast properties extended from Vilnius to the eastward into areas of the North and South. This family (their Polish branch later called themselves Radziwills) was largely responsible for the spread of the Reformed faith in the 16th century. As elsewhere in Europe, the new religion enjoyed great success at first until the Counter Reformation arose. Due to activities of the Jesuit Order, Lithuanian Protestantism eventually lost its power, and the number of adherents declined.

Kedainiai was a small town on the bank of the river Nevėžis. It had once been a bustling center of Calvinist cultural life. The Radvila Dukes founded schools and libraries here as well as printing presses for issuing church materials and learned books. Visitors from abroad were frequent as there were connections with Protestant countries. In the days when the Dukes, like other magnates, had their own private armies, Scottish guards in Radvila service were stationed in Kėdainiai. In the year 1756, the annals of the local Reformed church listed numerous Scottish names, including a pastor named Jacob Inglis. Few reminders were left of these times and Father said that so far, little historical research had been done.

In Biržai, tales were told that some of our people, particularly the Yčas family, were of Scottish ancestry. Some of these Scots might have settled in Radvila lands in Biržai by way of Kėdainiai, a possibility interesting to think about. The Yčas family name, unusual in any language, turned up in New York in a different spelling, but was pronounced exactly the same, i.e., "Eachas." However, when contacted years later, this American family had no information as to where their forbears came from.

When we visited there, the only reminder of the past glories of Kėdainiai was the great church building erected by the Radvila family. Certainly the largest Reformed church in Lithuania, it was now much too big for the few parishioners remaining. Once in a while it was used for a concert or for a public meeting. A few steps below the church floor, many leading members of the Radvila family were interred. It was eerie to be in that underground burial chamber, the first I had ever experienced, and some indelible memories remain. The occasion for our visit was an important anniversary attended by many people. Duke Jonušas Radvila of

174

Biržai, a famous military leader and perhaps the best known of the clan, had signed a treaty of mutual assistance with Sweden three hundred years ago. It was an effort to escape the pervasive influence of Poland. As to be expected, Duke Jonušas was highly praised by Lithuanians and much maligned by the Poles.

The historical implications were of great interest to the grownups, but were well over my head. I was much more impressed by the mummified corpses in the mausoleum. Some of them were not properly entombed but were lying in open coffins and crumbling away into dust. One of these was a later Radvila from Vilnius, also named Jonušas. Like his ancestor, he was a great champion of the Calvinist religion. The corpse, now just dry skin and bones, had a deep gash on the skull. I was told that this Duke had died of a hatchet blow to his head, doubtless the work of some religious fanatic. Little was known about the circumstances of his death or who the murderers had been. When I asked my elders, I got the answer that for sure it had been someone in the pay of the Jesuits. To me, this was a fascinating murder mystery that had me wondering for a long time afterwards.

By the Bend in the River. Sometimes we went south to Prienai near the Nemunas, a town famous for its flavorful beer. The owner of the brewery, B. Šakovas, was an old family friend. There were two children, a girl my age and a younger boy. They were brought up by a nurse who liked to take them with her to the Roman Catholic church. To the horror of the Jewish parents, their daughter was baptized into the Christian faith without their knowledge or consent. Considered a calamity at the time, it turned out to be a blessing in disguise. When the Nazi German occupation came, none of the family survived except the daughter who had been baptized a Christian.

In the vicinity was Birštonas with mineral waters supposed to have healing qualities. Some springs smelled of sulphur and were bitter to the taste. Birštonas was becoming a popular summer resort. There was a long avenue of swaying birch trees on the river bank. Here the Nemunas made a series of curves. There were many inlets and isles to explore. One day, Father hired a boatman to take us around. From the rowboat, we saw a cloud of wild ducks flying toward the sky. Another rowboat emerged unexpectedly from among the reeds with several men sitting in it. They were completely naked and were preparing to dive off the edge to go for a swim. Far from being embarrassed at seeing us, a couple of them stood up in the boat and waved at us in the greatest good spirits. It must be mentioned that many people thought nothing of going in and out of the water without a stitch on. Country folk were not likely to even own a bathing suit. At any rate, nudity did not seem to shock anyone.

At the famous Bend in the River, the river makes an almost perfect circle surrounding a peninsula much like an island. Here we saw a "forest primeval", almost untouched by the hand of man. This area, called *Punia*, was a wildlife preserve with rare varieties of birds and animals like boars, deer, moose and wolves. This was a remnant of the vast forest that once covered most of the land. It was said that some centuries ago, the Grand Dukes of Lithuania used to have great hunting parties here. Among the beauties of the peninsula was the avenue of ancient oak trees with a view of the river and the tumulus, or castle-mound, on the opposite bank.

This hill was known by the name of Margeris, a folk hero of olden days. This may or may not be the actual site of "Pilėnai" where Margeris led his people in an act of defiance against the enemy. This was a castle on the hilltop, built of wood like others of the time. When surrounded by the Teutonic Knights, with no prospect but certain defeat, Margeris and thousands of his followers set fire to the castle and leaped into the flames. Romantic poems, novels and even an opera were written about this noble deed.

Further around the bend was the forest of Balbieriškis where we went on mushroom-hunting expeditions. It was a wooded area of pine and fir where mushrooms, like the ever-popular *Baravykas* (or Boletus), grew among the moss. Mushrooms are much enjoyed

176

by the people of Eastern Europe in contrast to the suspicion with which the Anglo-Saxon world regards them. People around us ate mushrooms without fear, always watching out for the poisonous varieties that might mean certain death. Father knew much about mushroom lore and taught us how to distinguish between the good and the bad. Besides the delectable *Baravykas,* there were yellow *Vovieriuškos* (Chanterelles) and the *Ruduokės* (Brownies) which were good for salting away for the winter in wooden barrels. Some varieties could be dried for later use. Most mushrooms we found were for eating right away and were often served fried or baked with plenty of onions and sour cream.

When mushroom hunting, we generally went in a borrowed car with a chauffeur at the wheel. This driver was called Kirejevas, so knowledgeable and well informed about everything and everybody that we called him "Mr. Know-it-all". Petrusia, the housekeeper, liked to join the party as did any tutor who happened to be around at the time. Needless to say, everything tasted wonderfully good at our outdoor picnics. One unforgettable day we brought a bucket of hand-cranked ice cream. Adding to our pleasures were visits to the gypsies who were fond of camping in these woods. They had their playing cards ready to tell our fortunes. There were games to be played after lunch. One that was a great favorite was called "Last couple join hands." Everyone lined up in pairs, separated and then ran as fast as possible trying to get together before the one who was "It" could catch them. Exhausted by all the exercise, we would stretch out on our rugs for a nap amid the rustle of the forest.

Chapter Twenty-Two
Getting Ready for School

There were several governesses and tutors to instruct us before we actually entered school. Miss Vivian E. Saunders arrived from Birmingham, England soon after we moved to the country. She was needed to teach us proper English, since our Mamma's attempts to teach us the language had no success. Miss Saunders was unbelievably thin, wore her dark hair cut in a short bob and constantly wore glasses. I thought she even slept with her glasses on, the better to see with in her dreams. This interested me since I had just begun to wear glasses myself. Eye glasses were so unusual at the time that they were a definite drawback as far as good looks were concerned. I found this out later when my classmates at school teased me about wearing them, but I would have been helpless without glasses, so that was that.

Miss Saunders taught us entertaining English rhymes and also introduced us to a wonderful book called *French Without Tears,* which was my earliest contact with this language. Miss S liked to talk about characters from romantic novels like *The Scarlet Pimpernel.* She also liked to talk about illnesses that she either had or might have in the future (now, what exactly were "Chilblains?") Miss Saunders was thrifty and tried to teach us that it was not necessary to have too many possessions, especially underwear. One of her favorite sayings was, "All you really need is to have one on, one in the drawer, and one in the wash."

She was a great needlewoman and made some of her clothes by hand, like frilly voile dresses sewn in tiny little stitches. Miss S had me embroider dainty little gifts and was a firm believer in Christmas presents for everybody (which was not our custom). I still remember the astonishment of great-aunt Dèdina when we called on her one Christmas Eve to present her with my laboriously embroidered doily. After she left us, Miss S did not go back to England, saying she had no family to go home to. She got herself rooms in Kaunas and made a good living giving private English lessons as she said "to some of the best people in town."

Another governess also stayed on after leaving our employ but in somewhat different circumstances. Mademoiselle Moutier was a striking looking woman with a mane of long black hair. She came from Switzerland to teach us French but soon left. She met a "sugar daddy," or man of wealth, and set up housekeeping for him in Kaunas, supposedly enjoying a life of luxury. Such an arrangement was considered scandalous in our society. None of the adults wanted to talk about Mlle. Moutier.

Such foreign language studies ended when definite plans were made to send us to school in town. There would be many stiff examinations to pass, and we had to be given the proper preparation in the native language. There were tutors available from among the students at Kaunas University. Tuition fees were high and some students gave lessons to supplement their income. The first such tutor was Jurgis Strazdas (his name means thrush in English). He was studying chemistry and later achieved distinction in his chosen field. Though Martynas, Jr. was a couple of years older than I, we had our lessons together.

Mr. "Thrush" was exceptionally kind and patient with us. We studied at a wooden table with a removable top with space inside to store copybooks, pencils and other supplies. Our teacher introduced us to school procedures new to us, like the bells rung at intermission-time. Our rowdy songs accompanied by a clatter of the tabletop always greeted the sound of Mr. Strazdas' bell. He encouraged me in my leanings toward history and literature and took real joy in instructing my brother in the natural sciences. When I met him years later in Toronto, Canada, he said he was not a bit surprised to hear that Martynas, Jr. was a distinguished professor of Microbiology. Mr. Strazdas added, "I am sure he is well on his way to getting the Nobel Prize."

As school examinations drew closer, we had serious preparation over a longer period of time by Juozas Lieponis (a name derived from *liepa* or linden tree). He was a student of Liberal Arts and an excellent teacher in a variety of subjects. After helping us over the hurdles of the examinations, he tutored the Twins when it was their turn to go to school. The goal for Martynas, Jr. and me was to enter the Fifth Class of a public school called by the name of *Aušra* (Dawn or Sunrise). These were separate institutions for boys and for girls, coeducation not being the general rule. This kind of secondary school, termed *gimnazija* had eight classes following four years of primary school and was like a preparatory school for university studies. The term *gimnazija* will be used here as this was more than a high school and was really like junior college. There were no American-style colleges and no Bachelors degrees. The first degree obtainable at the Lithuanian university was the equivalent of a Master's diploma.

In the *gimnazija* one selected either the classical or the commercial course, each with a set program in the subjects for study. Our choice was the Classical or A section, emphasizing Latin, foreign languages and the arts rather than the Commercial or B section, stressing business subjects, accounting and practical mathematics. There were tuition fees to pay in the *gimnazija*, and examinations were held at almost every step of the ladder. Students who could not meet the requirements had no alternative but to go to a trade or vocational school. This might be considered an elitist or undemocratic system by American educators, but the system worked well, and it was what was needed at that particular time and place.

Mr. Lieponis introduced us to reams of subjects, some of which had no practical application to everyday life. The examinations could not have been too terrifying, as I have only a vague recollection. For some reason I remember the natural sciences exam. I was required to give a detailed description of the eye of the common housefly, a complex structure enabling it to see in many directions at once. The examinations were in the spring, leaving time for one glorious summer of freedom before school began September first. There were the school uniforms to attend to. These had to be made to order. Boys wore black pants and high collared jackets, rather like those that military people wore. Girls wore dresses with long sleeves and finely pleated skirts. Over the dress one wore a black voile apron or pinafore, which extended from shoulder to hem. Both boys and girls wore visored caps displaying the school emblem. The boys' uniforms were always black whereas girls had dresses in blue, burgundy red, brown, etc., according to the school they attended. Mine happened to be a nut brown. A white collar and cuffs had to be sewn on fresh every day. Looking forward to putting on the uniform was a really exciting prospect.

Exactly when important events happened is not always easy to remember. The coming of Anne Crawford from Scotland was a milestone because she had a formative influence on our lives. She probably arrived during the hassle of getting our school uniforms, i.e., in late summer of 1932. Known as "Crawley," she found something pleasant to say to everyone and made herself right at home. She was interviewed for the position of governess by a Scottish friend, Prof. J. Y. Simpson, and was a credit to his judgement. A graduate in English of the prestigious University of Edinburgh, she took pride in her degree and liked getting mail addressed to "Anne Crawford, MA." Anne had a great sense of an individual person's capacities for self-improvement and firmly believed in the value of education. Added to these qualities was a sense of humor and an ability to enjoy new experiences, which made it easy for us to absorb some of her teachings. Many of them remain with me to this day, but a careful selection must be made of what now seems to be truly important.

Crawley's main task was to instruct the Twins, but she also conducted an informal "Great Books" program for all of us. The books she introduced us to included Margaret Mitchell's *Gone with the Wind* and *The Seven Pillars of Wisdom* by T. E. Lawrence. She was a diligent reader in many areas. Being adaptable and remarkably fast on the uptake, she could help Martynas, Jr. and me with our schoolwork in a way our Mamma never could. Anne tried to understand the requirements of our educational system, whereas Mamma could offer us no guidance in school subjects and even had a hostile attitude. She would say "Nobody in an American high school would be required to know anything about this." Crawley had an open mind and had an explanation of the value that some of these impractical school subjects might have for us in later life. In Crawley's opinion broadening our horizons and enabling us to hold our own in discussions with people smarter than ourselves could be a possible answer,.

She was much more than a governess or teacher and was always buzzing around doing household tasks in the kitchen and the farmyard, baking cakes and casseroles, gathering chicken eggs, milking cows, etc. When asked, "Why are you, an educated person, doing all this?", her reply was, "One should vary intellectual activity with physical work. And besides, exercising the powers of the mind enables us to perform any task better and faster." Crawley met every new learning challenge with joy, was endlessly curious, and even tried to learn Lithuanian. Her pronunciation was atrocious, however, like saying "zhibalou" for *cibulis* (onion) or "pigininny" for *piniginė* (purse). She did not have an ear for languages or for music either. She found many words unpronounceable but went ahead and spoke anyway. Crawley was a master of the difficult art of speaking out without hurting peoples' feelings, e.g., when correcting our manners ("don't put your elbows on the table…don't go clomp, clomp, clomp down the stairs…never make sandwiches at the table…be self-reliant and hang up your clothes…don't wait for the maids to do everything for you…"), Even when telling Mother in our presence, "Mrs. Yčas, I have never seen such selfish children," the good-humored way she did it offended no one.

Anne remained in Lithuania for a long time after she left us and remained a close friend of the family. She went to Klaipėda to teach English at the Commercial Institute and was remembered for years as one of its most popular professors. Wherever she went, she upheld the glories of the British Empire, on which she claimed the sun never sets (and carried with her a pocket-sized rotating map of the globe to prove it). She said, "I am British first and Scottish second, and woe betide anyone who tries to call me English." She knew a few words in Gaelic, and Sir Walter Scott and Robert Burns were her favorite writers. Though she admitted the greatness of Wordsworth and Keats, Robert Burns was supreme in her judgment. Among her heroes was Bonnie Prince Charlie, prevented by the English from occupying the throne he should have inherited. Crawley loved to sing Scottish folk songs, but did not pretend to be well versed in music. She said, "Grand Opera is all right, but I much prefer the compositions of Gilbert and Sullivan."

When visiting Crawley some decades later in Scotland, I learned that the years she spent in Lithuania were among the happiest of her entire life. This was the way she explained her real reasons for embarking on this adventure, "I wanted to learn new things and escape from a dull life in "Auld Reekie." (Reekie was her pet name for the capital of Scotland). Born into a family of nine children, she remembered how her gentle and loving mother had steered all of them into an academic education. Her father, by contrast, was always talking about lack of money and said that girls did not need to be educated. Crawley never married and said that an old maid aunt of hers was to blame for her single state (for which she had absolutely no regrets). Aunt Jessie helped bring her up and told her, "Anne, you have that certain look about you which does not appeal to men. You will never get married." We always thought that Crawley must have had a few love affairs though she did not talk about them. Clearly remembered is a humorous (and enigmatic) statement of hers on male-female relationships, "I have no intention of going to my grave guessing."

Crawley valued her position in our household and was not willing to surrender her rights to our affections to any governess past or present. She never was very friendly with Miss Saunders and discouraged her visits to us. The last of our French governesses, Mademoiselle J. Lys, who arrived in late 1938 and went home early because of gathering war-clouds, also did not get cordial treatment from Crawley. Mlle. Lys wanted me to go on a European trip with her, but Crawley talked me out of it. In the few months we had together, Mlle. Lys taught me to love poets of another day like Ronsard, plays by Molière, Racine and Corneille, the manifold works of Victor Hugo, novels by Balzac, etc. Her knowledge of French literature was quite remarkable. From her I heard that the literary and artistic achievements of the era of Louis the Sun King in France were certainly no less than those in England during the Elizabethan Age.

One of Crawley's gifts to her Lithuanian family, as she called us, was a replacement for those terrible old rafts that we still used for floating around the pond. She actually bought us a rowboat as a surprise, laboriously transported from points unknown. The fact that it had a hole in the bottom and needed bailing out whenever we went for a boat ride did not diminish Crawley's pleasure or the sparkle in her eyes. That was the way she was, always ready for fun and laughter. Perhaps she was not the one who dreamed up the experiment of the "motherly" tom turkey who was made to sit on eggs, but she thoroughly enjoyed our daily visits to see whether any little turkeys were hatched yet. The tom turkey was fed a rich mash spiked with vodka. He was quite comfortable sitting in a drunken daze in his straw-lined doghouse under the jasmine bushes. Whether it was the effect of the vodka or not, father turkey would take his brood out for a walk after the babies hatched, just as a mother turkey would.

As previously explained, the name "Turkey Lurk" had nothing to do with turkeys. However, there were actually quite a few turkeys there, mostly white in color. One ferocious snow-white tom turkey hated the peacock with a passion, and the two would engage in combat, like a pair of Roman gladiators fighting to the death. They often had to be separated before they did each other in.

This same male tom turkey was possibly the one involved in one of Crawley's jokes. Our parents wanted to send exhibits to the Agricultural Fair in Kaunas. White turkeys being a rarity, there was the chance of getting a prize. Then it was discovered that this magnificent bird had a black feather in his tail. Crawley would not hear of his being disqualified and amid much laughter she cut out the offending feather with a snip-snip of her scissors. The tom turkey went on to heights of fame and won the first prize.

On looking back, it seems that one of Crawley's greatest gifts to us was teaching us to appreciate and enjoy what was going on around us. In other words, she gave us a heightened awareness of living. We must have been a very unimaginative and self-centered bunch, taking everything for granted. As Crawley said, we children were like white rabbits brought up under glass seeing little outside our immediate environment. We shall be meeting Crawley again. She was one of the last people to say farewell to us when we left Lithuania forever.

Chapter Twenty-Three
School Days

The long-awaited day came at last when we donned our school uniforms for the first time. It was the custom to mark such milestones in life by a visit to the photographer. One of these photos of Martynas, Jr. and me standing proudly in our uniforms still survives (in black and white as there was no color photography then). Our teachers told us that school uniforms were a great leveler, or equalizer, no matter whether you were the son or daughter of a former mayor, a doctor, a farmer or a janitor. This was an explanation that did not interest me at the time, but I understood its full import later on. For the same reason, any kind of showing off at school was discouraged. Wearing of jewelry beyond a wrist watch or using any cosmetics whatever was not allowed, and there were many other restrictions. Our school uniforms were a holdover from the old Russian Czarist system as was the program of education at the *gimnazija*. Strict discipline rather than freedom of self-expression was emphasized. Lithuanian schools resembled the German *gymnasium* and the French *lycée* to some extent.

In fear and trembling I started the trip on the first day of school, riding in the Victoria carriage with the black pair of horses named Thunder and Lightning. We went through the suburb of Aleksotas down the hill and over the bridge across the river Nemunas. We had to pass City Hall with its tall tower and the whole expanse of Old Town before reaching the *Aušra* school building. This three-story structure was once occupied by the Seimas, or Parliament, and had a large assembly hall including a stage. As was to be expected, I felt like a fish out of water on first entering the classroom. Being thrown together with girls of my own age was a shock. I tried to keep my cool and not show anyone that I had butterflies in my stomach. Very little remains in my memory of those first few days and weeks. The home room teacher received me with great kindness, but of course I was a real curiosity to my classmates. In Class 5A there were about thirty students, seated two by two at their desks arranged in several neat rows.

There was another girl who was new and strange like me, and we were seated together. She was a Jewish girl named Anna Kaganas. Seat-mates were chosen by the students either because of personal friendship or for other reasons, the really clever or gifted girls being in greatest demand. Later, my seat-mate was Rita Vileišytė, a playmate of childhood days at Palanga. We stuck together because she, too, was also somewhat of a square peg in a round hole. It is amazing how Rita kept coming in and out of my life at some of its really important moments. We never lost touch even when we were far away from the country that was home.

Our class monitor was Birutė who was a straight A student rivaled only by her assistant Jovita. They were held up as examples to the rest of us in the competition for good grades. Both girls were so kind and helpful that their obvious superiority did not irritate us at all. A short period of prayer started the school day, usually with a hymn to the Virgin Mary. Non-Catholics were not expected to attend. This gave me a few minutes of leeway in case I happened to be late. Everyone was obliged to take religious instruction in one of the four main faiths: Roman Catholic, Protestant, Jewish and Moslem (a tiny minority). We were highly amused to see the visiting Orthodox Jewish rabbi put on his hat when he entered his classroom. There was absolutely no consideration for freethinkers or atheists. Being of a different religious persuasion did not prevent us from making fast friendships at school nor was there any discrimination to my knowledge.

The grading system had no A's or B's. It was on a downward scale from a five (excellent) to a one, which was so abysmal that it was hardly ever used. Three was a barely passing mark, and two signified failure. You could be asked to take an exam in a subject if your grades were poor or even to stay in the same class for another year. Everyone would stand up in respect for the teacher when he or she entered the room (we did not change classrooms; the teachers came to us). Teachers would bring the class journal from which names would be picked for oral recitation that day. Suspense was in the air as the teacher mounted the raised dais and got to the right page in the journal. You never knew when it would be your turn. If the lesson was not prepared, could you get away with it and not be called on to recite?

From time to time there would be written examinations in special copybooks for essays and mathematical problems. Some years later, when we were all really too old for such practical jokes, we played an April Fool's trick on the mathematics teacher. We wrote the required material into our copybooks, then substituted exactly similar, and blank, copybooks, which he gathered up after the written exam. As he marched out into the hall, laden with the wrong copybooks, we almost split our sides laughing. Our class monitor was chosen to run after him and succeeded in catching up with him before he reached his desk in the Faculty Room. She reported that the look of sheer astonishment on his face when informed of his mistake was easily worth a million dollars.

Mr. Remėza was a rare teacher who could enjoy a laugh with his students. Most teachers were not approachable as human beings and kept their distance, just as if they had been gods from Mount Olympus. Teaching was a highly respected profession. Most of our teachers were university educated and well paid. Their word was law and the Parents' Committee had little chance of winning in the case of a dispute about an unruly student or some point of school procedure. There was one instance, however, that was a major victory for the parents, and Mamma led the attack. At school dances no modern dancing was allowed. The waltz, the polka and folk dancing were the rule, but positively no fox trots or seductive tangos. Mamma was a free American spirit and convinced everyone that such restrictions were nothing short of ridiculous. This incident could not have occurred at a better moment. At this very time a pop singer of sentimental modern dance music, named A. Šabaniauskas, was becoming all the rage among young people.

For quite some time, I was somewhat of a loner. For one thing, I arrived and departed by horse and carriage instead of walking like many of my classmates. After school they tried to go via Main Street even if it was not the shortest way home, looking for interesting adventures. Some of them, scarcely older than I, met their boy friends on Main Street who might even carry their book satchels for them. These were briefcases, standard equipment for the high school crowd. Living in the country was definitely a drawback. Also, I did not fit in with those girls chattering about experiences I had not had, or books I had not read (mushy romantic novels were prime favorites with them). I was not a loner for very long. Later on, in the Sixth Class, I started to feel that I belonged, especially when I was accepted into the company of an "in group" of tall and attractive girls. Several of these remained my friends for life.

A common interest in defeating teachers at their game of stringent rules and regulations helped to meld us into a cohesive group. When teachers arrived in class, we were expected to be sitting quietly at our desks. Our classroom happened to be on the third or top floor. Sometimes there was lots of horseplay going on, mad racing around or even dancing in the hallway at intermission time. Some of us would lean over the balustrade to warn school mates that the teachers were coming up the stairs. Then we would scatter like birds in flight, diving back to where we belonged and sitting as pretty as you please. Another game was evading the rule about leaving the school building during school hours. Between classes it was such a temptation to run out to see what was happening around the *Prezidentūra* (Presidential Residence, like the American White House), which was just across the street. Sometimes important-looking guests would be arriving in limousines or in horse-drawn carriages. Equally tempting was the nearby Market Square where delicious fruit, cakes, smoked fish and other goodies were for sale. Racing back to the classroom after such adventures was considered very daring.

190

One could be expelled if caught too often in undisciplined behavior. Among many reasons for expulsion were smoking cigarettes, using alcohol or appearing in public places without wearing the school uniform, for example at dances, lectures, concerts or theatrical performances. Infringement of rules of conduct occurred much more often at the *Aušra* school for boys than at ours, especially in regard to alcohol or cigarettes. My brother loved to disobey rules of all kinds. One time, when the school Inspector (or provost) lectured him about appearing at the theater without the uniform, he was told that his behavior was that of an anarchist. "Well, maybe that is what I am" was the impertinent reply, whereupon our Father was summoned to the Inspector's office to explain. As for uniforms, defying this rule was a risky venture because some teachers, especially the much dreaded Inspector, frequented likely places in the hope of nabbing wrongdoers in action. We used to joke that the only safe place for hiding was in the darkness of a movie theater.

There was nothing we schoolgirls enjoyed more than a good juicy scandal. Imagine our feelings when there was one involving our teachers. Our Inspector was a middle-aged Roman Catholic priest who was observed far too often in the company of a pretty young Lithuanian Language teacher. There was no show of affection or any holding of hands, but soon they both disappeared from the scene. The Inspector left the priesthood and married the girl of his dreams, which to us was incredibly romantic. Romance of a different kind, involving British royalty, i.e., Edward, Prince of Wales, and Mrs. W. Simpson, was heart-rending and brought us to tears. Who could forget that emotional radio broadcast about "giving up the throne for the woman I love?" In our opinion, it was indeed a noble sacrifice. It sparked many discussions on the rights and wrongs of the case and about the invincible power of love, quoting the Latin saying: *"Omnia Vincit Amor"* (Love conquers all).

Our teachers encouraged us to attend cultural events, notably opera and ballet matinées at the National Theater. A few times we were taken to theatrical performances at the National Theater as a group, and I remember attending the opera *Faust* starring the world-famous Russian basso F. Chaliapin as Mephisto. There, of all places, I would have loved to get all dressed up in a pretty gown, anything but that drab black and brown school uniform. By the way, the opera *Faust* was a great favorite of schoolboys, but not because they appreciated fine music. The ballet sequences, according to my brother and his friends, were likely to be performed by female dancers very scantily clad in filmy and revealing costumes.

Sometimes the school organized outings to places and events of interest. I vividly remember a trip on foot to the ruins of the castle of Kaunas, which had marked the founding of the town in medieval times. A great sports and folk dance festival in Jurbarkas, where we went by steamboat down the river, stands out in the memory. There were trips to museums and art exhibits, agricultural fairs and parades on various holidays, where students marched and carried flags. However, such occasions were few, because nothing was as important as our school studies, and they always came first. One activity thoroughly endorsed by our school was the Scouting Movement. No less a personage than its founder, Britain's Lord R. Baden-Powell, came to a great Jamboree in Palanga by the sea in 1933, which did much to enhance the popularity of scouting. Martynas, Jr. got to go to this event but I did not, which was a big disappointment.

Outdoor camping experiences with the Girl Scouts are among the best memories of my school years. We put up tents lent by the Army and attended to our daily needs ourselves without any hired help or sophisticated cooking facilities. Open camp fires were the rule, and many were the pots burned coal black that we had to scrub. There were song fests, writing and acting of impromptu plays and compiling of a daily newspaper to which I was able to contribute. The appetites we developed from breathing the aroma of the pine forest were unbelievable. The dining table was a rectangle with knee-high trenches dug around it where we put our feet.

On every hand were woodland decorations or paintings made of sand and varicolored mosses, pebbles, twigs and pine cones. Taking turns at doing night patrol, going two by two around the camp while listening for the hooting of owls and the stirring of other nocturnal creatures, was always an exciting adventure. In such conditions of living together in close intimacy we learned things about each other that we had not known before. It was easy to make new friendships or to cast off the old in those carefree days of youth. Some of the skills learned through scouting proved very useful in later years. The same can be said about much of what we learned at school.

Of all these learning experiences perhaps the final examinations left the greatest impression. For *gimnazija* students, doing the required school homework was hard enough. Preparation for tomorrow's lessons could take two hours or more after the evening meal. The State Board examinations every potential graduate was subjected to remain in the memory as truly appalling. Some students actually became ill with worry and anxiety and begged to be excused from the examinations for reasons of impaired health. We were let off school for some weeks to prepare for the June examinations. These were in both oral and written form. Proficiency in the Lithuanian language was a prime requirement. No one could graduate without knowing the grammar and syntax backwards and forwards, not to speak of the final essay that had to be written in faultless prose and in acceptable style, with a clearly defined "Introduction," "Body of the Work," and "Conclusion."

Some students engaged tutors to coach them in their areas of weakness. Mine was mathematics which was no joke. Mastery of trigonometry, analytical geometry, differential calculus, logarithms and higher mathematics in general was required. During those balmy spring days, bees were buzzing around the apple blossoms as I sat in my favorite place for cramming for the tests. This was a crooked bough in an old apple tree, making a natural arm chair. There I would read my school books, repeating over and over again the facts that I would have to know. The finals were held under supervision of representatives of the Ministry of Education. Anyone caught copying a classmate's paper or in any shenanigans whatever could be instantly expelled.

There was a lottery system for the oral exams. We all hoped against hope that the ticket we drew would be on a question we were prepared to answer. We joked about practicing telepathy, thought transference and the like. After all these years, I remember my World History orals. I was certain sure I would have to report on how Napoleon III became Emperor of France, and this was exactly the case. Giving oral reports was no more difficult than writing essays as this was part of our everyday classroom procedure. As for myself, I had a natural facility for self-expression, both verbally and in writing, and there is no doubt that high school teachings helped me to develop this talent.

After the hard work for the Finals, the graduation exercises were a real letdown. Mr. K. Jokantas, the principal of the school, simply handed us our diplomas, and that was it. If there were speeches or a musical program, I do not remember them. Graduation ceremonies were a big disappointment to me as not a single member of my family was there to witness my proud moment. Not having my parents there made me feel rather like an orphan in a storm. My graduation present from Mamma and Father was a long string of yellow amber beads to wear with my national dress. I was having one made up to wear at the last and final dance.

Each graduating class at *Aušra* tried to do something different. Our graduating class, especially the Classical section (Section A), felt that we were something special and should do something unusual to enliven our last dance in the school hall. For one, we were the tenth class to graduate since the school's

194

founding, and for another, we each thought of our classmates as being remarkable for their character and originality of outlook. So how to celebrate our farewell party? Graduates of previous years had decorated the hall in special ways, served exotic foods or presented concerts or plays. Everyone was still talking about the skit given the year before, called "Eighth Class Princess," which had been so remarkably successful. Our graduating class hit on the idea of dressing in Lithuanian national costume.

As in most other European lands, our national dress was usually worn only by peasants in remote country villages. In our time, there was a revival of interest in ancient folkways, folk dances, songs, artifacts and also in national costume. This was sometimes worn by townsfolk instead of evening dress at dances and other social occasions. Much research was being done in those areas, and many fine illustrated books were available. Material for national dress had to be handwoven on looms; no part of it was machine made. We, the graduates of classes A and B, all tried to have ours made up in the colors and styles appropriate to the region where our families had their roots. The assemblage of about sixty of us made a colorful array of costumes when we sat down to have our picture taken to mark the end of our school days.

Graduation day may not have been marked by great pomp and ceremony, but the diplomas we held were much more than just pieces of paper. Many years later, some classmates agreed with me on their value. The Lithuanian *gimnazija* document remains one of the most precious of our possessions, no matter what else we may have achieved or the other diplomas we may have collected in going out into the wide world.

Part III

The Widening World

Vilnius Panorama
(Lithuanian Evangelical Reformed Church
is the building at extreme left)

Chapter Twenty-Four
Some Curious Encounters

As I grew older, I began to take more interest in what was happening in the world around me. On looking back, it seems that there were people in our society who were somewhat unusual, to say the least. A few personalities who impressed me had unique and hard-to-forget qualities of character and behavior. These include public figures as well as friends and neighbors with less claim to fame. They were not the usual run of people and could almost qualify as eccentrics, to a greater or lesser degree. Surely, they deserve separate mention.

A curious character who left his imprint at Turkey Lurk was J. Gabrys. We had never met in person, but I felt I knew him because of the tales told about him by Father. Something belonging to this person was stashed away among Mamma's precious souvenirs, stored in some eleven steamer trunks. Among them was a round plaque of white plaster, measuring perhaps 25 inches across. It was a bas relief of the face of President Smetona, but it had a broken nose. Why keep such a damaged piece of goods? Father told us the story of why he had kept it, "until the owner came and called for it." The owner was well known to him from gatherings in Paris, Lausanne, and elsewhere. This was J. Gabrys, a sworn enemy of the President. His hatred ran so deep (or was it fear of retaliation?) that he became an expatriate, preferring to live abroad.

On one of his visits to Kaunas, Gabrys became enraged at seeing President Smetona's plaque at an art exhibit. In full view of a crowd of onlookers, he broke the nose with his fist, which naturally caused a public furor. He said that he was not liable for damages, loudly exclaiming,"I purchased the bust with my own money and can do whatever I like with my own property." From this, one may gather that here was an eccentric personality. A man of many talents, he was well educated and fluent in many languages. Being fond of associating with the "Rich and Famous," he played the *grand seigneur* in French society by giving himself the imaginary title of Gabrys de *Garliava* (the latter being the name of his native village). Gabrys wrote many books and pamphlets, some of genuine historical value. Naturally, he had enemies and was suspected by some people of being a secret agent in the pay of the Germans or worse. Father, however, liked him and was amused by his antics. He gave Gabrys full credit for publicizing the Lithuanian cause through his information bureau at the Paris Peace Conference of 1919 and elsewhere. Father said that Gabrys had changed his name several times. His real name had been Paršaitis from the word *Paršas* (or piglet), which he was not at all proud of.

Another joke that appealed to Father's ever-ready sense of humor also concerned pigs. A signature in large letters of a soon-to-be famous person was done in whitewash on the wall of the pigsty. A budding poet named Vytautas Sirijos Gira wrote quantities of unsuccessful poetry. He once spent his summer vacation with us as a young student and wanted to be useful. Saying that manual work was good for his mind and body, he insisted on white-washing what he called "the palace of the pigs," leaving his large and flamboyant signature for posterity. This was considered sacrosanct and never to be removed. In those days, nobody talked about mental depression, and there is no way of knowing whether he was bothered by this condition. In case he was, he seems to have discovered a cure. I vaguely remember that Vytautas visited us once or twice and that he went to the "Pig Palace" to see if his signature was still there. This poet had a father who was unusual to say the least. Liudas Gira was a distinguished literary critic, a poet and a man of letters. He was known to be highly undependable and not to be trusted. He kept changing his mind and his political opinions according to the needs of the moment. Father called him a turncoat, and he was certainly no friend of ours. Sure enough, when Soviet rule came to Lithuania, L. Gira was one of the first to advocate collaboration with Moscow.

More than just a little eccentric was one of our rather frequent visitors, Prof. J. Balčikonis. He was a scholar in linguistics and a lexicographer who had spent years compiling a dictionary of the modern Lithuanian language. Only a few volumes came out in his lifetime, but the completed work published in the 1970s serves as a model for years to come. He lived in the suburb of Aleksotas and would always come to Turkey Lurk on foot because he said he liked the exercise. Being a bachelor, he had his nonconformist ideas and was very much of a health addict subsisting on home-grown vegetables, goats' milk and honey. In his garden he kept goats and had a number of bee hives. He was very knowledgeable about bees and would come to our home to take the honey out when the time came. Clouds of bees would swarm all over him without ever stinging him. He would talk to them to keep them calm. The Prof. knew many fascinating stories about their life and habits. He was just one of the friends from old days in Voronezh, Russia, who would come to see us. Many of them kept in touch. There were bonds of friendship very hard to break between people who had lived in this renowned Lithuanian refugee center in the years of the Russian Revolution.

Perhaps one of the most unusual people I ever came in contact with was the famous statesman A. Voldemaras. He was an associate of Father's in the early days of national independence. A man of small stature, he was of unprepossessing appearance but of brilliant intellect. He wore his hair clipped very short, standing straight up in "hedgehog style," as people called it. He was always attracted to women much taller than he was. Our Aunt Aldona, a chestnut-haired beauty close to six feet tall, had amusing stories to relate about Mr. V. In the early 1920s, he was one of her admirers, though she said she gave him no encouragement. He brought gifts of fine chocolates and bottles of his favorite liqueur to her home. He would talk, talk, talk, while sitting on the sofa, drinking most of the Benedictine himself, which Auntie said was reason enough for not liking him. Not knowing what else to do, Aunt Aldona used to entertain Mr. V by playing the piano. He made a good audience and seemed to know all about music. He was very adept with compliments and what she called sweet talk. Voldemaras was so well informed about many things that there was hardly a subject he could not talk about.

A. Voldemaras had advanced degrees in history and philosophy. He seemed to be all set for an academic career, but became President Smetona's first Prime Minister instead. He was also in charge of the country's foreign affairs. Representing Lithuania's cause in the League of Nations, he had a memorable confrontation with Poland's Marshal J. Pilsudski. Dressed in full military uniform, the angry Marshal rattled his sword on the floor in exasperation when Voldemaras got the better of the argument.

Mr. V plotted to overthrow the Smetona regime and developed a following among military officers. This would-be dictator, described in some European newspapers as a "little Mussolini" was sentenced to imprisonment and later sent to the provinces, being barred from setting foot in Kaunas. President Smetona considered him so dangerous that, in the late thirties, Voldemaras was exiled and forced to live abroad. Although I never met him personally I did ride the same train with him on one of his attempts to return to Lithuania. This was in the last days of August 1939, just before the start of World War II. Mr. Voldemaras happened to be in the same railway coach in another compartment just down the hall. I had a good look at him when the train stopped at the border.

Border police had come after him and were trying to carry him forcibly out of the train. All the while he kept shouting, "I protest! Let me go! I have the right to return to my country that is in danger!" The policemen told him that he was forbidden to return. His struggles were to no avail, and I saw him being hauled away by force, still protesting loudly. To add a postscript, Voldemaras did eventually return to Lithuania, but chose the wrong time to do so, when Soviet troops were already in occupation. He was captured and immediately deported to the Russian interior, where he died. Some people still cannot understand why a man of such intelligence chose to return, not realizing that he was "putting his neck into the hangman's noose." He wrote books and memoirs, but the most intriguing aspects of his life are not explained.

And now, to return to matters closer to Turkey Lurk, here are some totally different people who lived in our vicinity. Despite the generally accepted notion that Jewish people were not interested in farming as an occupation, two well-run farms near us had Jewish owners. Well known to us were the Šeinas (pronounced Shaynas) and the Frenkelis families. Šeinas had a brother who had a butcher shop in Old Town in Kaunas. The farmer was tall and the storekeeper short in stature, thus everybody called them Big and Little Šeinas. They hated each other with a passion (nobody knew why) and were not even on speaking terms.

We had good relations with both. Sometimes we went horseback riding with the son of Big Šeinas. It was always a pleasure to buy meat at Little Šeinas' store because he had such a welcoming attitude. There were times when Father, so widely known as a peacemaker, would be called upon by one or the other of them to take messages back and forth. They said, "Oh, Mr. Yčas, can you please tell my brother this or that. You know I cannot talk to him," and Father never refused to be the go-between. However, his efforts to make peace between the brothers were always a dismal failure.

The Frenkelis family, as stated earlier, was the owner of Turkey Lurk before the big estates were broken up by the land reform. All that remained to them was a farm called Freda, close to Kaunas, where we visited once in a while. The older brother, named Volka, became Father's partner in various business enterprises and lived in town. He was rotund in face and figure, had a great sense of humor and was a real character. He had played madcap tricks in his youth, like riding a horse up the stairs to the second floor of his high school building. Volka married into a wealthy family. His wife and daughter liked to dress in outlandish gypsy style in long beads, shawls and hoop earrings. The wife's brother liked to read and write philosophical works and saw no reason to go to work. Maybe the three of them could be called the "hippies" of their day.

The younger Frenkelis brother named Manka liked to stay home and run the farm. I can still visualize his tall, athletic figure in high boots with a riding crop in hand. Freda had been left in equal shares to the two Frenkelis brothers and their two sisters. They, too, lived in town but would come to the farm with their husbands for extended summer vacations. Manka said that they never contributed a thing but just came to enjoy the songs of the birds and the perfume of the flowers. One sister married a physician with a practice in Kaunas. The husband of the other, named Mizrochas (pronounced Mizrokas) said he did not need to have a job. He was a natural born "boulevardier" who lived on his income.

Mr. Mizrochas paraded on Main Street under the linden trees, always elegantly dressed, carrying a cane and tipping his hat to his acquaintances. He spent much time in cafes including the famous Konrad's Café, a great meeting place for all who mattered in society. Here he picked up the latest gossip and chitchat, priding himself on being well informed. Alas, the whole family was liquidated by successive Communist Russian and Nazi German occupations. However, Mr. Mizrochas managed to escape and joined relatives in Paris. He was seen walking on the Champs Elysees. Some said they saw him at the roulette tables in Monte Carlo. Later he was reported to have been seen, elegant as ever, on Fifth Avenue, New York,. Was it Mr. Mizrochas himself or only his specter, walking blithely along twirling his cane?

Father had many friends among Jewish people. One winter, he came down with a severe case of pneumonia. This could well have been fatal as fast remedies like sulfa drugs were yet to be discovered. The chief rabbi of the Kaunas community called to ask about Father's health, and I was the one who took the message on the phone. The rabbi said that prayers for Father's recovery were to be said in Jewish temples all over the city. Who is to say that prayers are not effective? Father did get his health back, although it took many weeks.

A person who could qualify as an original was a chance acquaintance on Main Street. This was a visitor from the USA named Akvilė (Aquilla), an unusual name to be remembered forever, meaning "eagle"in Latin. At this time, we had a number of what was called "Lithuanians from America," the accepted term for returning emigrants. Like many others, Akvilė spoke Lithuanian well. She expressed opinions I had not heard before. Here she was, complaining about the lack of public toilets in Kaunas. She said to me, "I have been going crazy looking for a toilet. Can you direct me?" True enough, public toilets were scarce. The only one I knew of was in the Theater Gardens, so I took her there.

"Don't tell me this is the only one in the whole city! ," said Akvilė, and she launched into an angry tirade about the lack of culture, or "culchah," in Lithuania. Her anger was no less, even when she discovered that the facilities were free. No payment was required to enter "the place where even kings must go on foot," according to the old saying. Her way of measuring a country's cultural level was new to me. Later I learned of the great importance Americans attach to plumbing facilities. On going abroad, they heap scorn on those countries where bathtubs and especially toilets do not come up to par, and never mind the rare cultural treasures they came to see.

Some of the visitors of Lithuanian heritage may have been critical of the lack of progress, but there were plenty of others more tolerant including members of my own family. They were not just tourists on a flying visit. They came to stay, bringing their expertise and their dollars with them. Grandpa Šliupas , his son the prof. and his daughter the physician, were among those who tried to help the Old Country get back on its feet. Grandpa invested his life savings into of commercial concerns, such as steamship and railroad companies, sawmills, financial associations, etc. Alas, they failed to show a profit. One enterprise financed by emigrants from the USA was a department store, then unique to Kaunas. It was popular at first because it carried goods hard to obtain elsewhere. However, the employees gave notoriously bad service. Mamma said, "Evidently they have never heard of the grand old American principle—the customer is always right!" After the early enthusiasm had worn off, we generally shopped at the "tried and true" Jewish stores so numerous in town. Here we found people who had a natural talent for making the shopper feel welcome and maintained a genuinely customer friendly atmosphere.

Having tasted the freedom and amenities available in America, few returning emigrants could settle down forever. Ships carried people to and fro across the "Big Pond" as some called the Atlantic ocean, while they made up their minds where they wanted to live. The government encouraged emigrants to return because they brought financial benefits and a lively cultural exchange. Business people with money to invest, as well as artists, writers and musicians came to try their luck in the Old Country. An association for strengthening relations with overseas Lithuanians was founded and enjoyed considerable success. A great congress of this association was held in Kaunas shortly before the outbreak of World War II.

Chapter Twenty-Five
Musical Notes

Mamma missed the country of her birth and the chance to hear American music, so very scarce in our town. She had a sweet small voice and liked to sing, accompanying herself on our Knabe piano. Old-fashioned melodies from the turn of the Century like "Love's Old Sweet Song," "Juanita" and Stephen Foster's "My Old Kentucky Home" were top favorites. Mamma could hardly sing the latter without tears coming into her eyes, and I learned to do the same. It must be one of the most touching songs ever written about the pain of losing one's home. Mamma's voice was not the greatest, and she knew it. One of her comic tales from the past was about the time when none other than the famed Mikas Petrauskas told her she could never be a real singer. This renowned music teacher put her through rigorous exercises. He had her repeat "LA-LA-LA-LA" at the top of her voice fifty dozen times. However, the Maestro's verdict remained negative, and Mamma's voice did not get a passing grade.

Mamma had no interest in Lithuanian songs. I never heard her sing any but those from a "Favorite Songs for School and Home" songbook, published in America. Years later, things changed. When she reached the USA, she developed a great nostalgia for the Old Country and preferred everything that was Lithuanian. Yet during her Lithuanian years, she longed for everything that reminded her of America.

Father could play the piano by ear and knew a few simple chords to accompany folk songs. Unlike Mamma, he did not read a note of music. Father appreciated music enough to serve as President of the Philharmonic Society, but that did not make him a musician. Incidentally, the years of his presidency (1932–1934) were a success, according to some critics, in bringing some great programs and artists from abroad to the Kaunas stage.

Ours was hardly a very musical family. None of us children were really talented. However, it was part of the custom of the times that we should take piano lessons, for which Martynas, Jr. and I went to the Kaunas suburb of Šančiai. Getting there was more fun than the actual lessons. We rode a tiny choo-choo train along the banks of the river Nemunas from the Aleksotas bridge, all the way to the railway bridge and beyond. This was called *Žaliasis Tiltas* (Green Bridge) because from time immemorial it had always been painted green. The narrow gauge train was a leftover from Russian Czarist days and was called by the old name of *Kukushka*. It went on its merry way, sounding a long drawn-out "toot toot" on its whistle and blowing clouds of steam.

There was plenty of music in my soul but I made little progress because my fingers were clumsy and my coordination was poor. I struggled with exercises by Czerny and daily practice was an unpleasant chore. My downfall was a piece called *Für Elise* by Beethoven, which I never mastered. I got so far and no further, and my parents were persuaded to stop my piano lessons altogether. To this day, it gives me the cold shivers to hear someone play this piece, which I remember as pure torture. It is hard to understand why young people then and now are forced to play it. However, music lessons with the accomplished Mrs. Čiurlys were really beneficial. From her I gained an appreciation for music, a lifetime interest that has never flagged. Eventually, I came to realize the value of music as a means of communication, a language understood by people in every part of the world whether they can talk to each other or not.

Other impressions remain from those music lessons. Our teacher's elder daughter Janina sometimes flitted in and out of the room, always in a hurry to go somewhere. Dressed in her brown and black high school uniform, she seemed like a superior being. I was a long way off from going to a regular school at the time. Janina talked about school doings and boyfriends, using big words that were hard to understand. A remarkable item in our piano teacher's house was the handwritten menu for daily meals hanging on the kitchen wall. You could learn what day of the week it was by seeing what the family was having for dinner. If it was Tuesday, it might be beef croquettes with mushroom sauce. It could be sausage and sauerkraut on Thursday and, of course, fish in some form on Friday. This kind of planning in advance was an orderly arrangement which did not exist in our household.

Mamma could get some of the ambiance of the America she missed by going to the movies. There were many movie theaters where she liked to go, though she was not really a movie fan. Most of our young people were affected by movie mania and followed film showings with avid interest. Perhaps more films from America were shown in our town than the ones which were made in Germany, France or elsewhere. During the time when we were growing up, Mamma enjoyed movies featuring Greta Garbo, Gary Cooper, Douglas Fairbanks and others. At the time, only quality films were being exported to foreign countries. The "Best of Hollywood" and none of the "B-Pictures" (or movies of inferior variety) were shown in Kaunas.

Although movies from the USA were everyday fare, American stage plays were hardly ever seen. Mamma was overjoyed to hear that real live American actors were coming to present a musical play based on *Uncle Tom's Cabin* by Harriet Beecher Stowe. Here was something that Mamma called a classic, which the entire family had to attend. At the box office, our parents were surprised to find that it was practically a sellout. An eager audience filled the summer theater on Main Street. How does one attract an audience to a production in another language on a subject as alien as slavery and issues of the American Civil War? Hardly anybody could have heard of the author, whose work had stirred up so much sympathy for the oppressed.

So why were people anxious to buy tickets? First of all, it was the novelty of the thing and second, it was advertised as having black performers. Who had ever seen a dark-skinned person in our town? This aroused much excitement. The black actors caused a sensation when they went for a walk under the linden trees on Main

Street. Crowds of curious onlookers followed them, especially the girls. I have no clear memories of the play, except the scene of Eliza's daring escape to freedom and the fierce dogs barking at her heels. Forever to be remembered is the haunting music of Stephen Foster's plantation songs, accompanied by the pleasant twang of a banjo, an instrument I had never heard before.

Most people were in agreement that the National Theater, particularly the opera, was one of our greatest cultural attractions. The Drama, Ballet and Opera theaters were housed in the same building, which had the only really large auditorium in town. It was the locale for other public gatherings like concerts and sometimes political meetings. The musical debut of Algis, a great friend of my brother's, took place there. I was among the friends assembled to cheer him on as he performed Beethoven's Emperor Concerto. Even today, whenever I hear this concerto, I can still feel the excitement of the occasion. It was a big thrill to have our friend play the piano to the accompaniment of a full orchestra.

The National Theater had no financial worries since it was supported by the Government. Performers and theatrical personnel were considered employees of the State. Opera singers, especially the star performers, could command high salaries. There was no need to charge exorbitant prices for tickets, which were only a little more expensive than those for movie theaters. Going to the Opera was a status symbol, but it was not a dress-up occasion for showing off evening gowns, furs and jewels, unless it was a special event like a premiere or a gala performance.

Waiting for the curtain to rise was an interval filled with delicious suspense. The curtain of burgundy red velvet was decorated with a huge branch of the *Rūta* (the Lithuanian national flower called Rue in English) embroidered in gold thread. The orchestra would start tuning up, and many were the jokes about people who knew so little about music that they thought that this was the start of the performance. Some might have had trouble understanding what was happening on the stage, but this was unlikely. Every opera was presented in Lithuanian translation, which made it all the more enjoyable. Translations of the librettos were made by several leading poets like F. Kirša and S. Santvaras who were well versed in many languages. Their words were so well chosen, and so eminently singable, that some arias achieved the status of popular songs sung in the streets. A saying of the day was, "Even my dog can howl the Drinking Song from *Rigoletto!*"

La Traviata was liked for its own sake as well as for sentimental reasons. It was performed when the curtain went up for the first time at the grand opening of the opera theater on New Year's Eve in 1920. At this time, some capable singers were still stranded by revolutionary conditions in Old Russia, but enough were on hand to make such a performance possible. The moving spirit was K. Petrauskas who sang the lead role and also acted as stage manager. Our parents were in the audience of almost one thousand people who crowded into the hall, glad to stand up if no seats were available. Mamma said that it was such a joyous occasion that many obvious flaws were overlooked. Costumes for the lead singers were inadequate and hastily assembled. There were no funds and no sewing materials to make proper costumes. Members of the choir appeared in ordinary street clothes. The scenery on stage was old and patched together. The orchestral music sounded rather thin because only two or three dozen musicians were playing. By the time I was old enough to go to the theater, such early difficulties were a distant memory. Costumes were splendid and so was the scenery, generally painted by leading artists.

The opera was our well-loved land of make believe. Our remote corner of northeastern Europe had a surprising taste for the exotic. Of some fifty operas in the repertoire, one of the most popular was Bizet's *Carmen*, a tale of sunny Spain. Also much appreciated were Rossini's *The Barber of Seville*, Verdi's *Aida* and Gounod's *Faust*. Even though things Russian were not too popular, Mussorgsky's *Boris Godunov*, Tchaikovsky's *Eugene Onegin* and his *Queen of Spades* were well liked. There were new composers attempting to present operas on patriotic Lithuanian themes. One I saw was about a woman warrior, heroine of medieval times. It was said that you had to be really patriotic to sit through the opera *Gražina*, and truly it was very long and very dull. This work by J. Karnavičius contained melodies of dozens of folk songs, seemingly unrelated to the text. There were plans for rewriting and shortening *Gražina*, but the author died before this could be accomplished.

The more heavy-handed German operas were not performed. Only two works by R. Wagner were really popular, *Tannhäuser* and *Lohengrin*. Who could forget the knight in shining armor stepping out of the swan boat, as portrayed by star singer Kipras Petrauskas? He knew he was irreplaceable and had supreme self-confidence. A handsome man over six feet tall, he was endowed with marvelous acting ability and had an expressive lyrical tenor voice. He was so highly esteemed that the Government presented him with an estate in the country at taxpayers' expense. When a cosmetics company started selling their product with Petrauskas' picture on the wrapper, advertised as the "favorite soap of the acclaimed star singer," his stature did not diminish. Such blatant commercialism was quite unknown in Lithuania, and many people thought it quite absurd. Petrauskas himself had no objections. His celebrity status was assured, and it would have been a wonder if it had not gone to his head.

In 1934, there was a gala performance when the famed Russian basso F. Chaliapin came for a visit. Petrauskas took pride in having started his career as a protegé of this singer in the old Czarist days at the Marinsky Theater in St. Petersburg. The two old friends were on the Kaunas stage together in the opera *Faust*. Petrauskas was in the title role, and Chaliapin gave a gripping performance as Mephisto. I was lucky enough to be present to witness the sheer joy of the singers and the enthusiasm of the audience. Petrauskas, like other colleagues, sometimes went on tour to opera houses of Europe and South America. While abroad, he began to call himself by his Russian title "Star of the Marinsky

Theater" and hardly mentioned the opera of Lithuania. O course, Lithuanians were deeply offended and started suspecting that their idol had feet of clay . Indeed, there were flaws in his character that surfaced years later. After the Soviet occupation, he chose to remain and to collaborate with the invaders. His golden voice was now failing, and his further performing efforts did not bring him success.

Another star singer whose schooling dated back to Czarist times was the statuesque dramatic soprano Mrs. Valerija Grigaitis. She was so tall, even in sandals, that it was rumored Petrauskas had to wear elevator shoes when singing with her in operas such as *Aida* or *Cavalleria Rusticana*. No less important was the mezzo soprano, Vincė Jonuškaitė, who headed a rising young generation of operatic singers. She was a country girl who began her musical studies in the city of Berlin, a student on a scholarship. She was always appreciative of the financial aid given her by Father and others who believed in her talent. One of our more thrilling experiences was when the whole family received invitations to attend the gala performance marking her 300th time on stage as Carmen, one of her most successful roles. By this time Vincė, a real go-getter, had engaged the affections of a wealthy and prominent man. She became the wife of D. Zaunius, Minister of Foreign Affairs. This, of course, did not hurt her operatic career. Besides being a great performer, she was certainly the most magnificently dressed person on stage. Unlike others who wore costumes supplied by the company, Vince was attired in her own gleaming silks, satins and lace.

Opera singers from the USA—many from the Chicago area, a great Lithuanian center—performed at the Kaunas National Opera. Among them were sopranos Marijona Rakauskaitė and Barbara Darlys. I happened to see both on stage in Puccini's *La Tosca* and Verdi's *Aida*, respectively. In the final scene of *Tosca*, Marijona caused a sensation because her long dress got caught on a nail. She was to leap to her death over the parapet of the castle where her

213

lover had died. She hung over the edge motionless, and finally the curtain came down without the problem having been resolved. We never got to know the standoffish "Miss Rack," as some called her, but Barbara Darlys became a close friend. She was fond of Mamma's exotic vegetables. Many times we drove to Kaunas with baskets of root celery, asparagus and American style corn for Barbara to share with friends who were homesick for such delicacies.

There were loyal fans who came to see their favorite operas performed over and over again. None was more faithful in attendance than Mrs. A. Kutkus, a friend of our mother's. She was a wispy blonde in nondescript clothing who wore hick glasses. The poor lady was gradually losing her eyesight, and nothing could be done for her since surgery for cataracts and the like was not yet known. Mrs. Kutkus resembled a nervous and somewhat bewildered hen. Her husband Alexander was a second-string tenor at the opera. She adored him and tried to attend all of his performances. She thought he was the greatest singer that ever lived and that he should have the leading role every time. Sometimes, Kutkus got such roles in the absence of better singers. Mrs. Kutkus was an intelligent woman of refined tastes and she also possessed a university degree in law. She was very much in love with her husband, despite the fact that he was carrying on a longtime romance with a much more flashy lady. His paramour was an opera singer and, like him, was not of the first rank. One can imagine Mrs. Kutkus being moved to tears while watching the dimly seen shadow of her husband behind the footlights. Did she know about his faithlessness? As the saying goes, the wronged wife is often the last one to find out.

Perhaps Mrs. Kutkus and Mamma became friends because she needed a shoulder to cry on. In any case, the friendship started with a Maltese cat that Mamma gave her as a gift. Maltese cats with short-haired coats of bluish grey were very popular then. The cat became the joy of Mrs. Kutkus' lonely life and was followed by another gift. This was my favorite pet, a miniature Pinscher. I came home from school one day, and Pongo was not there, bounding down the stairs to meet me. Mamma, without asking me, had given Pongo away telling me that Mrs. Kutkus' need was greater than mine. This explanation did not prevent me from shedding torrents of tears and caused me great pain.

Through Mrs. Kutkus, I was taught a great lesson about unselfishness in sharing with others less fortunate. Of course, she could not know about her influence or that she had also shattered some of the illusions of my adolescence. Up until then, I had firmly believed that the bonds of love and marriage went on forever. The prince married the princess and they lived happily ever after. How could another woman steal somebody's husband? Such things occurred in the movies, in books or on the stage, but somehow they had a fairytale quality. Having them happen to someone we knew was a shock. This classic case of the wronged wife brought me face to face with some harsh realities of the world.

Chapter Twenty-Six
Storm Clouds Gather

In the late Thirties, life went on just the same. Nobody realized that this could be the calm before the storm. At Turkey Lurk there were signs and portents of coming events, if only we could have understood them. Some people said it was a bad omen when the oak tree in the orchard was struck by a bolt of lightning. During electric storms the rumble of thunder would frighten many people including Petrusia, who might even hide in the closet. She half-believed the tales that this was Perkūnas, ruler of the gods, riding the skies in his chariot. Despite the wide use of lightning rods, homesteads in the countryside around us were sometimes set on fire. When this happened people would say, "Perkūnas is angry," that is, he was using thunderbolts to show his power.

Besides beliefs connected with the thunder god, oak trees were the object of special veneration. This was partly the heritage of old pagan days when the forces of nature were worshiped in sacred oak groves. It seemed a miracle when the oak tree in the orchard managed to withstand the bolt of lightning. It could have continued to live on for years to come. However, visitors to our old home in 1992 reported that there was no oak tree and no orchard, only a multitude of dwelling houses where trees had once stood. Right then, I realized that I never wanted to see the old home place again. Instead of this senseless destruction, the new masters of Turkey Lurk could have made a splendid park for everyone to enjoy. I do not know exactly when Kaunas started expanding into our property or when the oak tree perished. I could only sigh, alas for the oak tree, the storks' nest, the lilacs and the lindens!

After that splendid oak was wounded by a bolt of lightening, the second and larger oak tree on our southern borders also fell. This giant was so ancient that it started to rot inside, forming a cave big enough to shelter a human being. Some vagrant made his home there and started to build fires to do his cooking. One day, the entire cave caught fire and spread into the branches. A black column of smoke arose and was seen for days. There was no way to put out the blaze. The smoke could be seen for miles as this "King of the Forest" burned down, an event deplored by the whole neighborhood.

A third omen for those of poetic imagination could have been the sullying of the crystal clear water in the round pond near this same oak. People had come here from miles around to get pure drinking water, supplied by an underground spring. Now it was opaque and colored pink like clay. It was clear no more and could never be restored to its pristine state. There were traces of horses' hooves and wagon wheels in the mud. Some unknown scoundrel must have driven into the pond with his wagon for reasons unexplained. Could the defilement of these sparkling waters have a meaning for the future?

In a few short years there would be great world happenings that would shake our lives to their very foundations. But meanwhile, it was "business as usual." Perhaps some political leaders were concerned but the general public did not worry, leaving such things to those who were in charge. There were disturbing events in foreign countries, but at first they seemed too remote to cause concern. Then came the Italian attack on Albania and Ethiopia. We sympathized from afar with what we called the poor benighted people. How could they resist the onslaught of Benito Mussolini's modern war machine? I was not too interested in international affairs, but there was so much "political palaver" in our household that I could not help being affected. Father, Martynas, Jr., and their friends listened to the daily international news on the radio and avidly read the newspapers. Father preferred discussing world news rather than local events, perhaps because he found current trends of the Smetona regime rather disturbing. In the beginning, everyone had worked together in a friendly manner without regard for party affiliation. And now, people who did not belong to the dominant or Nationalist Party were being brushed aside. Furthermore, as an experienced parliamentarian, Father could not see how a country could be run without a *Seimas* (Parliament) as had been the case for over a decade. No parliamentary elections were held until 1938.

There was talk of imposing sanctions on Italy by the League of Nations. Lithuania, a loyal member, was also involved. The joke went around that our refusal to export any more potatoes to them was hardly the way to stop further Italian aggression. At first, Mussolini and Hitler were dismissed as a couple of clowns or paper tigers using scare tactics. Hitler was then making a determined rise to power in Germany. Once we actually saw him in person when Father took the entire family on a trip to Koenigsberg, East Prussia. After dining at our favorite restaurant, we unwittingly ran into a Nazi military parade. There was Adolf Hitler, a most unimpressive-looking little man riding in a tank. An obviously mesmerized crowd was shouting *Sieg Heil* (Hail to Victory) and *Heil Hitler* (Hail to Hitler) amid the blare of band music and a great waving of swastika-decorated flags.

We liked going to Koenigsberg, former seat of the Prussian kings, partly because of its aura of history. There were quaint medieval buildings around the river and ships going out to sea. The ancient university held interest as so many of our compatriots, including several Protestant ministers, had studied there in times past. East Prussia was a land once inhabited by the old Prussians, who were relatives of the Lithuanians. These had been practically wiped out by the Teutonic Knights of the Cross. In later ages, masses of German-speaking settlers had been imported. Only the geographical names remained as a reminder, like *Eitkūnai* (called *Eitkuhnen* by the Germans), *Trakėnai* (which became *Trakehnen*), *Isrutė* (which became *Insterburg*) and even *Karaliaučius* (meaning city of kings, was Germanized into *Koenigsberg*). For us, the *Blutgericht* restaurant deep down in the dungeons of the Castle of the Teutonic Knights was better than all such historical associations. Here you could get a local specialty: tasty dumplings called *Koenigsberger Klops* and delectable frankfurters (who but the

219

Germans could make them taste so delicious?). The meal would be accompanied by pickled herring, sauerkraut and potato salad with tankards of beer if one so desired.

We were to hear a great deal more about that unimpressive little man in the tank. When making speeches on the radio, Adolf Hitler seemed to have become a raving madman, shouting threats filled with hatred. Sometimes he spoke so fast and furiously that he tripped over his words, making some of his listeners laugh. Even people who knew German well had trouble understanding his rantings and ravings. His speeches were mostly about alleged mistreatment of Germans in other countries, and it was not long before Lithuania also became a target.

A sizeable German minority lived in Klaipėda (Memel), and trouble could be expected from that quarter. The situation had aroused the wrath of Hitler some years before. A Nazi-instigated plot for a German *Anchluss* (takeover) was uncovered. The culprits were brought to trial by Lithuanian courts of law and found guilty of treason. Hitler got into a towering rage and declared an embargo on Lithuanian exports to Germany, at that time a large item in our trade. However, this was a blow from which we could recover. New outlets were soon found in England, which was glad to import our high grade butter, bacon and other foodstuffs. British tastes, however, did not run to the geese so much enjoyed by the Germans. For a while there was a great surfeit of geese in our markets, giving rise to what outside observers called "the Lithuanian Goose Story." The solution devised by the Government was to compel every public employee to purchase a certain number of geese, whether they liked goose meat or not. Father's cousin, John Yčas the engineer, a bachelor with a good job at the Post Office, complained that he was forced to buy five or six geese. "What shall I do with them?" he asked. The only thing possible was to give them away, but nobody he knew would take them.

At about this time, our guests at Turkey Lurk were enjoying a real delicacy, but it was not goose. It was home-smoked duck sausage, an experiment dreamed up by Mamma. True, the Government had encouraged everyone to raise geese for export, but Mamma simply preferred ducks. She raised such multitudes that the only solution was to make them into sausage. One visitor, loud in his praises, was our guest several times that year, hoping to take duck sausage home with him. This was an affable Roman Catholic priest named V. Mironas, well on his way to becoming Prime Minister.

Meanwhile, there was disquieting news from abroad. After Hitler's outcries about mistreated German minorities, the next step was to grab the territories in which they lived, notably Austria and Czechoslovakia. National boundaries started to collapse, and nobody could feel safe any more. Everywhere the Nazis went, they liquidated their opposition with the utmost cruelty and brutality. Hitler's misdeeds are only too well known and do not need repetition here. But what was happening in the Soviet Union should not be forgotten. Outrageous crimes against humanity were being perpetrated by dictator Stalin and his Communist cohorts. Germany's nefarious record, even taking into account the Jewish Holocaust of the 1940s, was equaled, if not surpassed, by Russia. Stalin left a bloody trail of victims behind him. The exact number of his victims can never be known because there was no one there to count them or to compile statistics. The facts show that the figure could well reach many millions. There was a cartoon we saw in those days, as apt today as it ever was. It showed Stalin trampling on a mountain of corpses and was captioned, "Twenty years of murder, brutality and savagery." This was no surprise for those who, like us, lived right next door to the USSR. Our general feeling about the Bolshevik horrors has already been told.

The mid-thirties was the era of the Great Purges staged by Stalin to get rid of his enemies. The innocent perished with the guilty. The purges began to have meaning for me when I heard that someone I had known and liked was a victim. This man was in the diplomatic service of the USSR. His title was chargé d'affaires at the

Soviet Embassy. He was dark-haired, wore rimless glasses and had a German-sounding name. Strangely enough, our Kaunas house at Laisvės Alėja No. 4 had been the Soviet Embassy for quite some time. I had occasion to visit my childhood home when I accompanied my parents there for a dinner invitation. It seemed much smaller than the house I remembered, and the garden had none of the trees and flowers of previous days. The house looked very different because the Russians had the walls of the reception rooms painted a Revolutionary Red, like their flag, but the fat white columns supporting the ceiling were still white.

Our host, Mr. Fekhner, was nothing like the fearsome Bolshevik type I had imagined. He was a gentle and very cultured person. Maybe the fact that he was a "gentleman of the old school" and a popular member of the Kaunas diplomatic circle was against him. He was soon recalled to Russia and was said to have been "liquidated" there. In view of the many similarities between the Russian Communist and the German National Socialist (or Nazi) regimes, a joke then current had a real point. The right answer to the question about the difference between them was "It's colder in Russia."

This sketch of world events may give an idea of the concerns and attitudes in Lithuania in those few years of freedom that remained. For us, the high school graduates of the late 1930s, what was happening abroad was not of much concern. These events were rather like a backdrop to the play that was unfolding before us. There were only a few more acts to go, as it were, before the performance ended and Fate would ring down the curtain.

After receiving our *gimnazija* diplomas, my classmates and I were considered young ladies. We were overjoyed to appear at public gatherings, theaters, lectures and so on, without those everlasting black and brown school uniforms. We were well on our way to being grown up. Our parents and/or chaperones no longer supervised our parties (formerly they would look in to make sure all was in order). Even though we thought of ourselves as young ladies, we continued to go to some of our favorite high school hangouts.

The Italian Ice Cream Parlor at the end of *Laisvės Alėja* made an excellent meeting place and certainly served the best such refreshments in town. Known as *Itališki Ledai* (Italian Ices), it was said to have been founded by a real Italian from Italy. Still remembered with pleasure is the *Pieno Centras* (Milk Center) vegetarian restaurant with dairy products that tasted far better than those you could get at home. This was run by a major company of great importance to Lithuania's export trade. Where else could you get such delicious clabbered milk with boiled potatoes or golden brown potato pancakes, all topped with mounds of sour cream? Or *pieno šampanas* (milk champagne), a mildly sweet and sparkling yellow beverage, so refreshing on a hot day?

Places that had been forbidden territory—like *Konrado Kavinė* (Conrad's Café), a gathering place for VIPs, posh restaurants, and occasional night clubs—were now open to us. However, only the most sophisticated of my classmates ever went there. The most popular boys were, of course, the ones who had a car (very few and far between). There were some young professionals, mainly engineers as I recall, who were very eligible bachelors to take us around. Much in demand was a rather unexciting young man who drove a shiny new Packard, loaded with as many girls as possible. Incidentally, my brother always got a warm welcome when he appeared in our green Chevrolet.

Turkey Lurk became the scene of what we thought of as wild parties which, of course, were pretty mild by the standards of today. One of my classmates named Yadwiga, a prime mover in the cause of freedom for young people, told me later, "I shall remember one such party to my dying day." This old school friend is among the dozen or so from our graduating class now living in the USA or elsewhere in the Western World. Some of them are still among my dearest friends and share with me a great love for our old school days. Yadwiga was romancing her admirer of the moment behind the rosebushes (very innocuously to be sure) at an all-day get together one summer's eve. Anne Crawford, peering through the curtains at an upstairs window "accidentally on purpose" saw it all. She ran to tell Mamma "Mrs. Yčas, evil things are happening in the garden," and she was not entirely joking.

Many youngsters then growing up had to leave Lithuania forever without enjoying any of the pleasures of social life. I consider myself lucky to have received my high school diploma before the fateful year of 1940. I was old enough to have danced at balls and to have been invited to a few parties by people who really mattered in our society. For some time we had been decked out by our mothers in party dresses and long evening gowns, so we could make a proper appearance. Sometimes they were made at the atelier of the famous Trejienė, the leading dressmaker in town.

My first long dress was made of daffodil yellow tulle. Not having the figure for it, I was never much interested in clothes. It is no wonder that I was no match for my tall and willowy classmates in their lovely gowns. Three of them literally stole the show. Irene was dressed in wine red taffeta with many ruffles. Sally was in navy blue satin, trimmed with clusters of pink apple blossoms. Rita was in a gown of pleated white chiffon in classical Greek style. A custom one could call quaint was having a bevy of girls escorted to the ball by some willing mother acting as chaperon. It was not very proper to have a gentleman escort you to the dance, but it was quite all right for him to see you home.

Our parties were mostly in private homes where we danced until the wee hours of the morning. Sometimes we went to fancier places. One evening George Zabielskis, a young man about town who got invited everywhere because he was such a great dancer, gave a large group of us a grand entertainment at the *Versalis*, one of the really elegant places in town. There was dinner and dancing, and I thought it most outstanding. However, when reminiscing later with my friend Rita, far more sophisticated than I, she said she had not been impressed because she had been wined and dined there several times before. In all these activities, I was at a disadvantage because I lived in the country. It was not always convenient to ask a friend in town to put me up for the night in case of a really late party.

Chapter Twenty-Seven
Nothing Lasts Forever

Practically every one of the girls in our class, including me, went on to university studies. Among my classmates, the most popular areas of study were medicine, dentistry, Liberal Arts and the teaching profession. As for me, my dearest dream at age 18 was to be a judge. In our conservative society, there was no "ultra feminism" or "war between the sexes." It was understood that the man was the head of the family. No one felt the need for emphasizing women's rights. Women were free to take jobs or to enter the professions and were not excluded from political life. There were women lawyers, doctors and dentists. Our family dentist was a lady, and so was our ophthalmologist. In 1920, a woman, the talented writer G. Petkevičaitė became a member of the Constituent Assembly and was elected to preside at its very first meeting. This was the body that laid the legal foundations for the fledgling Republic of Lithuania.

After we graduated from high school, we had the freedom of being university students. The Latin words of the medieval academic anthem that we sang *Gaudeamus igitur, iuvenes dum sumus* (let us rejoice while we are young) had real meaning for us then. There were none of the stringent *gimnazija* requirements. You could go to lectures or not, just as you wished, and even take examinations at your own pace; in other words, you were treated as an adult.

Rita and I enrolled at law school together. Time did not permit me to complete the requirements, but Rita, who left Lithuania later than I did, obtained her degree. Some subjects of study were rather dry, like the subdivisions of Civil, Criminal, Commercial Law, etc. Very enjoyable were courses in legal philosophy, logic and many aspects of Lithuanian law (an unbelievably complicated subject due to the heritage left by foreign occupants over the centuries). Our special joy was a two-year course in Roman law. This was the legal basis for areas where the Napoleonic Code was in force. When

I met Rita in the USA years later, we revived long forgotten memories of our student days. We had been close pals in preparing for examinations together. Rita showed me snapshots preserved in her album. "Who are these two young girls," I asked, "sitting under a willow tree surrounded by piles of books?" "Why, that is you and I, by your house in Turkey Lurk," she replied. "We were cramming for the test in Roman law." Quite enamored of the civilization of ancient Rome, we are wearing wreaths of white roses, which we must have thought appropriate.

We were enchanted with our professor, truly a great instructor. In fact, many of our professors could have made a good showing at any university abroad, as we who have studied in other lands can attest.

Prof. A. Tamošaitis, knowledgeable in International Law and educated in France, wrote original works like *Ancient Roman Family Relationships* and translated the monumental works of his teacher, Prof. P. Girard. Prof. V. Jurgutis wrote authoritative works on financial theory and was also a wizard at practical aspects. He organized the Bank of Lithuania and originated the *Litas*, the country's first stable currency. His lively lectures attracted such crowds that sometimes there was standing room only. Prof. V. Stanka, a scholar in legal philosophy, was one of the few whose books appeared in English translation. He gained a reputation in the USA with his own philosophy, published as *Ethical Humanism,* centered around individual joy and harmony with nature. It was full of ideas from the Orient, especially those of Asoka, Buddhist King of ancient India.

A whole new world opened up to us when we became university students. We really enjoyed ourselves as never before both on and off the dance floor. Father was in great demand, just as he had been in my early years, to direct the ever-popular "waltz with figures." This was somewhat like the country dancing in the USA today. Some of the balls took place in the Neo-Lithuania Student Building up the hill near *A žuolynas* (Oak Park). Others were at the very posh *Karininkų Ramovė* (Officers Club), a general favorite because it had one of the best parquet floors anywhere. Another great place was the Military Academy ballroom. My brother Martynas, Jr. had many friends among the cadets. It was a pleasure to bask in the attentions of the future officers dressed in their elegant white-belted uniforms.

Very early in my dancing days, I had to discard the shiny pumps of gold leather that were especially purchased to go with my gauzy evening dress. I had been assured that the shoes "came straight from Paris," but they were much too tight right from the start. Only vanity could have made me wear them to my very first ball. The joy of the occasion, mingled with the excruciating pain in my feet and the terrible blisters, is something that will always stay in my mind. Besides dancing, there were other things to do. By this time, I had learned to be a fairly good typist and could be of help to Father in his writings. He encouraged me to write articles and several were published in *Lietuvos Aidas* (Lithuanian Echo), the main newspaper of Kaunas. Not everybody knew how to use a typewriter, and it was considered quite an accomplishment. Father always wrote in longhand. I really appreciated the opportunity of typing some of his memoirs and learned much in the process.

In the meantime, Germany's aggressive acts in Europe had made the ultimatum an effective way for Lithuania's neighbors to get what they wanted. Emboldened by the generally lawless atmosphere, Poland chose to present an ultimatum to Lithuania in March 1938, threatening military retaliation if it did not open up its borders. The Poles, who had no intention of giving up Vilnius, felt that Lithuania's unforgiving attitude deprived them of certain economic advantages, like access to the Baltic Sea via the River Nemunas and the port of Klaipėda. The crude and cold-blooded way Poland tried to push us around caused great indignation. Our Government gave in to the demands and there were public demonstrations. We students were all fired up to join the demonstrators in front of the National Independence Monument in

Kaunas.   Lithuanian university students, like those in other European countries, took great interest in political happenings. We thought of ourselves as responsible citizens capable of telling the Government what to do. There were angry speeches, shouting and singing of patriotic songs. Finally, the police came to disperse us with tear gas, which we thought was very unfair. After a lapse of nearly 20 years, a Polish flag with the emblem of the White Eagle was raised over the newly opened Embassy building.

People made fun of the emblem and asked each other, "Have you seen the White Chicken yet?" The popularity of the Poles sank to a new low. Many people were happier than ever that Lithuania had chosen to be a separate country and had resisted Polish blandishments to revive the joint Polish-Lithuanian State of former days. After World War I, many Poles thought this was desirable and were even ready to take up arms to enforce their plan. Oddly enough, some of the newly arrived Polish diplomats and their entourage could not understand why their flag was not greeted with joy and why they were not welcomed into society. They were actually offended that few of our people wanted to associate with them.

Another event later in the year was the national elections, the first in many years. President Smetona had been in office for a long time. I was under the required voting age of 21 and did not participate, but I have vivid impressions. People all around me might have liked a change, but many said they could not think of a better candidate for President. As expected, the incumbent was elected by a landslide. The remarks made by a simple laborer at Turkey Lurk are worth remembering. This unlettered cowherd stopped me in the farmyard one day to ask how the elections were coming along. "You have been to school and may know something I don't," he said. "Who is likely to make a good President?" I had to reply that I had not heard any other name but Antanas Smetona. The cowherd said, "Now isn't that strange? So many thousands to choose from, and they can't think of anyone else." He thought for a moment and added, "If anyone asks me to vote, I am sure that my opinion won't make a bit of difference."

During this same year of 1938, I had some trips abroad, my chance to get acquainted with the outside world. The usual way to reach Western Europe was by taking the overnight train to Berlin, Germany. I shall always remember this city as my enchanted gateway to foreign lands. At times, I was my Father's chosen companion when he attended international conferences representing our Reformed Church. Since that first meeting of the Presbyterian alliance in Pittsburgh, Pennsylvania, in 1921, he had been going to such gatherings, especially those of the World Alliance for Friendship Through the Churches. In 1938, he took me to a meeting in Larvik, Norway, a place of which no one had ever heard. We got tired of being asked if we were going to N a r v i k in the Arctic Circle. Visiting all three of the Scandinavian capitals, especially Oslo with its Ship Museum, was a delight. The best thing about Larvik was meeting Barbara von Richthofen who became a lifelong friend.

Hitler was still on a rampage in 1939. German armed forces arrived in Klaipèda (Memel) in March. Germany's ultimatum carried a veiled threat that their troops might not stop at the Lithuanian border if we did not comply. According to people who saw the German takeover, war planes were buzzing in the air as ships steamed into the harbor. Soldiers, sailors and brown-shirted Nazis paraded in the streets. Swastika-decorated flags were everywhere and there was a carefully orchestrated welcome from local inhabitants. The statue of the German Kaiser Wilhelm, removed by the Lithuanians, was again put in place in the city square. Hitler arrived triumphantly in an open automobile and made the usual fiery speech about bringing happiness to the liberated German population.

The loss of Klaipèda was a great blow at the national as well as the personal level. For the Easter holidays that year, some of my brother's friends from the Klaipèda Region came to stay with us.

231

They were cadets at the Military Academy, cut off from their homes and families. Now they literally had no place to go. This resulted in some fast friendships with several members of the Gailius and Brakas clans. They enjoyed home-cooked meals, always asking for omelets made with unlimited numbers of eggs available from Mammas's chicken farm. It was quite an occasion for excursions on horseback, games and sports. The boys would put up targets on the wall of the old gray barn and use them for pistol shooting practice. I was deathly afraid of all firearms, but they urged me to try. However, when I tried to shoot, they laughed at me. The boys said, "Far from hitting the target, you could not even hit the barn!"

Speaking of sports, one of the great diversions of 1939 was the basketball games that brought teams from many countries to Kaunas. Lithuania was trying to keep her European championship title obtained the previous year. It was won again this time after a hard struggle. Everyone in our circle, sports minded or not, tried to attend this event. I can still remember the shouts of joy and the boos during the match between the Latvians, the chief contenders, and the Poles, an exciting game as neither team was too popular. For us, the stars of the show were our high school friend, A. Visockis, who made such an excellent radio commentator, and the three Andriulis brothers, all brilliant basketball stars.

In August 1939, I was allowed to travel all by myself to the World Conference of Christian Youth in Amsterdam, Holland. After envisioning an ideal future of universal peace and love, it was disillusioning to "come back to earth." Weapons were already being brandished, and there was talk of war. Despite gathering storm clouds, I lingered at Barbara von Richthofen's baronial estate near Liegnitz in Silesia. Barbara said, "I don't want to be inhospitable, but don't you think you should be going home?" True enough, uniformed troops were filling the trains and military planes were droning overhead. Without knowing it, I was a witness to history in the making. World War II was about to begin. Somehow there was room for me on the train to Berlin. Soldiers in battle dress crammed the aisles of the train to East Prussia and Koenigsberg. The train proved to be the next to the very last one permitted to cross the so-called Polish Corridor. I felt lucky to have reached home safely.

On the way back I witnessed another kind of historical event. There was a long stop at Virbalis on the border. A. Voldemaras, the erstwhile Prime Minister of Lithuania, was on that train. He had been exiled abroad by the Smetona Government. On my return to Kaunas in those last days of August, I was greeted at the station by the whole family wondering why the train was so late. This of course was because of the Voldemaras incident. Everyone was interested to hear about the brave fight he had put up in his struggle with the police.

As the Thirties were ending, some people had a feeling of foreboding. Superstitious old folks said that some misfortune was bound to come. They said that skies "red like flame" would tell the world that war was coming, just like a similar phenomenon had heralded the Great War of 1914. In the summer of 1939, on a buggy ride homeward from Kaunas, some of us noticed that the Northern sky was an unnaturally bright red. As we watched, scarlet tongues of flame-like lights moved ever so slowly upwards from the horizon. Someone suggested that this could be the Northern Lights (Aurora Borealis) seldom seen in Lithuania and usually white in color. Whatever it was, it definitely was a most unusual display.

When World War II erupted on September 1, the Lithuanian government declared neutrality. Lithuanian leaders hoped to steer clear of the conflict between the Big Powers, but this was not to be. Two partners in crime—Hitler's Nazi Germany and Stalin's Soviet Russia—were already sharpening their knives to carve up Lithuania and its Baltic neighbors Latvia and Estonia. Their plans were a closely guarded secret for a very long time, but there were rumors going around even then about the Ribbentrop-Molotov Agreements. The actual documents whereby Germany and the USSR eliminated the Baltic countries by a stroke of the pen were signed in August.

233

They were not found until years after the Second World War had ended.

Our country home had visitors the like of which it had not seen before. As German armies smashed into Poland, the Russians attacked from behind and the whole land was squeezed as in a vise. Polish military people and civilians fled in all directions and several thousand found a safe (however temporary) haven in our country. Among them was a group of military men at Turkey Lurk. They found a warm welcome in our house, or in the great barn where the overflow slept on the straw. The officers slept in our house. Arriving with the refugees was a stray black and white dog, an obvious aristocrat, maybe an English setter. He seemed to belong to no one and had the saddest eyes ever seen. We took care to feed him well but, when night fell, he would disappear. Evidently he was searching for his master, probably lost somewhere with the Polish Army. One evening the dog went off and never came back.

To our surprise, among the refugees was a relative in cavalry officer's uniform, a cousin of our grandmother's. He spoke Lithuanian quite well like other members of his family whom we met in Vilnius later on. Jasius Dovoina had trouble removing his long riding boots. He explained that his orderly who had always taken care of him was no longer there to do the job. Jasius had a good sense of humor and was very good natured. He smiled so charmingly that we girls could not refuse to help him with his boots when asked. He was a welcome guest and told us comic stories about our relatives living across the border which included some strange sounding characters.

Meeting these Polish refugees was a good lesson for us all. As Father so wisely told us at the time, refugees should be treated with compassion because one never knew when we ourselves could be in their shoes. It certainly came true for us when, barely one year later, the time came to flee our home. After we lost our home and country we, in turn, were fortunate to be given a helping hand wherever we went.

Chapter Twenty-Eight
Vilnius is Ours!

Of all the exciting events in 1939, none was more stirring than the return of Vilnius in late October. The ancient capital had been under Polish occupation, and now it was in Lithuanian hands again. No force of arms was required because the Soviet Union handed the Vilnius Region to Lithuania, so to speak on a "silver platter," but there was a price tag attached. The USSR had seized the area from the Poles and wished to station military bases there. Lithuania, now somewhat experienced with ultimatums, was presented with yet another. This was the first time something was offered in return for Lithuanian concessions, even though it was really "Stolen Property."

As one may imagine, this caused serious misgivings. Again there were public demonstrations against our government's decision to accept the demands for military bases. I felt I was getting to be an old hand at the game of political activism when I joined a student group of demonstrators. This was at the same place as before, by the National Independence Monument. A prestigious military leader named General V. Nagevičius, of unusually great stature both physically (well over six feet in height) and figuratively, made a speech to pacify the crowd. His conciliatory words, "Our giant neighbor to the East means well and can bring only good to our people," convinced none of us. Again the police descended on us with their tear gas which caused our eyes to burn. However, we felt this was a small price to pay for doing our patriotic duty.

At this time, there was another international event causing us concern, since it was happening not far from our borders. Finland was brutally attacked by the Soviet Union in a conflict widely known as the "Winter War." Some of our young men spoke of joining the Finnish Army as volunteers, but the war ended while they were still talking about it. It lasted only a few months, and the province of Karelia was wrested from Finland. For this dastardly deed, the Soviet Union was ousted from the League of Nations,

235

which we agreed was a very good thing. There was great public sympathy for heroic little Finland defending itself against an enemy many times larger and stronger.

Introduction of Soviet military bases turned out to be a Trojan Horse in which more armed men were hiding. It was only a matter of time until the Soviets demanded total occupation of the entire country. There was a satirical couplet going around, "*Vilnius mūsų, o mes—rusų*" (Vilnius is ours, but we belong to Russia). In the meantime, however, people could not help rejoicing. Government dignitaries arrived from Kaunas to watch Lithuanian troops make a triumphal entry into the city. If there was talk of transferring the Capital from Kaunas to Vilnius, there was no time to put such plans into action. Again, like so many times throughout its history, Vilnius had been the scene of battle. A feeling of great sadness pervaded the city. Some of the buildings were in shambles, and there were numbers of refugees and homeless people. There were many more Poles here than ever before, since many had come from Poland itself to escape the ravages of war.

Vilnius had always been at the crossroads of many cultures and nationalities. There were halfhearted attempts by those in charge to make everybody in Vilnius speak the Lithuanian language, but this was not realistic. Much more important was provision of food for the starving population. When I got to Vilnius later that fall, the local Lithuanian Evangelical Reformed Church and its leader, the Rev. K. Kurnatauskas, were deeply involved in providing food and shelter for the homeless. This old friend from Biržai days took our family to see the kitchen operated by the Church and taste some of the soup dished up from a big pot. From a distance we saw railroad cars standing at the station, loaded with the food supplies, arriving almost daily from Kaunas. On looking back, it seems the Soviets were doing themselves a real favor by getting Lithuania to cope with the many problems in administering Vilnius.

Part of the University of Vytautas the Great, where many of us were students, was transferred from Kaunas to Vilnius, including

236

the School of Law. As we wandered around the tree-shaded courtyards, the colonnades and the arched hallways of Vilnius University, we felt there was no comparison with the starkly utilitarian University buildings in Kaunas. Some of them had been hastily constructed and were quite devoid of charm. Here was a great university that had started its career in the 16th century as a Jesuit Academy in what later became the heart of Old Town. The square in front of the Baroque style church of St. John had been the scene of public meetings and outdoor theological debates in the days of the Reformation. According to legend, a bonfire had consumed Protestant books in this very place in an *"auto da fe"* incited by the Jesuits. Some famous scholars and literary lights had studied at the University including the first researchers of Lithuanian history and poets like Adomas Mickevičius (Adam Mickiewicz).

It was interesting to visit the antique shops of Vilnius, filled with curiosities, works of art, books and paintings. Many people in need of money were selling their treasures right out in the street. In fact, the city itself resembled an antique—everything was rather neglected and run down. The Polish rulers who said that Vilnius was so important to them had done little for the city in the way of improvement. It was now a provincial borderland. In former times, it had been the capital of the Lithuanian Grand Dukes when their territories reached far out into Slavic territories in the East. There were plenty of reminders of its glorious past. For us to see our tricolor flag flying from the Castle of the 13th Century Grand Duke Gediminas high on the hilltop was a great thrill. The house where our Declaration of National Independence had been signed in 1918, not to mention other buildings with historical associations, was an inspiring sight. In a sense, we felt that we were coming home to a place we had always known and loved.

Though I had never been here before, Vilnius seemed strangely familiar. I took the train from the Kaunas railroad station and arrived at a station very like the one I had just left. Indeed, there were many buildings here in very similar architectural style.

237

Like Kaunas, Vilnius was set on the banks of a river called the Vilija (or Neris) not very different from the Nemunas, flowing by hills and dales lined with evergreen woods. There were familiar looking steamboats, all paddle-wheelers, which could take you on a day's excursion. One day, a group of us students went by steamboat to Verkiai, once an archbishop's palace, full of art treasures of bygone days. Kaunas had nothing to compare with this profusion of palaces, churches and ancient buildings filled with works of art. We could see why Vilnius had always attracted an endless stream of visitors.

It may be that much looked familiar because of the tales told by our parents. It will be recalled that the Yčas couple had lived here as newlyweds when World War I was ending. In a sense, I was following in the footsteps of Father and Mother as places they had talked about came to view. Across the river from the Cathedral and the center of town was a park where they often had picnics with their friends. This park was named *Žvėrynas* (Zoo) although there had been no wild animals there for years. The story was that some forgotten nobleman had kept a zoo here once upon a time. Mamma treasured her memories of a picnic in the rain in 1918. Everyone got sopping wet but refused to go home since they were having such a good time. Father and a friend named V. Stašinskas, in high spirits despite the weather, grabbed umbrellas and started to dance the cakewalk, singing merrily like a couple of song-and-dance men. A photograph of this scene was kept for years among Mamma's precious souvenirs.

As one approached the city, one saw innumerable church towers etched against the skyline. There were enough churches here to bedazzle the pilgrim, the majority of them Roman Catholic, but there were temples of other religions as well. It was said that there were enough churches here for a pilgrim to visit a new one every day of the year. The great wall that had once surrounded the city had disappeared long ago during some foreign invasion. Some centuries ago, non-Catholic believers like Protestants, Jews,

238

Moslems and others were forced to build their places of worship outside the city walls. One last segment of the wall still remained near a famous shrine called *Aušros Vartai* (Gates of Dawn) where there was a so-called miraculous picture of the Virgin Mary. Her face was black, whether darkened with age or deliberately painted that color, as were some Russian and Polish icons. I marveled at the arms, hands, legs, etc. made of solid silver that were hung all around the altar by former invalids grateful for being healed.

Among the many splendid churches was that of St. Peter and Paul's in grandiose Baroque style with sculptures like those to be found in Rome. Not far from the University was my personal favorite, the small church of St. Anne, a light and airy red brick building in exquisite Gothic style. It was said that Emperor Napoleon, who stopped here on his way to conquer Russia in 1812, had been enchanted with it. According to popular legend , he had expressed the desire to take this church back with him to Paris,. There were mementoes of Napoleon all around us. He was courting Lithuanian and Polish support for his Russian adventure. When we first came to Vilnius, there was a place called Napoleon Square as well as others named for historic figures like Russia's Marshal Kutuzov. Many such names were changed in a frenzy of "Lithuanianizing" the streets, squares and buildings, so perhaps they are now called something else.

For some people, the white columned Cathedral was the most splendid of all. The interior was white with glittering crystal chandeliers. It was full of tombs and shrines decorated in silver. Many famous figures were buried there. We were told that one of them was the beloved wife of King Sigismund, Barbara Radvila, who died young, reputedly poisoned by her jealous mother-in-law. Even more interesting was a trip down some dark steps to an underground altar to Perkūnas, ruler of the gods. This was said to be an authentic remnant of pagan times. A curious fact is that Christian missionaries spreading the Gospel in Lithuania and in other countries tried to defeat the "Powers of Evil" by building churches directly over remnants of pagan temples. The Cathedral, like our Reformed Church, was built in the classical Greco-Roman manner, a style which was a rarity in Vilnius. Many of us thought our Reformed church, so much smaller and far less ornate, was better proportioned and more appealing than the Cathedral. For one thing, our Church had no gap in the center of the row of columns, which gave the Cathedral facade the look of a row of teeth with some of them missing.

The trip from Kaunas was so short that my brother and I went to university lectures by train, returning home late in the evenings. This got to be tiresome, so Father said we should rent rooms. The three of us answered an advertisement for accommodations by the riverside, near Gediminas Street. To our vast surprise, the door was opened by a white-haired gentleman who knew our father. He had been a Polish member of the Russian Duma in days gone by. They immediately recognized each other, although they had not met in years. Like many others in the city, this gentleman had fallen on hard times. He was resolved to make ends meet by renting rooms in what had once been a luxury apartment. Everything there was worn and threadbare, but clean and comfortable. The owner was glad to rent to us on condition that there would not be any wild student-type drinking parties. This became an ideal gathering place for our friends who would bring their own refreshments and sit for hours in the interminable conversations of youth.

Winter was coming on, and it was so severe that people said it was reminiscent of the unbelievably cold spell we had in 1929. At that time, the cherry trees newly planted by Father had frozen, and snow drifts several feet high lined our garden fence. That last winter in Vilnius (who knew it would be our last?), everybody wore their heaviest winter clothing. There was no hot water. Keeping houses properly heated was a problem, and sometimes students wore their overcoats when attending classes. One day, when out for a walk in the snow near the remnants of the city wall, I had a surprise

240

encounter with Anne Crawford, and it was a pleasure to see her. She had a contract to teach English at some college or other and generously offered me a place to stay at her apartment if I wished.

There was another surprise encounter, far less pleasant, when I had a "brush with certain death," as I called it. Around the corner of a winding little street, some place in Old Town, I almost met a horse, nose to nose. There was no sound of bells to warn me. The driver of the sleigh did not see me, and for some reason the horse was not wearing the usual sleigh bells on its harness. Luckily, no harm resulted, but I was all shook up. For years, I remembered that due to my own carelessness, I had been almost run over by a horse.

Among other activities was skiing on the hills near the monument called the Three Crosses. Skiing was rarely possible to do at home since our countryside was so flat. Never confident on skis, I had a few tumbles but got up none the worse for wear. These were days of perfect winter sunshine. Sometimes going to lectures seemed a terrible drag. There was a professor, a friend of Father's, whose feelings would have been deeply hurt if we did not put in an appearance. This was K. Šalkauskas, whose lectures on Civil Law were so dull that they could put you to sleep. We would come at the beginning of his lecture and slip away to play hooky until close to its end. Then we would come back so that he would be sure to notice that we had been there. Our refuge was a café directly across the street called *Štralis*. Here we sampled delicious French pastries in the warm glow of candles covered by pink lamp shades, enjoying the childish prank we were playing on our instructor.

In January 1940 came an event of importance for all who loved the Reformed Church. The last synod of those days was held here, where it had always met before the well-known closing of the Polish-Lithuanian border. In the intervening years of national independence, synods had been meeting in Biržai. Our Church, founded by Duke M. Radvila in this city in Reformation times, had been cut off from its brethren for two decades. Now the two severed parts joined together with great rejoicing, and I felt privileged to be present with my parents. Within the Church in Vilnius, there were people of various nationalities, including the Polish. We celebrated this occasion in our own church of the white classical columns on *Pylimas* (Embankment) Street which had once been outside the walls of the city. The Church owned several buildings including a library housing treasures like the originals of letters by John Calvin, written from Geneva, Switzerland and many rare books. Alas, in later years the Library was a casualty of bombs of World War II and many of the priceless materials perished.

Before saying farewell to Vilnius, I witnessed another impressive event on February 16, 1940, in Cathedral Place. This was the last celebration of Lithuanian Independence Day that we would see. It was exceptionally cold. A platform had been set up among the snowdrifts for speakers and guests, all dressed in heavy overcoats, mittens and fur hats. Among them was our President, Mr. Smetona. He spoke on a note of rejoicing about being able to celebrate the anniversary in our own capital city. Also present were the commander of the Soviet military detachment and his staff. He offered congratulations in a most friendly manner and wished the Lithuanian Republic long and happy years. This was the first time I had a good look at a Russian uniform, gray in color and of sinister appearance. It must be said here that Red Army troops were kept well hidden at their military bases somewhere far away from the center of town, and we seldom saw them. In a few short months we would rue the day that they ever came this close. Soviet troops soon engulfed us like a "Red Tide."

Chapter Twenty-Nine
The Red Flood

When summer came in 1940, there was another ultimatum from the Soviet Union demanding total occupation of the country by Russian troops. Putting up a fight against this show of brute force was hopeless. People were stunned into silence. I do not remember any demonstrations or outward resistance to the government's decision to accept. From this point on, the sequence of many unexpected events becomes blurred in my memory.

A great blow to us and to everybody we knew was losing our country's President. Just before the Soviet invasion, I happened to be in town with my parents. We were parking the green Chevrolet in front of the Automobile Club when a friend named P. Vileišis came up and told us that the unbelievable had happened. Only the day before, we had all listened to Mr. Smetona's radio address urging all citizens to keep calm and fearless in the face of the crisis. Now he had left us for "some place across the border." As it turned out later, this was a wise decision for him personally. He would doubtless have been arrested and deported as had happened to the presidents of Latvia and Estonia. At the time, the general feeling was utter disappointment and dismay because our captain had abandoned his ship and his people as well.

Soviet troops flooded the entire land on June 15, at a time of turmoil in Western Europe. The outside world neither knew nor cared. The German seizure of Paris, France, had all the attention and the publicity. Red Army troops moved into Kaunas from an easterly direction. The main highway was close enough for us at Turkey Lurk to hear the ominous clatter of the Russian war machine. We girls had an idea of what it was and did not want to hear it. All the same, we could not resist climbing up to the third floor of our house to find out the source of all that noise. Anne Crawford was with us at the time. She said, "Let's open the windows wide." Nothing unusual was to be seen, but we could clearly hear the rattle of wheels, the clank of tanks and artillery and the muffled tramp, tramp, tramp of the innumerable feet of horses and men on the main highway going north. All this weighed like a stone upon the heart for it meant that we were no longer masters in our own country.

Strange visitors started coming to Turkey Lurk. A truck, manned by communist agents, arrived at our house to round up people by force to vote in the new parliamentary elections. Everyone knew they were rigged and not free in any sense of the word. This was to be a puppet parliament which would do the bidding of the Soviets. Our Mother told the agents, "I am an American and have no right to vote here. As for my daughters, they are much too young." And then the truck went on its way. In July, the parliament was made to vote under duress for incorporation into the USSR.

There were indications that soon we might lose our home. The new rulers started to confiscate private property. Homes were searched for weapons, and people were arrested for keeping firearms. We were fortunate to be warned a few days early that agents of the new Communist government were coming to Turkey Lurk. In case something besides weapons would be seized, we started to pack part of our valuables and succeeded in sending them by rail to our Biržai relatives. This was a fruitless venture. Far from being grateful, the Yčas cousins said that these possessions only caused them endless trouble. Our sterling silver dinner service was secretly buried under a tree on the lake shore near the old Biržai parsonage, and today nobody can remember just where.

As for the Knabe grand piano, which we considered a treasure, it had a remarkable adventure. By some miracle, we managed to store it with a friend, Stasys Šimkus. He was a noted musician and composer who lived not far from us and already owned several pianos. However, someone gave the secret away. One day, two government agents arrived and demanded to know just where the piano had been hidden. They told us with pride that they had just been released from prison where the Smetona regime had confined them for Communist activities. Mamma was gravely concerned when I asked that the horses be harnessed and rode off in the Victoria carriage with the two jail birds. Mr. Šimkus happened to be home. I said very nonchalantly, "Hello, Mr. Šimkus! I brought you some guests." He was greatly surprised to see me and to hear that he had to give up the Knabe as it was to be placed in some public institution in Kaunas. There was no way he could refuse.

In the absence of our father and brother, we girls rounded up an assortment of hunting rifles (including a Winchester) used by our menfolk and managed to spirit them away into the hands of a close friend called Vladas Šimoliunas, an officer of the Lithuanian Army. One revolver remained for which various hiding places, like the chimney flue, were tried and rejected as being too obvious. We sewed it into a waterproof bag of yellow oilcoth. One dark night my sister Evelyna and I had the exciting adventure of throwing the revolver into the green pond, so named because it was covered by a blanket of bright green duckweed. Sometimes we wonder whether the revolver could still be there after all those years.

Arrests and deportations of so-called "Enemies of the People", i.e., anyone who might think of resisting the invaders, started in July. Father managed to escape quite unobserved by taking a regular train to Šiauliai and then buying another ticket to Klaipėda. He was traveling ostensibly on official government business. Father had a diplomatic package with him, supplied by his friend J. Aukštuolis in the Foreign Office, just in case anyone should stop him at the border. Soon, Father was followed by Martynas, Jr., who slipped across the border on his bicycle. His flight had several comic aspects. Our green Chevrolet had been parked in Kaunas at his place of work and played an important role. It was confiscated by the Russian Secret Police (NKVD) while Martynas, Jr. was out to lunch. They were not very clever, leaving word that they were coming back to talk to him, but he knew better than to wait. My brother telephoned me at Turkey Lurk He asked me to come to a meeting place in town and bring him some clothes "and don't ask the reason why." I must have looked a sight wearing my brother's shirt, his jacket, his cap and his sweater and carrying his underwear in my handbag. I also wore a pair of his shoes and socks as I felt he was going on a long, long journey.

But what of our last weeks at Turkey Lurk? Father had plenty of political savvy but nonetheless delayed his departure as long as he could. When a Soviet tank appeared practically on our doorstep, he still could not bear to go. One day the tank, a rather small one, got stuck in the mud in front of the great wooden barn. Evidently the driver had lost his way and was now in a hurry to catch up with his detachment. Some of us came out with Father to see this most unusual sight. The tank driver was getting angrier and more frustrated by the minute, and it was hard not to show our amusement. All offers of help were proudly refused. The answer was always, "*Nyet, nenada*" (No, not necessary). After quite a while, the driver saw it was hopeless and he might be stuck in the mud forever. Several of our horses were harnessed and with a mighty heave-ho he was out of the rich black mud. The tank went triumphantly on its way toward Kaunas. As soon as it was safe, we burst into hilarious laughter at this rout of the Red Army. We laughed and laughed again until the tears came to our eyes.

There were other tears to be shed very soon, this time on a much more serious occasion. One day, Father gathered us all into the library, sat down at his writing desk and asked our advice about his projected flight to the West. Our brother's immediate reply was, "Let's all go together while we can, load a few things into the Chevrolet and drive southward to the border." Our ever-sensible Mother, who had seen mortal dangers, separations and hurried journeys in her life, thought that Father must go right away. "If you stay," she said, "we may all perish. But if you go, you may be of help to us." Father, who never cried that we knew of, took out his handkerchief to wipe away his tears. "It breaks my heart to leave you," he said, "but I know I must." We girls could only weep and

246

said not a word. Our brave Mamma did not cry but said, "I am sure we shall all meet again soon." In a few months, her words came true, and the family was together again.

Soon after the departure of Martynas, Sr. and Jr., a truck with perhaps ten Red Army officers drove up to our door. They informed us that they were moving into our house. They graciously allowed us an hour or two to remove our belongings. What to take, and what to leave behind? Many precious possessions had to be abandoned. Among other things now forgotten, I decided to take two small oil paintings and a handwoven belt and buckle plucked from my brother's artillery officer's uniform. Such is brotherly gratitude that when I presented the belt to him much later, he wanted to know why in the world I had not thought to bring him something else. He wanted the enameled *Vytis* emblem (the Lithuanian coat of arms) that had been attached to his uniform pocket bearing the date of his graduation from the Military Academy.

The two miniature oil portraits of ladies in the 18th century Russian court dress, decked with exquisitely painted pearls and diamonds, were given for safe-keeping to a dear friend. By some miracle, Algis handed them to me when we met many years later in the USA. Remembering our fond farewells—it was hard to say goodbye—at the orchard gate, he had kept those portraits with him through all the wartime evacuations and bombardments. Algis was among the men friends who came to Turkey Lurk to see how we were getting along despite the dangers involved. Drafting young men into the Red Army or arresting them as "Enemies of the People" was always a possibility. Like some others, Algis ran around in ragged clothes, hoping he would not be mistaken for a "rich bourgeois," a favorite Communist swear word at the time.

Our new lodgers were mostly *Politruks*, or officers entrusted with "political supervision" of their comrades, an interesting institution of the Red Army of those days. They minded their own business and treated us well enough. They probably had orders from above not to molest the local population, leaving the "dirty work" to the NKVD or secret police. The *Politruks* at our house seemed to have little to do except to polish their weapons and go to town on buying trips. They would come back from Kaunas loaded with "luxury items" such as clocks, watches, soaps, toilet articles and shiny new bicycles. They acted like people on an extended vacation.

Some of them wanted to talk and be friendly, for example, a married couple who were both lieutenants. The woman told us, "I am a medical doctor and my husband is an engineer." They both looked far too young to have received their diplomas, but they said that professional training in the USSR started at a very early age. For those of us who knew some Russian there were opportunities to learn something about Soviet life. The Red Army people exaggerated about everything in Russia being the "biggest and the best." One told me in all seriousness, "We have fine homes, plenty of good food and even factories for manufacturing oranges."

Our conversations generally took place in the kitchen where we took turns preparing our meals at the same wood-burning stove of white tile. The Russians liked to eat well and enjoyed our produce including poultry, meats and vegetables. The plentiful supplies of fresh creamery butter never ceased to amaze them, and hot water coming out of the tap seemed a marvel. One dark-complexioned charmer with mischievous black eyes was anxious to talk to us, offering to marry any one of us three sisters and take us to a "new life" in Russia. The "new life" would take some getting used to, he said, but there was no way we could escape from the Soviet system. Anywhere we went, Communism would be sure to follow, even if we went to the USA. How well I remember his words, *"Vi nikuda udrat nebudite"* ("You will never get away").

The Communist era was a disastrous time for our poultry and livestock. Their numbers were getting noticeably fewer. At night, under cover of darkness, poachers came out to chase the white turkey, the gander, the rooster and their flocks. The birds had to run for their lives (were they chased by Red Army people, or farm laborers wishing to put them in the cooking pot?). Some of our workers believed the government propaganda about everything now being common property. They looked forward to having land seized from the rightful owners and given to the laboring classes. Our gardener, usually so meek and timid, was now boldly stealing bags-full of Mamma's giant Spanish onions and selling them at the market. We had to grin and bear it as the saying goes.

Life with the *Politruks* was not without laughter. Somehow they discovered a copybook that I had used for studying the Russian language (a requirement for University law studies). In it there was an article in my handwriting copied from a Soviet military paper *Krasnaya Zvezda* (Red Star). It was about the heroic acts of a *Politruk* in what to us was that cruel Russo-Finnish War. "'Forward', this hero cried, as he urged his soldiers on. Red flag in hand, he led them across the snow and ice." Our Russian lodgers were very pleased with my work. They did not know that I had copied the article purely for its comic value and not because I was an admirer of the Red Army.

Another amusing episode was the famous "Attack of the Bees." You could hardly say that our bees were to blame for stinging several of the *Politruks*. They had been stirred into fury by one of our visitors called Anzelmas Gailius, a military school pal of our brother's. He tried to take honey from the hives without knowing what he was doing. Swarms of bees rampaged all over the farmyard, and anyone in their path had to run away and hide. The culprit himself took refuge in the woodshed and was afraid to come out. One *Politruk*, riding the garden path, fell off his bicycle and dove into the bushes. He was badly stung and demanded to know who was responsible. I had to tell him that our friend, cowering in the woodshed, was a mass of bee stings himself. Should he come out and apologize? The *Politruk* said, "I don't want to see him but tell him that he is a *Bolshoi Durak* (a great fool)," and I certainly did tell him just that. We were lucky that the episode ended with no tragic consequences.

The pump broke down one day and everybody had to get water from a neighbor's well. A lieutenant sometimes accompanied us, carrying a bucket just as we did. Our conversations were mostly on the evils of religion and the lies told by churches and their agents, the priests. Another subject was so-called equality for every citizen of the USSR. Never clarified was the fact that ordinary Red Amy soldiers slept in tents on the grounds of the Fort whereas the officers lived under our roof with all the comforts of home. The major, who was their commanding officer, a kindly older man with a graying beard, told me one time that he had every sympathy with us in our present situation. In Czarist times, he told us, his uncle had lost everything in the Great Revolution. "He learned to live without possessions," he said, "and so will you."

Our good times, such as they were, had to come to an end. Quite unexpectedly, a second Red Army truck drove up some weeks later with many more officers. This time, they were taking over the whole house. "Where shall we go?" Mamma asked their commander. He said that he did not know and added, "Just like you, we of the Red army can get marching orders any time to move to who knows where." It did not take long for us to get ready. We already knew of an empty apartment we could borrow from the Yčas relatives in Kaunas.

One of our farm workers, now remembered only as the good hearted Andrew, offered to hitch up a horse and cart. He said, "I will take you wherever you want to go." We were allowed to pack a few clothes and small possessions as well as some provisions for the journey. Leaving Turkey Lurk was not a shattering experience for any of us at the time. The weather that afternoon was unusually fine. It was August, but already there was a tinge of autumn in the air. We took our comfortable seats on the hay at the bottom of the cart. As Mamma told her three daughters, we were fortunate to be alive and well. She urged us to be courageous and to strike up a song, thus putting up a bold front. We sang a merry ditty to the clop-clop of the horses' feet and the rattle of the cart wheels. And so we took the road from Turkey Lurk to Kaunas for the very last time.

Chapter Thirty
Last Days in Kaunas

We drove by horse and cart with what little was left of our possessions to a suburb of Kaunas called *Žaliakalnis* (Green Hill). As we said farewell to Andrew, the driver, we realized that we did not even own the horse and cart any more. There was no one to greet us as we entered the Yčas cousins' apartment, since they were all away in Biržai. They had left us the key and told us to make ourselves at home. A strange feeling overcame us as Mamma turned the key in the lock. She said, "This is not our home and we won't be here very long." For quite a while, Mamma had been investigating various ways of escape from the so-called Soviet paradise, but nothing was clear as yet about what was coming next. The only things that were sure was that we had been turned out of Turkey Lurk and that Kaunas was not a safe place for us to be. The town was full of rumors that apartments and other private dwellings were being sequestered for military purposes.

There was now a puppet government carrying out orders of the Communist rulers of Russia. In countries under foreign occupation there are bound to be collaborators, and Lithuania had its share. A delegation of prominent people, among them an Army general and several distinguished literati went to Moscow, "begging to be allowed to bring back Stalin's sun," in the words of a well known woman poet. Later on, excuses were made that they were forced to do this despicable deed, acting under duress, and some of them fled the country later. What their true sentiments were is hard to determine. As far as I was concerned, V. Krėvé-Mickevičius, a renowned writer, was to be regarded with suspicion. When I was introduced to him years later in the USA and he extended his hand in greeting, I politely shook hands with him, but it was with a feeling of revulsion.

Red Army troops started to bring their wives from Russia at about this time. I never saw any of them, but funny stories were told about them. Madly shopping at the stores for what to them

253

were luxury items, they were buying up cosmetics, soap, clothing, hats (the more feathered and be-ribonned the better) and especially underwear. Among the latter were nightgowns that the Russian army wives mistook for evening dresses. They appeared at the National Theater dressed in nightgowns and hats.

The atmosphere in Kaunas was certainly changing. *Laisvés Aléja,* or Freedom Avenue, once such a lively place, now had a dreary look. Few familiar faces were to be seen. Gripped by fear, many people were not sleeping in their own beds at night, and some had left town altogether. They were supposedly visiting relatives in the country. During our final stay in Kaunas, we avoided Main Street. People told us it was not pleasant any more and not even safe. The Avenue was no longer alive with happy crowds out for a stroll under the lindens. Gentlemen used to doff their hats greet their acquaintances and bow to the ladies. Father, who had conservative ideas, would not dream of appearing without a hat. When my brother refused to wear one Father said, "In the old days, only lunatics and serving-maids would appear in public without their hats."

The very last time we were out on the Avenue, coming in from Turkey Lurk on some errand, we found it depressing. Mamma, fearless as ever, said, "I am an American. What can they do to me?" and insisted that we girls all be properly dressed, complete with hats and gloves. We met people, usually so elegantly turned out, who now wore ragged clothes. One was Mrs. Merkys, wife of the Prime Minister, wearing no stockings, her hair all askew, in a faded cotton house dress, probably hoping that she would not be recognized. As has been said before, people dressed this way so nobody would think that they belonged to the bourgeois classes and thus be labeled "Enemies of the People." Active opponents of Communism were the first victims, but it would not be long before others, merely suspected of being hostile, would be imprisoned and deported. Oddly enough, the most violently persecuted were believers in the wrong kind of Communism, like followers of Leon Trotsky, a sworn enemy of Stalin.

Our neighbor, Army Col. K. Skučas, whose daughter was a classmate of my youngest sister's, was arrested right away. In the first year of the Soviet invasion comparatively few people managed to escape abroad. Perhaps they hoped that they could lie low and not be noticed. Those who remained behind were exposed to the full fury of the mass deportations of June, 1941. Thousands of people of all walks of life were packed into cattle cars and sent to remote areas of Siberia.

In the summer of 1940, droves of would-be Americans surrounded the American Legation in Kaunas at this time. The rumor was going around that the US Government would send a ship to rescue them. There was nothing Mamma wanted more than to get on board and sail away, and we girls looked forward to this great adventure. Alas, it was not to be. The American Minister (there was no Ambassador in Kaunas), a personal acquaintance, played the heavy handed bureaucrat who made no exceptions. He turned Mamma away because of legal technicalities. It appeared that she had not been going to the US Legation every two years to declare her intention of remaining a citizen (a law that has since been repealed). So Mamma did not get her birthright and had to wait until she got to the USA, where she regained citizenship through the courts. One of the great disappointments of our lives was this decision made by Dr. O.J.C. Norem, the American Minister. We were utterly devastated when we were left behind as the ship called the "American Legion" departed from Petsamo, Finland, on August 8, 1940. It arrived in New York some twenty days later.

Besides the Americans, there were British citizens who had to be evacuated. German forces surrounded us on every hand. Norway was a prime target of the German military machine. War had erupted, and there seemed to be no way out. We were greatly interested in the British evacuation since our own Anne Crawford was very much involved. Crawley was like a member of our family.

After she ceased being our governess, she was always coming back to spend vacations with us and trying to help out in emergencies. We thought we already knew how resourceful she was, but she surprised us in this time of turmoil "rising magnificently to the occasion" (one of her favorite phrases). When the British Minister and his staff left Kaunas, Crawley was appointed to take charge of the evacuation of her compatriots. This was a feat she accomplished with courage and great ingenuity. It took several months before the trip to Australia, a most unexpected destination, could get underway.

Crawley was one of the first people we contacted when we came to the Green Hill apartment. She had been able to smuggle out some of our things from Turkey Lurk, saying that they were hers and she had her rights as a British citizen. The Red Army men asked no questions as Crawley marched out on foot, carrying a small suitcase containing some of our clothing and family photographs. Getting transportation to and from the apartment was no problem since Crawley had made friends with a young man who drove a car. Lithuanian-born Joseph Kagan had lived in England for years but had property in Lithuania to take care of. He was glad to serve the transportation needs of Crawley and her friends. As it turned out, Joseph was to play an important role in our Great Escape.

Somewhat earlier we had received our first message from Father. He had found a haven with friends in Klaipėda across the border and our brother Martynas, Jr. was also safe and sound. Father outlined plans for our future such as getting separate Lithuanian passports for each of us through our Embassy in Switzerland (like most others, it was still in operation). The message came via a friend in Koenigsberg, Professor Arseniew, who was to be an intermediary in case we lost touch. Exactly how the message came I no longer remember, but it was not by ordinary letter. Mail services could not be trusted because of possibilities of censorship. The term "Iron Curtain" had not yet been invented, but we were being walled off from the world.

Crawley was in a predicament and asked Joseph Kagan to help her out. At this time she was plotting and planning the escape of dozens of her British compatriots out from under the Soviet peril. For anyone to have motorized means of transportation in these times was really something. People affluent enough to have cars were losing them right and left. All sorts of private property was being confiscated under the guise of "liberating the bourgeoisie from their possessions." Joseph liked excitement and adventure and took pleasure in driving people around.

Crawley also had an adventurous spirit and enjoyed dodging dangerous situations. The British subjects in her charge were mostly teachers of English, chauffeurs, secretaries, nannies, tutors and governesses employed in Lithuania and in neighboring Latvia and Estonia. In many cases they had stayed at their jobs for years and were no longer young. They came to the British Legation in Kaunas and took shelter under its roof, hoping that their Government would rescue them.

For reasons difficult to fathom, the British Minister, Thomas H. Preston, found it necessary to retreat eastward to Russia before the evacuation of these stranded citizens was completed. Maybe he was in a hurry to get away from Kaunas. For years he had represented Britain in the glory days of Czarist Russia and never got used to Lithuania, a place he considered to be a provincial backwater. His contempt for his present surrounding was quite evident. Furthermore, he chose to use the Russian language when speaking to local people. All things considered, Mr. Preston was not exactly the most popular diplomat in town.

Of all people, Anne Crawford who had no training in affairs of state, was selected to lead the expedition. She performed the task "as to the manner born." Crawley had true qualities of leadership and brought the matter to a successful conclusion. She had a sense of humor and above all, plenty of courage. She was outspoken in defense of her own and other people's rights, relying on her status as a British subject to keep her safe from harm. This she defiantly announced to anyone who would listen, stating that she had the might of the entire British Empire behind her!

The British envoy had left instructions and some money for the evacuation but could not foresee the exact date to get moving. The stranded Britishers would have to reach their homeland in a roundabout way. The people in distress had to be housed and fed. In the hurry of departure, many of them did not bring sufficient clothing or provisions, not to mention money, which in this chaotic financial situation was likely to be of little value. When the funds left by Mr. Preston ran out, Crawley gleefully started selling Legation property in the absence of any authority. Furniture, office supplies, typewriters, fur coats, etc. started disappearing into the Black Market. Years later in Scotland while reminiscing with us about these events, she said her conscience did not bother her a bit as "these abandoned objects would have been confiscated anyway."

Unforeseen circumstances delayed the evacuation until October, 1940. The travelers had to cross Russia by train going eastward to Siberia and the port of Vladivostok. There they took a ship and reached safety at last. Some remained in Australia for good but others longed for their homes in Britain half a world away.

A participant now living in England named Ruth Marshall Jenkins shared her memories in an unpublished memoir entitled "The Only Way Out." She celebrated her 21st birthday when she came to Lithuania as a governess just before World War II. Ruth was young enough to enjoy the trip to the fullest. There was much singing and dancing, both on board and on the platforms when the train stopped. Most of the 170 Britons played cards or other games to pass the time and had hot water going so they could drink tea day and night. They departed from Riga, Latvia, and changed trains in Moscow. They were thrilled when the British Ambassador stationed there came to the train to wish them Godspeed. After the lonely expanse of the steppes came the Ural Mountains and the unforgettable Sea of Baikal. Most of the time, the train went slowly. But sometimes it picked up frightening speed, going recklessly around the hairpin curves, supposedly to make up time. Ruth was shocked to find out that the bold engineer was a woman. Surprisingly enough, the train arrived in Vladivostok exactly on time, to the day, the hour, and almost to the minute. The travelers were marched two by two aboard the waiting ship. As they stepped across the gangplank, they felt they had reached safety since the ship was British territory. After some years in Australia, Ruth managed to return home to England.

Chapter Thirty-One
The Great Escape

As anyone who has ever been in a similar situation knows full well, leaving your home to go off into the unknown is a big decision. One of my high school classmates said, "I would never leave my country, which is a most unpatriotic thing to do." Years later, she came to the USA as a refugee. When we met, it was hard for me to hold my tongue and not say, "I told you so." There were others seeking a way out who did not speak so grandiosely about patriotism. Irene, another school friend, found a novel way to leave by marrying a much older man who was in love with her. He happened to be a citizen of Switzerland, and promised to rescue her entire family if she became his wife. I remembered that I had been born in that country and investigated the possibilities of getting a Swiss passport. The Swiss Consul gave me a firm refusal since there was a residency requirement of five years. American citizenship laws, however, were very different. It was said that to be born in that country was enough.

For people like us, there was a way of getting out by applying for German help as *Volksdeutsche* (persons of German origin), that is, by pretending to be what we were not. At the time, the Stalin-Hitler friendship was at its height, (which lasted until Germany attacked Russia in June 1941). Germans and those of German blood were permitted to leave the Soviet orbit. It was not necessary to speak their language, but a number of blatant lies about one's ancestry had to be told. Getting your name on the list was easy if you were a Lutheran (deemed to be a German religion) and sometimes being a Protestant of any kind would do. Mamma was totally against this procedure, and how right she was. We had not a drop of German blood and might have been marooned forever in a country alien to us, not to speak of falsifying papers and losing our peace of mind. In Mamma's opinion, other ways of escape would be sure to open up. In the meantime, important information had come through my sisters' playmates, two girls who by a strange coincidence were also twins of about the same age. Their mother, Mrs. Bražėnas, gave us the name of someone who could put us in touch with people taking refugees across the border. This was Father J. Kipas, an administrator of the Jesuit High School. The smugglers, far from being patriots, were doing this for personal gain and would demand payment. Mamma did not ask for anyone's advice and handled this all by herself. It took several weeks before contacts for this dangerous venture could be made. The borders were under guard of Soviet troops, and they had orders to shoot any escapees on sight.

Finally, there came that long-awaited knock on the door. An unknown man stood outside saying he had an important message. Mamma talked to him only after he gave her a secret password that had been agreed upon. We learned that in a few days we were to meet the smugglers who would take us to the border. There would be some distance to walk and small bundles, like our Girl Scout knapsacks, would be all we could take with us. This would not be much, so making decisions on what to pack took some thought. We needed our overcoats, a change of clothes, a nightgown, a toothbrush and an extra pair of shoes, in case ours got wet. After all, how much does one really need? We lived very comfortably for six months with what we had in our sacks. I remember wearing several layers of underwear and a sweater over a couple of blouses, which was good protection in the cool fall weather. Mamma packed a wool "union suit" for Father, who had departed with only the lightest summer clothes. She also took title deeds to the Turkey Lurk property and other documents and insisted that I take my high school diploma. I did not tell her that I was taking a few treasured photographs, and she did not know that Violetta, probably the most patriotic one of us all, stuffed a handwoven Lithuanian flag into her sack.

We were told to keep our escape plans a secret, but surely we could trust our faithful visitors Crawley, our bachelor Uncle John Yčas, the engineer, and our new friend Joseph. These were the only people to whom we said our fond farewells. I wanted to say goodbye to my dear friend Rita, but there was no opportunity. Years later, she told me that she had gone to the apartment to see if she could catch one last glimpse of me. She shed tears when she found the place was empty, and that the birds had flown (and I was much moved to hear her tale). As for Joseph, he immediately offered to drive us wherever needed on the first stage of our journey. He gave me a box of chocolates to sustain us on the trip. It still remains one of the most memorable gifts I have ever received.

Joseph Kagan, a remarkable personality, deserves a few words here. He was a jokester who loved funny stories and also popular music. He was quite the ladies' man as I discovered when he would take me for a drive. He liked to quote a favorite saying that he learned from Anne Crawford, "Don't drive with one hand. Use both and take a taxi." The radio would be blaring the latest British hits from the BBC. ("The Lambeth Walk," "I've Got My Love to Keep Me Warm," etc.) amid our singing and our laughter. There was no inkling then, apart from Joseph's cleverness, suavity and charm, that here was a British subject of future distinction, one day to be a member of the House of Lords. His flamboyant, and sometimes scandalous career was based on knowing the right people at the right time in ways unknown and unattainable to most of us. Though Joseph did not succeed in saving his family's property from the Communists, he was eminently successful in other ways when he got back to England. This was after a series of hair-raising adventures. When the German occupation came, he barely escaped with his life.

Through manufacture of textiles and raincoats named "Gannex," Joseph drew the attention of none other than Prime Minister Harold Wilson. From then on, Joseph was on his way up, meeting the rich, the titled and the famous. It seemed everybody, even Royalty, wanted one of these raincoats, which were considered to be a great contribution to the British economy. As sometimes happens, Joseph needed only one little push to get elevated to

Knighthood and to the British Peerage. Mr. Wilson recommended him for a seat in the House of Lords in 1976 where Joseph served until his demise. Mamma wrote the new Lord Kagan of Gannex a congratulatory letter on behalf of the entire family. Joseph replied, saying that in spite of many intervening events, he still remembered us and was delighted that we too had not forgotten. A postscript should be added. When I visited London in the 1980s and 1990s, I met this old friend and had the good fortune to be invited to attend sessions of Parliament. In the House of Lords, I remembered how impressed Father had been with this grand old British institution when he first visited it in 1913. Joseph introduced me to some of the Lords and Ladies and soon had his audience laughing as he told of the adventures we had in what he called "running away from the Russians."

Now back to my own adventure. When the time came (it was Friday, the 13th of September), Joseph was there with his car. Driving us took a lot of courage because sentries could be shooting not only potential refugees but their helpers as well. Our chauffeur decided to drive by roundabout ways, not directly through the city. Over half a century later, I still shiver at the memory of the Red Army encampment we encountered on the way. We were driving through the Vale of Mickevičius (named in honor of the famed 19th century poet). Joseph was not fazed a bit at seeing Soviet tanks parked by the side of the road. He zipped by them with an amused and nonchalant air, and nobody stopped us. Joseph was so self-confident that not one of us was scared. Had he not said, "Leave the driving to me?" He took us safely to the designated meeting place. Near the Aleksotas bridge over the river Nemunas, we were to transfer to another car.

To ride with people we did not know was a bit scary. Two unknown persons were sitting in the front seat. Immediately they told us to keep silent and not say a word, and there was no talking whatever. There was a man behind the wheel, a cap shadowing his face, and a woman beside him with a peasant-type kerchief on her head. They were part of the underground network that smuggled people across the border for a price. We had already paid using a few valuables, of which I recall only a radio and Mamma's silver fox fur, plus a sum of money. We were taken south on the highway to a place near Kalvarija, where a farmer's cart and horses awaited. We spent part of the night sleeping, fully clothed, on the straw in this farmer's barn. I was tired and fell into a deep sleep, but Mamma later said she was worried and did not sleep a wink.

Suddenly I awoke to see a candle burning uncomfortably close to my face. A woman said, "Your guides have arrived, and it is time to move on." My watch said it was about two o'clock. I could dimly see articles of clothing and furs suspended from the rafters, evidently seized from people who had been running for their lives. Two men came and had us all walking single file across ploughed fields in the dark of the moon. Wide strips of borderland were ploughed over, as we later found out, so it would be easy for frontier guards to trace the footprints of escapees. It was dark, and the moon shone only fitfully through the clouds. Fortunately, we encountered no one. One of our guides led the way, and the four of us followed, each at a distance of a few hundred yards, and the other man brought up the rear. To my surprise, I was the one behind the leader and a great deal would depend on my eyesight (which had always been poor). I was so single-minded in my concentration on the man in front that I did not even think about who was behind me. That was my sister Violetta and directly behind her was Evelyna helping our Mamma over difficult stretches. Mamma, never the athletic type, might not have leaped the ditches and the stones if Evelyna had not been there to encourage her and hold her arm where necessary.

When the ploughed area ended, our guides explained that we had crossed the border. There was time for a little conversation, our first, since they had not said a word to us except "Keep silent! Someone may hear us!" They told us that woodlands were in front of us and the next town was Punskas. There we would have to surrender to German frontier police, but it was best to wait for daylight. The frontier made a wavy line here and we could easily wander back into Soviet-held territory again. The area we were in was formerly Lithuania, seized by Poland, now occupied by the Germans. Mamma made sure that one last handful of Lithuanian soil was securely tied in her handkerchief (for sentimental reasons, she took it with her everywhere on her later travels). Then it was time to say goodbye and thanks to the unknown men whose help was so important to us.

Mindful of what they had said, there was nothing to do but to catch a nap and wait for sunrise. As it had just rained, the grass was damp and soggy when we stretched out under a tree. By this time, we were all so worn out that even Mamma said she dozed off. Someone has said "It is always darkest before the dawn," and we found out how true this was. Having been a Girl Scout, I felt I had some experience in spending a night out in the open and drew comfort from the rustle of the forest. The guiding hand of a power greater than all of us had led us to safety, especially since I was not wearing my glasses during the entire time of our walk to freedom. Finding the forgotten glasses in my pocket—the glasses I thought I could not do without—was an experience shattering enough to last me all of my life. My eyes, though not of the best, had served me well when dire need arose.

Gradually, the sky lightened up and with the first rays of the sun came the chirping of songbirds. We started walking in the direction advised by our guides, through the forest and down a road hoping to reach a human habitation. The first sign that a village was not far away was the honking of geese. Evidently we were approaching a farmyard. Perhaps we would soon meet a farmer and his cart that would take us on the next step of our journey. With the sunrise came the dawning of a new day and adventures lasting many months before we reached the fabled land of America.

Chapter Thirty-Two
Road to Another Life

As a new day was dawning, Mamma, my two sisters and I walked a strange road to an uncertain future. The full impact of what had just happened—leaving our home and country perhaps forever—did not sink in until much later. Soon a farmer came by in his horse-driven cart and offered us a ride to the Frontier Police Station in Punskas. As we were rolling into town, he told us how the local population had been plundered and reduced to near-starvation by the greedy German occupants. Uniformed policemen were breakfasting at outdoor picnic tables near the Station. They immediately asked us, "Are you Jewish? Are you Polish?" Upon learning our true nationality, they said, "Good. Now we won't have to send you back."They congratulated us for what they called our courageous escape and then invited us to have some breakfast.

The police chief said we were under arrest and sent us to the local Lithuanian Roman Catholic rectory. The hospitable Father Želvys offered us lodging on straw mattresses on the floor, regretting that he had not even a scrap of food to give us. Next morning Evelyna and I went out foraging for provisions. Not having so much as a penny in our pockets, we planned to do some work in return for a bite to eat. But the local farming folk would not hear of it. Taking one look at our citified clothing, they said, "Young ladies, how could you be of help to us? We have little enough for ourselves, but are willing to share what we have." Munching bread and cheese, we returned to the rectory to find that we were expected to board the train for Suvalkai to be questioned by the Gestapo, or secret police.

The Gestapo was well informed and knew all about our family but depositions were required just the same. A handsome blond young man, clacking away on a typewriter, took down everything I was saying. We were sent to a refugee detainment camp near Goldap, East Prussia, accessible only by horse. A huge

Army wagon and pair took us there. At the camp, we were greatly surprised to meet some acquaintances from Kaunas days. For two weeks we stayed in wooden huts and slept on straw mattresses. Sometimes we went on jaunts to the woods to pick wild berries and mushrooms. After it was learned that our Father and brother were in Berlin awaiting us, we were released and allowed to board the train.

Father had rented rooms near the centrally-located Friedrichstrasse train station. One may imagine our joy on being reunited, chattering excitedly about what had happened since we parted. As I related some of my funny stories, I noticed that Father was mopping his eyes with his handkerchief. He had visions of my being deported to Siberia because of all these careless conversations with Russian *politruks* at Turkey Lurk. Our first good meal in days was supper at a nearby restaurant consisting of *Ostseescholle* (a type of sole) and a mound of boiled potatoes, in return for some required ration cards.

There was a job waiting for me, much to my surprise. Father had made contact with the local American Express Company. A typist was needed there to address envelopes. This was the first job I had ever held in my life, an exciting prospect. However, the work was rather dull and soon I felt like a prisoner chained to my desk for the incredibly long hours of 9 to 5. Actually, I was not always at my typewriter. Often, I was summoned to the front desk to act as interpreter. People of many nationalities were then stranded in Berlin, all waiting for financial rescue through checks coming from abroad. Among them I remember some Americans, many refugees from Lithuania or elsewhere, and even a few elderly Russians who had fled their country in the days of the Great Revolution.

Shortly afterwards we had a most welcome visitor. This was Barbara von Richthofen, bearing gifts from her country estate in Silesia. Never to be forgotten is that tasty bread, butter and salami sausage, as well as the financial support, to speed us on our way. Barbara's visit brought us cheer and served to brighten our days in

Berlin which at this time was a dark and eerie place. The British Royal Air Force had started bombing the city. Street lights were dimmed at night, window shades were drawn, automobile as well as foot traffic was almost nil. Policemen would appear, rising like ghosts out of the darkness in their phosphorescent coats of white. We had to spend many hours in bomb shelters. A little old man would come around, tapping on doors to waken us with his "Alarm, alarm" spoken in a feeble voice. The crash of explosives and rattle of antiaircraft guns never seemed to come too close. Finally we found the bomb shelter business so boring that even Mamma, who was afraid of bombs, was unwilling to make the trip to the cellars below.

There were other reasons for wishing to leave Berlin as soon as we could. In late 1940, German-Soviet friendship was at its height. It was entirely possible that the Russians might demand that refugees like us be returned. The Germans had no reason to detain us since the USA and Germany were not yet at war; the attack on Pearl Harbor being almost a year away. Mamma was American born so exit permits were granted as soon as we could get visas to go elsewhere. It would be a long wait until our American visas came through. We planned to move on as soon as our Argentinian and Brazilian visas were secured. I felt a little sad to leave Berlin and its cultural assets, hotels like the historic Adlon on the street called Unter den Linden near the Brandenburg Gate and splendid museum displays like the Egyptian collection. Above all, I would miss the Tiergarten with its extensive zoo, the best I had ever seen.

Six seats in the airplane being hard to get all at one time, my brother and I set off for sunny Spain to be joined later by the rest of the family. As we departed, we joked that we were moving South, like the swallows, because we had no warm winter clothes to wear. This was our first such trip. Neither of us had ever seen the Mediterranean Sea or the Pyrenees. After stopping at the wrecked and bombed-out airport in Lyon, France, the plane took us over the brown and yellow expanse of a mountain range. Then came the blue of the Mediterranean and ships like white specks on the water.

At Barcelona we were greeted by swaying palm trees and flowering oleanders. We found the *pensión* (rather like a small hotel) which Father had engaged for us on an avenue called Rambla de las Flores. It was full of flower stalls, making it a colorful paradise. The two of us spent a delightful few days, liberated from parental supervision. We took in local sights like the still unfinished Temple of the Sacred Family and the Royal Palace. We sat in outdoor cafés, savoring port wine with black olives and *almejas* (a kind of mussel). On the Catalonia Plaza, the main square, we saw a rustic scene in the middle of the bustling city. All traffic, including carts drawn by donkeys had to stop to let a shepherd and his flock of sheep go by.

We learned that we were in the capital of the Catalán people, proud of their heritage and chafing under the yoke of Spanish rule. A student who wrote poetry in the Catalán language became our friend (he even wrote a poem about me titled "Beauty from the Baltic"). This young man made it a point to enlighten us, explaining that the popular Spanish saying, *"España una, grande, libre"* ("One Spain united, great and free") was nothing but an empty farce.

Wounds left by the recent Civil War were still apparent. The city endured over two years of bombing raids by General Franco's forces. We saw ruined buildings, torn-up streets and masts of wrecked ships sticking up out of the water in the harbor. People were subsisting on meager food like chick peas, tomatoes, onions and sardines, when obtainable. Despite hardships the people, like those living in our *pensión*, retained their natural gaiety. There were parties almost every night, much drinking of a local wine called Manzanilla and dancing to guitar music. A pretty young lady would jump up on the table and perform Flamenco and other dances. My brother and I were captivated by the novel atmosphere. We told our parents that we wished to stay and explore Spain, and never mind the trip to America. We wanted to stay behind and absorb some of the fascinating local cultures.

My longtime dream to see the famous Museum of the Prado in Madrid was soon to come true. Father was impatient to get to Lisbon, Portugal, from whence we would be able to sail off into the New World. When I learned that we were to stay in Madrid just one night, I insisted on dragging the whole family to the Prado. Truthfully I was the only one interested. I won them over by the argument that we might never pass this way again. Fortunately our train arrived at a time when the museum was still open. There were magnificent paintings by Van Dyck, Murillo, Goya, Velasquez and others to admire, all hanging on dingy walls and very poorly lighted. There was an air of darkness and gloom, seeming to make an appropriate setting for the many rather forbidding portraits of Spanish royalty. Old-time kings and queens with their families appeared so stiff and formal that they did not look like people one would wish to know.

The train ride from the capital of Spain to the capital of Portugal lasted twelve hours. It was remarkable because it was the dirtiest and slowest train any of us had ever been on. There were people crowded tightly into our compartment. It was such a shaky and bumpy ride that it was quite impossible to sleep. However, everybody was good-humored and easily given to laughter. Things got to be quite chummy when it was discovered that we could communicate a little with our fellow passengers in our rudimentary Spanish. We had taken some lessons in Berlin in anticipation of a possible trip to Latin America. My sister Evelyna received a marriage proposal from a button salesman traveling with his 19-year old son. He said his son had a great future in the family business and that Evelyna would make him an excellent wife. Everybody was highly amused, but the young man just blushed and never said a word.

The only diversion was eating our sandwiches and talking to our fellow passengers. Martynas, Jr. reached into his pockets and discovered keys from our lodging in Madrid. He had failed to return them on our departure and sheepishly admitted that he had other keys unlocking doors to places we had stayed in since leaving home. This was just one joke, and soon there was something else to laugh about. Someone opened up a can of unfamiliar food called *calamares en su tinto* (squid in its own ink, or juice). It looked repulsive but the taste was not bad when we sampled it. Father said the slimy black mess should be thrown out of the train window, and he did so amid general merriment.

Chapter Thirty-Three
Last Sojourn in Europe

Lisbon was our last "jumping-off place" before leaving the continent. We were impatient to get away, but meanwhile Portugal was a charming place to be. Leaving Europe in the winter of 1940–1941 was no simple matter as the place was full of refugees of many nationalities, all with the same idea. Passenger space in ships, especially those bound for the USA, was booked for months ahead. The local American embassy held up our visas so long that we realized that we should try our luck in South America. Numbers of people, including many Jews, were trying to escape Nazi German domination. Those who (like us) were fleeing Soviet Russian oppression were comparatively few.

Local people were remarkably uninformed about the Soviet peril, judging by the naive questions we were asked, even by journalists who should have known better. Several came to take our pictures and write articles for the Portuguese papers while we were staying at our first haven, the Hotel of Two Nations. They were amazed to hear the true facts as we related our experiences. The hotel, recommended to us in Berlin, was run by a German in partnership with a Portuguese, thus accounting for its name. This was our first introduction to Portuguese hospitality and amazingly good food. We joked about gaining weight, and this happened to all of us in no time. Privations encountered elsewhere on our journey did not exist here. Tables were loaded with four or five courses: soups, salads, seafood and meats of many kinds, rich pastries and scrumptious desserts, all with plenty of wine.

While riding a streetcar on the main thoroughfare called Avenida do Liberdade (Liberty Avenue), we met a Portuguese Army lieutenant named Luis Menezes who became a lifelong friend. He delighted in taking us around and making us feel at home. Luckily, he spoke English very well indeed. When we got to know him better, we girls wanted Luis to take us out riding in a horse drawn carriage, but he refused. He said: "It would be undignified for me to be seen riding in a carriage instead of mounted on a horse." Luis, who served in a regiment of artillery, was a splendid horseman. Sometimes he would come on horseback to visit us, clattering along with his orderly (attendant) behind him. He often brought gifts of good things to eat like pastries or chocolates. It was always his orderly who carried the packages. At Christmas Luis brought us a turkey, a bird hard to obtain here. One time I met this cavalcade when out walking with my parents. Luis approached at a gallop, obviously showing off. He reined in his horse so sharply that it almost sat down on its haunches. He signaled to his attendant to hand me a big bouquet of roses. I had acquired an admirer but, with all the insouciance of my young years (and considerable cruelty), I merely laughed at him. Of course his attentions were flattering, and it is no wonder that the picture described above is etched firmly in my mind.

Luis was born and raised in Jesuit schools in Goa, India, then a Portuguese colony. He had exquisite manners but also had his pride as far as attentions to the ladies were concerned. He took a dim view of two young Lithuanian men, Paul and Vito, who appeared in Lisbon shortly after we came. My sisters and I were impressed partly because we had never met anyone like these two Naval officers. We were not even aware that Lithuania had a navy. It consisted of one ship, a German minesweeper left over from World War I. Paul had been the captain of the ship named "President Smetona" and Vito was his second in command. The two had acquired "spit and polish" at the Royal Naval Academy in Livorno, Italy, and were quite an addition to our social life.

Paul and Vito did not lack for self-confidence and thought of themselves as gentlemen of considerable culture. So did we, but this shining image got a bit tarnished upon closer acquaintance. When we moved into an apartment, Father and Mamma invited our compatriots to have their meals with us. The "two beauties," as we called them, managed to rent a room directly across the street from us. Now we had a pair of men willing to go marketing, carry our packages or run errands for us. We got to be great friends, and they joined us in many pleasant excursions. However, they were sometimes a source of annoyance and family dissension. Our parents, particularly Mamma, felt that two bachelors growing slightly bald were far too old to be constantly hanging around their daughters. Sometimes there were angry words, and it was not safe for the two to come "across the street." Our balcony was clearly visible from their window, and more than once we three hung up a towel or other "white flag of truce" signifying that all was well, and the storm had blown over.

It must be said that our Navy men were not always easy to get along with. Vito was a highly strung, nervous type, very easily offended, looking for insults where none were intended. Paul, not at all temperamental, was rather stolid and had little sense of humor. Often he did not understand when he was the butt of our jokes. We were living in a dilapidated building, directly above a store with a sign saying *Ovos Garantidos* (eggs guaranteed). It was a wholesale place selling eggs fresh from the farm. This became our name for the apartment and many were the verses I wrote here, either about the fun and laughter we had or sentimental trivia about the homeland we had lost. Unfortunately, my humorous "Ode to Ovos Garantidos," like the rest of my literary effusions, does not lend itself to translation. By the way, I was often made fun of because I was constantly scribbling in my diary or trying to compose so-called immortal poetry.

Conditions in our apartment were rather primitive. True, we had a bathtub and running water, though not always hot. The bathroom lock was so faulty that you might get locked in permanently if you were careless in turning the key. Sometimes it was unbearably cold because there was no heating whatever in the house. Portuguese homes got along "as is" the year round. In winter you sat at the dining table, warming your feet at a brazier placed under it. This was a flat pan holding burning coals, somewhat like a Japanese-style hibachi. A heavy tablecloth made sure that none of the heat would escape. All in all, it seemed like an ingenious invention.

We often walked down the Avenida do Liberdade to the landmark statue of the Marques do Pombal. He stood high on his column with a life-size lion, symbol of his prowess. As Prime Minister to the King, he had rebuilt Lisbon, which had been shattered by a mighty 18th century earthquake. Almost within the shadow of this monument, there was a lovely park to walk in, named after England's King Edward VII. This was a real joy when drifts of pink almond blossom marked the coming of spring. We had christened the Avenida our *Laisvés Aléja* (Freedom Avenue, after the one in Kaunas). Of course it was much more grand, having unusual sidewalks in black and white mosaic patterns. There were areas with statues and fountains, notably at the plaza called Rossio. Buses and streetcars existed, but we generally tramped the full length of the Avenida on our way down to the edge of the *Teijo* (or Tagus) river at *Praca do Commercio*.

We found a new home in the spacious apartment of the Raposo family. They were Protestant missionaries lately returned from Angola, Africa, then a part of the grandiose Portuguese Empire. Since we boarded at their table, cooking, dishwashing, and other chores were no longer necessary. Our hosts spoke English rather well and a new way of life began. I was a little sorry to give up those enjoyable forays to the open air market where I had learned to bargain for fish, fruit and other produce. A few words of Portuguese were sufficient to answer the calls of the sellers, *Muito barato* (very cheap). I would walk away exclaiming: *Nao, nao, muito caro* (no no, very expensive).

The advantages of our new abode were many. Some of our favorite spots were now much easier to reach. If we could get to the Port early enough, we might see fishwives with baskets on their heads, crying *Pescado! Bacalhao!* (fish, codfish) at the Tower of Belem. This was a monument to great explorers of the past, headed by Prince Henry the Navigator. A full scale model of the ship *Nao*

Portugal (New Portugal) was bobbing up and down at anchor in the bay. In this ship, Vasco da Gama, a contemporary of Columbus, made his historic trip to India.

The many cafés where some of our acquaintances liked to gather near the Rossio were now within easy walking distance. Among refugees of different nationalities were Polish people including some who had relatives in Lithuania. There were so many Poles here that they had set up their own Red Cross Relief station. We were cordially invited to stop in and get some much needed clothing and other supplies. Father did not like to moralize, but he reminded us of what he had said about good deeds coming back to us when we had received Polish military men at Turkey Lurk.

At the café we learned something of Portuguese ways. The way one summoned a waiter was amusing, i.e., by making a hissing sound like an exaggerated "Psh Psh." The waiter would bring you wine or other beverages, accompanied by sweet stuff, olives or other munchies. It seemed that local men left their wives at home when they went to the cafes. Their women seldom went to public places. Young girls were tightly supervised and had to have a chaperone when they left their house. The Portuguese language sounded strange and baffling, so similar and yet so very different from the Spanish. It had many hissing sounds like "Sh" and "Zh" which occur in Polish and Lithuanian as well. We had a good laugh when a Polish friend said that it sounded like Lithuanian when he heard it for the first time. Father replied: "No indeed, to me it sounds very much like Polish."

It must have been in this café that I was first introduced to the mournful sound of the traditional Portuguese ballad called the *Fado*. The singer, accompanied by guitar chords in a minor key, relates stories of a vanished love or similar personal loss. The Fado, a uniquely Portuguese creation can melt the heart of even the most unwilling audience. The national psyche seems to be romantic in the extreme. Perhaps this is well expressed in an untranslatable concept

277

called *saudade*, a feeling of deep melancholy and longing for days and places gone by.

Another milestone in our lives was reached when we started to attend services at the Scottish Protestant church on *Rua Arriaga*, a gathering place for British residents their friends. Britons were numerous here, as ties between the two lands were strong, fostered in part by business and trade in port wine, an English favorite, over the centuries. The Reverend Stuart Robertson and his lively wife gave us a hearty welcome. We started meeting others of our faith. This was a Roman Catholic country, and Protestants were few. Clearly remembered are some who said that their forbears had been Huguenots fleeing from France. The hospitable Robertsons gave a bang-up Christmas party at their home. There was plum pudding, wreaths of holly, pulling of "crackers" and jolly songs and games.

Our pro-British attitude could have been a key to our social success. One introduction would lead to another, and soon we had almost more invitations than we could handle. They were mostly to ladies' tea parties where our menfolk were reluctant to go. However, we women enjoyed them immensely. A highlight was a visit to the Perry sisters. They were called Pereira in the Portuguese manner because their family had resided here for so long. The three elderly ladies lived in a lavishly furnished home replete with souvenirs and had never married. Their father had been a sea-captain and had brought lovely jewelry, embroideries, paintings and porcelain objects from his voyages to the Orient. The sisters told us fascinating tales about the reasons why they had remained single.

An attractive spot to visit was Estoril, full of luxury homes in an attractive setting of parks and flowers. For years it found favor with aristocrats, like exiled kings and queens or other deposed rulers down on their luck. It was hardly a surprise to find our own President Smetona living there with his family. With him was his wife, his son, daughter-in-law and two small grandsons. Father used to visit their home and reminisce about the happenings since their last meeting. The President had not received a cordial welcome either in Germany or Switzerland. Their respective governments considered his presence to be an embarrassment. For President Smetona, Portugal was only a temporary haven and his heart was set on going to the USA. There was much discussion about where he should go. Father agreed with Julius, his son, that it might be wise to choose some country like Brazil, but the President insisted on going to America. He got there eventually, but his stay was not a happy one as he never found an agreeable milieu. In the year 1944, he died in a tragic fire at his home in Cleveland, Ohio.

Father went to Estoril not only to visit the Smetonas, but also to try his luck at the gaming tables at the Casino, said to be reminiscent of Monte Carlo. Almost invariably he came home with winnings. He smilingly said that he won often because he was gambling with a good purpose in mind, namely to support his wife and family. He had something like a remarkable sixth sense telling him when to stop. Only the more adventurous members of the family like Evelyna and myself would accompany him to the Casino. We never won anything and soon gave up. The rest of us, especially our brother (anything but an optimist), refused outright to go.

All this time Father (who had always thought it unpatriotic to have financial assets abroad, e.g. in Swiss banks) was appealing for help to friends and relations in the USA. This took a lot of writing in which I tried to help, beating the keys of a typewriter in poor repair, which somebody had given us. The President was told of my efforts at writing and translation, and soon I was honored by invitations to help in some of his paperwork. The Smetona house seemed to be always in a turmoil, what with Mrs. Smetona's bad relations with her daughter-in-law, her attempts to direct her husband's every move and her general state of disorganization bordering on panic. None of the packing was finished until the day the family was to leave for Rio de Janeiro. In early March, I was at the dock when the Smetonas sailed away on the ship named *Serpa Pinto* with their mountains of luggage. They almost missed the boat in a very literal sense. They were so late that the gang plank was already being raised when they arrived at the port. The Smetonas got on board only because the ship, like many Portuguese vessels, did not lift anchor at the appointed time.

We left a few weeks later. Taking off for the new world was a harrowing event. Passage had been secured on a small ship called the Angola that was bound for Brazil. Those American visas we had applied for months before were still not available and leaving without them seemed unthinkable. Attempts to contact the Embassy and consular officials by phone or letter were to no avail. Mamma decided to take matters into her own hands. She said, "I am an American by birth and will certainly give these bureaucrats a piece of my mind." None of us were allowed to go with her. She marched out accompanied by her big black umbrella. When permission to see the Consul was refused, she said she rattled the umbrella on the floor and screamed loudly, "You should be ashamed of yourselves" and simply walked in to personally state her case to the consul. In a few hours, she returned in triumph with the needed documents. However, the Angola was sailing the next day, and it was too late to make any changes in our tickets.

Shipping out was exciting and we, too, almost missed the boat. Packing was not the problem because we had few possessions to take. Our parents insisted that all six of us must arrive together and getting two taxis at once was not easy. We came to the dock barely in time for dear Mrs. Robertson to thrust bouquets of fragrant purple violets into our hands. The Raposos were there and, of course Luis. Luis later said he followed the progress of the Angola with his eyes down the broad expanse of the Tagus river all the way to the Atlantic Ocean.

Chapter Thirty-Four
Voyage to the New World

This was the first such trip I had ever taken. To this day, nothing ever equaled the impression made by the transatlantic voyage of the Angola, even though later there were other ships and other voyages. The Angola was tiny, only some seven or eight thousand tons at the most, but she was well run by a competent crew who did everything possible for the comfort and convenience of the passengers. On board ship it was still Portuguese territory and once more we experienced the kindness and solicitude associated with that nation. The whole trip had an ineffable charm that lingers with me still. Just like the country of Portugal, it keeps beckoning to me across the years.

We had traveling companions of whom we were not previously aware. Our two Lithuanian navy men were coming with us, without saying a word about their plans. It was very likely Paul and Vito's idea of a practical joke. Another surprise was one more compatriot on board, a young Roman Catholic priest, quite worldly and humorous, on his way to missionary work in Brazil. We all had our meals in the dining room sitting at the same table with our compatriots. The trip started out with smooth sailing, and fair weather continued most of the way. The Angola rocked very little, and none of us were much bothered by seasickness.

Sitting on deck waiting for land to appear was quite an experience, our first stop being the isle of Madeira. When it became visible, it was like a pearl of iridescent pink and blue rising up from the ocean. Sea dolphins were gamboling about as we approached what we termed an enchanted island. Women were standing on shore carrying baskets on their heads filled with bananas and pineapples as well as masses of roses and carnations. Warm and balmy breezes were blowing as we mounted the steep cobblestoned streets of Funchal. The way to get around was by ox-drawn carts with metal runners rather like sleighs seen elsewhere in winter time.

Women were sitting on their porches, busily embroidering table linens, towels and blouses for sale to tourists.

There were free samples of sweet Madeira wine to be savored from huge casks in the wine cellars. We could not tarry here as there were other attractions. A white villa on a hilltop, surrounded by bougainvillea bushes in full bloom, was where Poland's Marshall Pilsudski had kept a vacation home. We were told that he lived here for several months at a time, and we thought that he showed remarkably good taste. We had to hurry back so the ship would not sail without us. We were in the Azores, one of the earliest discoveries of Portuguese explorers. Beyond lay the Canary Islands belonging to the Spanish, but we did not stop there. The Capo Verde Islands were to come next. Landing at Santo Tomas, just West of the coast of Africa many miles south of Madeira, was a thrilling prospect.

Here the vegetation was entirely tropical and the weather was uncomfortably hot. It seemed that the entire population, all of them black, came out to welcome us. After stopping at the open-air market where there was little to buy, we found our way to the church. It was painted a stark white, but all the images of the saints inside had black faces, even Jesus and his Mother Mary. After leaving the Capo Verde Islands, our ship approached the Equator. Rather remarkably, at the very moment when we were crossing this line, Mamma felt chilly and asked for her coat. She said later that she would never have known that this event had taken place if it had not been for the Masquerade Ball that marked the occasion.

Perhaps in deference to the plight of the many refugees on board, the Angola's personnel saw to it that the passengers were lavishly wined, dined, and entertained. They roamed at will all over the ship without distinction between first, second and third class. When it became too hot for passengers to sleep in their bunks below, they could sleep wherever they wanted. A large group of friends regularly slept on mattresses on the floor of the bar next to the dining area. Every afternoon, at teatime, there was live music and everybody, young or old, could beat on drums, rattle the *maracas* (a kind of noisemaker) and join in the singing, if they felt so inspired. The good-natured musicians seemed happy when we made the rafters ring with songs like *Amapola, Tiro Liro* and *Bahia o - o - o Bahia*. For those wishing to dress up for the Masquerade Ball, bright colored crepe paper, ribbons, shawls, and other materials were provided. We put our heads together and dressed Violetta as a rose in a green hat and red paper petals covering her skirt. Evelyna was a mermaid with her long blond hair floating behind her and a fishtail decorated with green scales and real seashells.

There was so much going on that I remember wishing the voyage would never end. Among our many parties, one impromptu moonlit evening stands out in my memory. More and more passengers came out on deck to hear one of the ship's officers play his guitar. Argentine tangos like one called *"Medialuz"* ("Twilight") and snatches of songs of many nations soon had people singing, whether they knew the songs or not. When asked to make a contribution, our Lithuanian contingent surprised them with our own version of the tango, a dance quite popular where we came from. The melancholy tones of our song reminded a Portuguese gentleman of a *Fado*. This was rather far-fetched, but a compliment just the same. At intervals we gazed at the heavens and the changing panoply of stars. Familiar constellations had given way to those like the Southern Cross because we were in another hemi-sphere. It was getting late and members of the gathering disappeared one by one to catch some sleep. A few of us remained on deck until the moonlight faded away, hoping to get a glimpse of the Morning Star.

The magnificent harbor of Rio de Janeiro drew near sooner than we expected. Mountains, bays, and inlets came to view. It was said that there were 365 mountain peaks here, one for every day of the year, headed by Corcovado. At its summit was a giant statue of Christ with arms outstretched. There was a cemetery going down the mountainside named for St. John the Baptist with which we were to become well acquainted. Despite the beauties of Rio, our brief stay there was not a happy one. It was to hold grievous memories, and we were glad to get away when the time came.

We had arrived in the middle of the Brazilian summer. It was unpleasantly hot and sticky. When out walking, you easily got tired and soon your clothes were wet with perspiration. People here were fond of wearing white clothing so the laundries and dry-cleaning establishments must have been doing good business. Father's heart, weakened by diabetes, was not of the best. The damp heat was particularly hard on him. As head of the family, he insisted on handling all important matters himself. He would come home exhausted from many trips to the local police station where all foreigners had to have their documents checked. You could be heavily fined if you did not have your passport with you. Very often the police officials would tell Father that our passports had been lost and that it would take time and money to find them again. He hated to submit to what he called "this disgusting game of extortion," but finally did so much against his will.

In the Copacabana area we found rooms in a *pensión* with the help of Gibrail, a Brazilian friend we had made in Lisbon. This charming young man, so tall, dark and handsome, told us about places of interest and sometimes took us there personally. Among the excursions was one to the National Art Gallery with splendid paintings by unfamiliar native artists, also the Botanical Gardens where flocks of jewel-like hummingbirds flitted around the blossoms. In time, we met more people we knew at a nearby café. There was Julius Smetona who had hopes of finding permanent employment here but gave up later to join his father, the President, in the USA. We also met some former ship-mates from the Angola.

A few of our fellow passengers had met with good luck, like the French family who inherited a modest fortune immediately upon arrival. Not so fortunate was a blonde and personable refugee from Central Europe. She had traveled to Rio to join her husband, but he was not waiting for her as planned. He had completely disappeared, and she did not know if she would ever find him again. High on our list of social activities was the beach at Copacabana, only one of six or seven on the bays of the city. When going swimming, however, one had to be careful because there was a dangerous rip-tide that could carry you out to sea. I experienced this myself on one terrifying occasion. I barely escaped drowning while battling my way to safety. I remember thinking that much in the tropics was not safe and that even the waters could be treacherous.

Father soon discovered the Casino where he played roulette with his usual good luck. He seemed to be vigorous enough, holding fast to his dream of conducting us to America. One evening he went to the Casino all by himself, refusing my offer to go along. He came home in good spirits and even ate a red apple with a hearty appetite. That night he died in Mamma's arms of a massive heart attack. A doctor was summoned, but it was too late. He tried to comfort us by saying that the death must have been a painless one. We spent days in grief and mourning, too sorrowful at times to eat or sleep. True, we had our courageous Mamma to lean on, but no one could take Father's place. And especially not for me, who had always been so close to him. Even now, after all this time, I have difficulty in setting down the mournful details. The first to learn of this tragic event was the Lithuanian Consular representative in Rio and later the minister of the local American Protestant Church. Both were of immense help in making the practical arrangements, including burial in the cemetery of St. John the Baptist on Mount Corcovado. Soon afterwards, American friends and relatives in the USA made it possible for us to book passage on a ship bound for New York.

On our way to the dock where the S.S. Brazil was waiting to carry us away, we sighted something of interest. This was the wooden ship called The Bear, in which a modern American explorer, Adm. R. Byrd, had sailed to the Antarctica. The barking of sled dogs on board made me wonder if the ship would soon be on its way back there again. The Brazil, some three times the size of the

Angola, seemed like a true ocean liner. Everything was on a bigger scale, including the loud blasts of the ship's sirens. We had a good trip and met a few interesting traveling companions. First came the Australian showman with his boxing kangaroo. He had traveled the world with his act and people told tales that he was actually an international spy. Two Mormon missionaries returning from their stint abroad and some Mennonite ministers were among the friendly Americans. However, nothing could equal the impression left by some fifteen Belgian men from South America. They were on their way to join the army being formed in Canada to fight Nazi Germany.

For some reason, the trip on the SS Brazil was not as remarkable as the one on board the Angola, remembered with such fond affection. The cozy and homelike atmosphere of this much smaller ship was definitely lacking. In a way, I was getting to be a seasoned world traveler, not impressed with crossing the equator for the second time nor with the changing constellations of stars. Also, the people I met on board did not seem quite as interesting as before. However, I had a genuine shipboard romance with one of the Belgian warriors, a nineteen-year old native of Chile. We spent hours reading French poetry and dreaming impossible dreams. He was sure he would never come home from the wars, and the prospect would reduce both of us to tears. The only time Eugene showed some gaiety was at the Masquerade Ball held when we were crossing the Equator. The men dressed up as pirates in boots and cutlasses and chased the women all over the ship. When caught, we had to pay fines like a few stolen kisses, or else be thrown into the swimming pool.

The SS Brazil made its only stop on the island of Trinidad in the Caribbean, a short one because the captain was running behind schedule. It was memorable mainly because of a few souvenirs we bought there: articles made of coconut shells, and beads of seeds and berries. The rest of the voyage was uneventful and left few memories. We hit some bad weather off the coast of North America but all inconveniences were forgotten when we reached our destination. The skies were overcast and the rain was drizzling down on that memorable day of May 5th, 1941.

Everyone rushed out on deck, leaning on the railings to watch a remarkable sight. The Statue of Liberty was rising up out of the fog against the backdrop of the skyscrapers of a tremendous city. There was a long wait for the tugboat that would take the Brazil across the expanse of the East River and the end of the voyage. I tried to catch a glimpse of Ellis Island where so many of our friends and relatives had first set foot on American soil, but it was nowhere to be seen. There was ample time to admire Lady Liberty and to think of the words of a poet written in her honor "I lift my lamp beside the Golden Door." I thought later that we were lucky to have come in by sea and not by air, in which case we would have missed this majestic view of the world famous statue, symbol of American freedom. Mamma, returning to the country of her birth, was deeply moved on seeing the Statue of Liberty as well as the Stars and Stripes displayed by the ships passing by. She had no trouble convincing all of us that the American flag is the most beautiful in the whole world.

The blaring of sirens on the approaching tugboat and other ships in the harbor, answered by blasts from the Brazil, announced our arrival. Gradually the specks on the dock became the shapes of people on the landing dock. A distant blue speck gradually got bigger and bigger. This turned out to be an oversized sky-blue umbrella unfurled by our aunt, Doctor Aldona, Mamma's sister. She had returned to her native land years before. Long ago, the two sisters had agreed on that brightly colored umbrella as a signal in case they did not recognize each other from afar. After the immigration formalities were over, we were on our way to Aunt Aldona's home in the Williamsburg section of Brooklyn, New York. She had hung up her shingle and was practicing medicine as usual. New impressions and adventures awaited us, but reaching our journey's end seems the right place to end this story.

The Yčas family shortly before landing in New York
Standing (left to right): Martynas, Evelyna
Seated (left to right): Violetta, Hypatia (author), Hypatia (mother)

Index of Personalities

Aukštuolis, Jonas (1886-?)
　　Career diplomat, a victim of Soviet deportation who died in
　　exile
Bacevičius, Dr.Antanas, M.D. (1871-1937)
　　Brother-in-law of Liudvika Šliupas, part-time resident of
　　Palanga
Bain, Isabel (dates unknown)
　　From Scotland, first of several governesses of the Yčas
　　children
Balčikonis, Prof. Juozas (1885-1969)
　　Lexicographer and compiler of dictionaries of the modern
　　Lithuanian language
Basanavičius, Jonas, M.D. (1851-1927)
　　A leader of the Lithuanian national renascence, called "The
　　Father of his Country"
Birutė, Grand Duchess of Lithuania (dates unknown)
　　Wife of the 14th century Grand Duke Keistutis, associated
　　with legends of Palanga
Bitkevičius, Petrusia Grauslytė (dates unknown)
　　Longtime housekeeper for the Yčas family, victim of Soviet
　　deportation
Caldwell, Robert. J. (1875-1952)
　　American industrialist and humanitarian, active in European
　　relief work after World War I
Chaliapin, Feodor (1873-1938)
　　Renowned Russian opera singer, appearing on the stage of
　　the National Opera in Kaunas
Čiurlys, Elena Bilminas (1892-1986)
　　Professor at Kaunas Conservatory of Music, piano instructor
　　of the Yčas children
Crawford, Anne Jane (1909-1989)
　　From Scotland, governess of the Yčas children and college
　　professor of English

Darius, Steponas (1896-1933)

Aviator acclaimed for his transatlantic flight from New York to Europe with co-pilot S. Girėnas

Dembskis, Vladislovas, Father (1831-1913)

Catholic priest and freethinker, making his home with the Šliupas family in the USA

Fedoroff, Elena Nikitishna Timofeeva (dates unknown)

Nurse of the Yčas children, a refugee from the Russian Revolution of 1917

Frenkelis, Volka (dates unknown)

Friend and business associate of Martynas Yčas, Sr., owner of a neighboring farm

Gabrys, Juozas (1880-1951)

Author of books and pamphlets, active at the Paris Peace Conference in 1919

Galvanauskas, Ernestas (1882-1967)

Minister of Finance and Prime Minister of Lithuania

Gediminas, Grand Duke (1275-1341)

Early ruler of Lithuania and founder of a dynasty

Jakubėnas, Povilas, Rev. (1871-1953)

Head of the Lithuanian Evangelical Reformed Church and professor of theology

Jakubėnas, Vladas (1904-1976)

Composer of orchestral, vocal, and choral works; music critic, and journalist

Jenkins, Ruth Marshall (1917 -)

English teacher working in Lithuania, evacuated to Australia in 1940

Jonuškaitė-Zaunius, Vincė (1902-1997)

Opera singer, leading mezzo-soprano of the National Opera in Kaunas

Kaganas, Juozas (1915-1995)

Lithuanian-born British industrialist, later titled Joseph Lord Kagan

Kalpokas, Petras (1880-1945)
Portrait and landscape artist, a founder of the Kaunas Academy of Arts

Kazragaitė, Basia (dates unknown)
Maid in the Yčas household who left to become a nun in a convent in Belgium

Kutkus, Aleksandras (1889-?)
Opera singer of the Kaunas stage and frequent stand-in for leading tenor roles

Kurnatauskas, Konstantas, Rev.(1878-1966)
A leader of the Lithuanian Evangelical Reformed Church, professor of Reformation history

Lieponis, Juozas (dates unknown)
Student of liberal arts, tutor of the Yčas children

Maironis (Mačiulis), Jonas, Father (1862-1932)
Roman Catholic priest and a leading poet of the Lithuanian national renascence

Merkys, Antanas, Col. (1887-1955)
Minister of Defense and the last Prime Minister of Lithuania, victim of Soviet deportation

Mickevičius, Adomas (Adam Mickiewicz) (1798-1855)
Romantic poet, writing in the Polish language on Lithuanian historical themes

Mikelėnas, Jokubas, M.D. (1886-1966)
Director of Biržai hospital, a cousin of Martynas Yčas, Sr.

Milyukov, Pavel (1859-1943)
Cadet Party Leader in the Russian Duma, author of historical works

Mlynarski, Emil (1870-1935)
Director and conductor of the Warsaw Symphony Orchestra in Poland

Neimanas, Stasys, Rev. (1899-1995)
Minister of the Lithuanian Evangelical Reformed Church

Petrauskas, Mikas (1873-1937)
Music teacher, choral director, and composer of some of the earliest Lithuanian language operas

Petrauskas, Kipras (1886-1968)

Opera singer and leading lyrical tenor of the National Opera in Kaunas

Pilsudski, Marshal Josef (1867-1935)

Political leader of postwar Poland who played a role in the Vilnius dispute

Radvila (also spelled Radziwill)

Family of Dukes of princely title, active over many generations in Lithuania's Reformation movement

Šakovas, Benediktas (1892-1942)

Business man, brewery owner in the town of Prienai

Saunders, Vivian E. (dates unknown)

English governess of the Yčas children

Šimkus, Stasys (1887-1943)

Musician, choral director and composer

Simpson, Prof. James Y. (1873-1934)

Theologian and British diplomat, a frequent visitor to Lithuania from his native Scotland

Šleževičius, Mykolas (1882-1943)

Vice President and Prime Minister of Lithuania

Šliupas Family

Variant spellings used, as in Slupas, Szlupas, Šliupas, etc.

Šliupas, Jonas, M.D. (1861-1944)

Leader of Lithuanian national renascence; grandfather of the Yčas children; married Liudvika Malinauskas; mother of their three children: Aldona, M.D. (1886-1980), Keistutis (1888-1932), and Hypatia (1894-1987); later married Grasilda Grauslys (1899-1976), mother of their son Vytautas (1930 -)

Šliupas, Rokas M.D. (1865-1955)

Hospital administrator, president of the Red Cross Society, and brother of Jonas

Smetona, Antanas (1874-1944)

President of the Republic of Lithuania in 1919-1920 and again in 1926-1940

Sokolskis, Konstantinas (1878-1937)
> Veterinarian and friend of the Yčas family

Strazdas, Jurgis (1906-?)
> Early tutor of the Yčas children, student of physics and chemistry

Tubelis, Juozas (1882-1939)
> Minister of Agriculture and Prime Minister of Lithuania

Valiukas (first name, dates unknown)
> Coachman in charge of the horses belonging to the Yčas family

Vasilchikoff, Prince Ilarion (dates unknown)
> Russian aristocrat, owner of estates in Lithuania

Vileišis, Jonas (1872-1942)
> Minister of Finance of Lithuania and an early mayor of the City of Kaunas

Voldemaras, Augustinas (1883-1944)
> Minister of Foreign Affairs and later Prime Minister of Lithuania, victim of Soviet deportation

Yčas, Prof. Jonas (1880-1931)
> Minister of Education during Lithuania's formative years, brother of Martynas, Sr.

Yčas, Martynas, Sr. (1885-1941)
> Minister of Finance and Communications during Lithuania's formative years; married Hypatia Šliupas; mother of their four children: Martynas, Jr. (1917 -), Hypatia, (1920 -), Evelyna (1923 -), and Violetta (1923-1976)

Books for Further Reading

Daužvardis, Josephine J. Popular Lithuanian Recipes. 9th ed. Chicago: Lithuanian Catholic Press, 1986. Treasury of favorite Lithuanian recipes with notes on special holiday foods.

Eidintas, E., ed. Lithuania in European Politics: The Years of the First Republic, 1918-1940. New York: St. Martin's Press, 1998. Essays describing Lithuania's emergence to independence after World War I with information on the reconstitution of freedom in 1991.

Gerutis, Dr. A., ed. Lithuania: 700 Years. New York: Maryland Books, 1969. Essays on the origin and development of Lithuania from medieval to modern times.

Harrison, E. J. Lithuania 1928. London: Hazell, 1928. Information on the first decade of freedom. Includes Who's Who in Lithuania.

Kantautas, A. and F. A Lithuanian Bibliography. Edmonton, Alberta: University of Alberta Press, 1975. Comprehensive listing of books in libraries throughout the USA and Canada.

Simutis, A. The Economic Reconstruction of Lithuania after 1918. New York: Columbia University Press, 1942. Contains facts and figures on Lithuania's agricultural export trade.

Zobarskas, S., ed. Lithuanian Folk Tales. Brooklyn: G.G. Rickard, 1959. Over 40 of the most popular Lithuanian tales and legends.